PRESS CONTROL
AROUND THE WORLD

PRESS CONTROL AROUND THE WORLD

Edited by
Jane Leftwich Curry
and Joan R. Dassin

PRAEGER

PRAEGER SPECIAL STUDIES • PRAEGER SCIENTIFIC

Library of Congress Cataloging in Publication Data
Main entry under title:

All the news not fit to print.

Includes bibliographical references and index.
1. Liberty of the press—Addresses, essays, lectures.
I. Curry, Jane Leftwich, 1948-   II. Dassin, Joan.
PN4735.A4   1982   323.44'5   82-9837
ISBN 0-03-059869-9   AACR2

PN
4735
P68
1982

Published in 1982 by Praeger Publishers
CBS Educational and Professional Publishing
a Division of CBS Inc.
521 Fifth Avenue, New York, New York 10175 U.S.A.

© 1982 by Praeger Publishers

23456789   052   987654321

Printed in the United States of America

This book is dedicated to
our journalist friends in
Poland and Brazil
who taught us to read
between the lines

ACKNOWLEDGMENTS

We owe thanks to many.

First, to the publishers who granted us permission to reprint the following articles:

Gaye Tuchman, "The Exception Proves the Rule: The Study of Routine News Practices," originally published in <u>Strategies for Communications Research: Annual Review of Communications Research</u>, vol. 6 (1978), R. Hirsch et al., eds., reprinted with permission of the publisher, Sage Publications, Beverly Hills/London.

Philip Schlesinger, "Princes' Gate, 1980: The Media Politics of Siege Management," originally published in <u>Screen Education</u>, Winter 1980/1981, no. 37. We are grateful to Philip Schlesinger and to the editor of <u>Screen Education</u> for permission to republish this article.

Lu Keng, "The Chinese Communist Press as I See It," originally published in <u>Asian Messenger</u>, vol. 4, nos.2 & 3 (Autumn 1979 - Spring 1980) with permission of the Center for Communication Studies, Chinese University of Hong Kong.

Second, to the institutions that funded our original research in Poland and Brazil, and to those that gave us shelter upon our return:

For Jane Leftwich Curry, International Research and Exchanges Board, Rand Corporation, Institute on East Central Europe of Columbia University, and Manhattanville College.

For Joan Dassin, J. V. Kaltenborn Foundation, National Endowment for the Humanities, Social Science Research Council, Tinker Foundation, Institute of Latin American and Iberian Studies of Columbia University, and Communications Department of Fordham University.

Third, to the people who typed the manuscript:

Georgia di Bella, Nancy Demmon, and Ruth Artig.

Fourth, to the people who worked with and inspired us. We can name only some of them here:

Prosser Gifford, Jun Eto, and Ralph della Cava, who organized the "Evening Dialogue on Censorship" held March 1980 at the Woodrow Wilson Center, Washington, D.C.; Dr. A. Ross Johnson; Glen, Andrew, and Matthew Curry; Marvin Alisky; Grazyna Drabik; Georgia di Bella; Dr. Mark Pasmantier; Dr. Robert Clarke; and the Dassin family.

CONTENTS

INTRODUCTION

BY JOAN R. DASSIN

A reader of this volume might have three basic questions in mind. How did such a collection on world censorship come to be? What kinds of material does it include? Why is it of interest, and to whom? Some concise answers can guide the reader through the pages ahead.

Like all books, this one has a history. Stimulated by an "Evening Dialogue on Censorship" held at the Woodrow Wilson Center in Washington, D.C. in March 1980, the present editors were fascinated by the idea that a common analytic framework could possibly explain divergent cases of censorship and non-institutionalized information management. Although the cases presented at the Wilson Center were censorship in occupied Japan, military-ruled Brazil, and post-war Rumania, it was apparent that a wide variety could be usefully compared. While it has long been understood that censorship is more the rule than the exception, we knew of no volume that systematically examined and compared the development of censorship systems. Nor could we think of any that explained censorship in different national and regional settings in relation to diverse political systems and economic structures for media ownership.

So the idea of a collection on world censorship was born, and with it, a search for contemporary material. As tentative outlines proliferated, three major areas of concern arose. How could the material's currency be guaranteed? Might not political changes hopelessly date these studies before the volume could appear? Then, would the classification of censorship systems into a geopolitical mold of West, East, and Third World raise too many shibboleths of cold war politics, modernization theory, or the tired classification of press systems into Communist, authoritarian, libertarian, or socially responsible models? Finally, what of the predictable diversity of authors? How could a refugee Chinese journalist and a specialist in the subtleties of state media control in France, to cite just one example, reasonably be expected to cover the same points in their analyses? Would the very diversity that made the idea so attractive in the first place prove its undoing?

Some comments about the ten studies included here will demonstrate how these concerns were resolved. A look at the organization of the volume, for example, addresses the first. The book is divided into four parts: "Controls over the 'Free Press': Western Democracies," with studies of the United States, Britain, and France; "Controlling the Communist Press," which examines censorship in the Soviet Union, Eastern Europe, and Communist China; "Press Controls in the Developing World," with articles on one or more countries in Latin America, the Middle East, and black Africa; and "External Controls of Domestic Media," a case study of censorship by a foreign power. In addition, Jane Curry's concluding essay relates the systemic variables and media control patterns discussed in the preceding studies.

Two factors ensure the currency of this material. First, seven of the ten studies, as well as Curry's concluding chapter, are published for the first time here. Of the previously published pieces, Gaye Tuchman's study of news practices in the United States was amplified especially for this volume. Philip Schlesinger's analysis of media-state relations during the Iranian Embassy takeover at Princes' Gate, England, in 1980, appeared in 1980-81. Lu Keng's discussion of the Chinese Communist press was published in 1980. Second, all three of these previously published pieces are essentially new for a general American audience: Tuchman's piece appeared in a specialized American academic journal, and the other two articles were published abroad. Aside from these considerations, the solid empirical research fundamental to all ten studies is ample guarantee that they will long represent valid scholarship.

This is true despite the authors' varying distance from events and different disciplinary orientations. Lu Keng's piece, for example, is based on his personal experience as a journalist. It is, nonetheless, a wide-ranging discussion of press controls in Communist China, as seen in the context of the functions, organization, and operation of the Chinese press.

The other studies take the long view provided by several academic disciplines: sociology, history, political science, communications, and literary criticism. All seek to identify complex, multilevel patterns and mechanisms of information control. These in turn illustrate the subtle relationships between media institutions and political systems. Insofar as the media in every society are a major information source for social scientists and the public, and are acknowledged political actors as well, these analyses will withstand the fast pace of political change.

Sometimes these essays can even illuminate subsequent events. Munir K. Nasser's study of the Middle East press, for example, was largely written before the assassination of Egyptian President Anwar el-Sadat in late 1981. Its theme is the dilemma posed by Sadat's crackdown on the press in the midst of his supposed "experiment with democracy" after 1976. Despite the changes wrought by events of the last few months, Nasser's point that Sadat imposed press controls to counter rising opposition to his policy of rapprochement with Israel, on the one hand, and the suppression of Moslem fundamentalists, on the other, still holds true. Indeed, it may well help to explain the very pressures that led to the assassination.

The second area of concern, the volume's geopolitical organization, is justified by the same analytic dynamism that ensures its timeliness. The "Western press," the "Communist press," and the "Developing World press" divisions reflect convenience, not ideology. Although all the studies are interpretive, none falls back on old-hat political rhetoric, supposedly neutral models of press systems that in fact disguise a pro-United States bias or outmoded development theories. On the contrary, every case study — from the United States to the Soviet Union, to Brazil, and back in time to U.S. censorship in occupied Japan — considers information control such a complex, interactive process that no unidimensional model can serve as an adequate explanation.

Gaye Tuchman's and Jane Curry's studies illustrate this point. Thus Tuchman holds that "the suppression of information is built into the very organization of the U.S. news media," because the preservation of the status quo is part and parcel of the procedures used to define and process news. Curry, for her part, holds that there is no single Communist model of press control in Eastern Europe. Rather, Poland, Czechoslovakia, Hungary, Yugoslavia, East Germany, Rumania, and Bulgaria have a variety of formal and informal censorship mechanisms that reflect national priorities and differences. Curry's detailed analysis of Polish censorship further demonstrates that even in a highly formalized system, direct lines of state control over various media are difficult to establish.

Philip Schlesinger's analysis and Lilita Dzirkals's study also avoid ideological stereotypes. Schlesinger clearly demonstrates the participation of the British media in the siege-breaking operations of the British state. Dzirkals, as one might expect, outlines the many devices used by the Soviets to place the USSR's vast media potential totally at the service of state interests. But she also clearly notes that "the creative talent and vitality of the media profession in the USSR are as strong as anywhere in the world." Furthermore, she recognizes that the Soviet media are aware of audience desires and "frequently challenge the bounds that authorities impose."

Similarly, neither Charles Eisendrath's study nor Lu Keng's account provides pat answers to the complex question of press behavior and control in Western or Communist countries. Thus Eisendrath places the French system "squarely between the philosophies of Watergate and the Gulag," and Lu Keng sees the strict controls over the Chinese press as inseparable from the many elements in Mao Tse-Tung's conceptualization of the political role of the press in a revolutionary society.

xiii

The articles about the press in the developing world similarly avoid facile theorizing. They are all based on heretofore disparate or unexamined primary sources, and they all study the relationship between a censorship system and its larger political framework in a given regional context. Thus, Joan Dassin's piece examines Brazilian censorship in terms of information policy in Latin American national security states; Munir Nasser looks at Egyptian press controls in terms of changing Middle East politics; and Dennis Wilcox assesses political stability and economic development in black African countries by examining press controls in the various national press systems.

Special mention must be made of Jun Eto's study of U.S. censorship in occupied Japan, published here for the first time in English. It is the only piece in this volume that treats a discrete historical example of censorship. It is also the only study of internal censorship by a foreign power. Nonetheless, its research technique and analytic framework are in keeping with the rest of the studies in this volume. Eto's piece merits inclusion for another reason as well: by providing concrete data about a censorship system that is virtually unknown in the United States, the study sheds new light on both the American victory and the Japanese defeat in World War II, thus demonstrating just how much the analysis of a given censorship system can reveal about the historical process.

The studies included here share many common threads, although they differ in methodology, regional focus, and thematic emphasis. Our task as editors was not so much to ensure that each contribution address identical questions as it was to delineate a range of issues suggested by the central topic. Throughout the volume, there is a shared concern with the process of censorship per se, its development, functioning, and in some cases, lasting consequences.

This is true also despite the varying scope of the articles. Some, for example, are narrowly focused. They deal with specific cases of information control. Others deal more broadly with the features of censorship systems or media in transition and their changing relationships to larger political structures. Some are compendiums of legal, economic, and professional pressures on national press systems, while another examines cross-cultural censorship.

This focus on the censorship process sets this volume apart from other current research. As summarized by editor Robert A. White in Communication Research Trends (Summer 1981), two broad themes characterize censorship studies: the legal and institutional procedures for deciding what to communicate, and the debate over what disciplines are most useful in resolving this question — the behavioral sciences, the humanities, political philosophy, or some combination of these approaches. The

CHAPTER 1

The Exception Proves the Rule:
The Study of Routine News
Practices in the United States

BY GAYE TUCHMAN

Officially, except during some periods of war, there is no censorship in the United States. Rather, as editors and reporters are wont to explain, while ignoring some rather complex Supreme Court rulings, freedom of the press—or the right to disseminate information—includes the responsibility of self-censorship to protect the national interest and the public welfare. According to this interpretation, when the New York Times decided not to publish the plans of the Bay of Pigs invasion before its scheduled date, it engaged in self-censorship in the national interest. Or, to use a more common example, when a news medium does not disseminate the details of a notorious crime, it is protecting the public welfare by facilitating the tasks of the police. Significantly, this news-media view of self-censorship assumes that it starts only at that point where a newsworker makes a conscious decision not to include a newsworthy fact in a story or not to run the story itself. Similarly, the most adamant defenders of a strict interpretation of freedom of the press would claim that censorship is the government's deliberate refusal to give nonclassified information or its deliberate attempt to suppress a story.

But there is another view of censorship and self-censorship, one implicit in this essay. It holds that the suppression of information is built into the very organization of the news media in the United States—the marriage, sometimes harmonious, sometimes embattled, between the news media and the centralized

Originally published in Strategies for Communications Research: Annual Review of Communications Research, vol. 6 (1978), R. Hirsch et al. (eds.), reprinted with permission of the publisher, Sage Publications, Beverly Hills/London.

and legitimated institutions upon which reporters and editors rely for information and "facts." By discussing "exceptions" — occasions when newsworkers depart from organizational and professional routines — it explores the general rules through which newsworkers frame their stories to uphold the dominant hegemony. It discusses as well the implications of these exceptions for content analyses of news stories.

Folk wisdom proclaims, "The exception proves the rule." This common saying may be understood to have both popular and scientific meanings. An unusual circumstance highlights the ordinary and expected by providing a contrast. Read as a statement about methods in the social sciences, the folk saying stresses the importance of variation to the generation of social science laws. Especially for those using statistical methods, only the examination of variegated or contrasting categories can lead to generalizations about social order. Validating folk wisdom, Lipset, Trow, and Coleman suggest a use of exceptions by qualitatively inclined researchers.(1) By examining the structure and processes of an exceptional case, one may learn about the customary situation: Thus, Lipset et al. study a democratic union to learn why most unions are not democratic.

This article offers an additional use of the rule–proving exception. It assumes that important components of organizational routines are necessarily hidden from the sociological observer, for routines are built upon understood and frequently unexpressed knowledge of organizational structure, ideologies, and power. Sometimes that knowledge is ineluctable. Participants in an organization may take that knowledge so much for granted that they cannot express it succinctly. Or knowledge may be so embedded in routines that it is hidden from their view. Exceptions enable the observer to perceive and so to examine hidden structures, ideologies, and powers.

For the past few decades, this fundamental insight has been important to the sociological study of mistakes at work.(2) Recently, Molotch and Lester(3) have expanded this idea to the study of political power. They suggest that news routinely promotes occurrences that those with institutionalized power define as public events. It structurally blocks occurrences and information inimicable to those with power. "Only by the accident and the scandal" — the exceptions — "is that political work transcended, allowing access to other information and thus to a basis for practical action . . . directly hostile to those groups who typically manage the political state."(4) By studying how accidents and scandals are made into routine events, Molotch and Lester suggest, one may study the processes of political power.(5) To take an example still unfolding when they published these articles, the Watergate scandal was transformed from an accidentally uncovered and illegal occurrence to a lesson in democracy. First viewed as an illustration of corruption and the abuse of power, it was later interpreted as proof that the news media, courts, and Congress protect the integrity of the American system of government.

Molotch and Lester's work emphasizes the importance of routines in constituting the everyday world, including the world called "news." Incorporating Garfinkel's(6) analysis of a clinic's account of suicides as a "bad record" and Tuchman's(7) analysis of news as a routinely constructed account, they stress that events are formed by the way they are processed. The rest of this article will develop that insight. First, I will describe how the everyday activities of professionals working in organizations make news. Second, I will apply the use of exceptions to portrayals of power. Throughout, I will discuss the use of exceptions to the rule by engaging in sociological analysis, rather than by making explicit comments about methods. The third section of this chapter is explicitly methodological, raising questions derived from the use of exceptions as an analytic tool.

Throughout this article, I draw upon examples gathered at three news organizations at which I was a participant-observer and upon a set of extended interviews at other news organizations. These are: a television station in a major market observed from 1966 to 1968; a daily newspaper with a circulation of over 200,000 observed from 1967 to 1968; the press room at New York's City Hall, with emphasis upon the City Hall bureau of a major New York daily, observed in the fall of 1975 and winter of 1976; and interviews with reporters covering the women's movement for major New York City daily newspapers undertaken in summer of 1975.(8) Throughout the discussion I will distinguish between occurrences and events. Following Molotch and Lester,(9) "occurrences" are amorphous happenings in the everyday world. "Events" are occurrences given meaningful structure as news or potential news.

HOW ROUTINES MAKE NEWS

The professed goal of any news organization is to provide accounts of significant and interesting events. Although apparently a straightforward aim, like many other seemingly simple phenomena, this goal is inextricably complex. The everyday world — the source of news accounts — is composed of a "glut of occurrences," many identifying themselves as significant news events for some individual or group. News organizations must sort these claims of occurrences. Minimally, sorting entails recognizing that an occurrence is an event and not a random happenstance the shape and character of which elude capture. The task of sorting is made more difficult by an added demand of occurrences.

Each occurrence can claim to be idiosyncratic — a particular conjunction of social, economic, political, and psychological forces that formed an occurrence into "this particular occurrence" and not into any other existing or having existed in the everyday world. Accepting this claim for all occurrences is an organizational impossibility. Like any other complex organization, a news medium cannot process idiosyncratic phenomena. It must reduce all phenomena to constructed classifications, much as hospitals "reduce" each patient to sets of symptoms and diseases, and teachers view individual students in terms of categories pertinent to learning. Any organization that sought to process each and every phenomenon as a thing in itself would be so flexible that it would be unrecognizable as a formal organization. Some mean between flexibility and rigidity must be attained.(10)

Together, these demands of the glut of occurrences suggest that news organizations must fulfill three tasks (among others) in order to provide news accounts: (1) they must be able to recognize that an occurrence (including an exceptional one) is a news event; (2) they must facilitate modes of reporting events that discount each occurrence's demand for idiosyncratic treatment and processing; and (3) work must be scheduled in time and space so that recognizable news events can be routinely encountered and processed. These tasks are inter-related. Modes of reporting are tools for revealing an occurrence to be a viable news event. Conventions arising from the scheduling of work call forth different modes of reporting. Accordingly, by enabling the second and third tasks to be accomplished, routines simultaneously recognize and reconstitute everyday occurrences in the everyday world as news. They make news.

Scheduling Work

The news organization's scheduling of work in time and space is an institutionalized news net.(11) It scatters reporters at civic, state, national, and (sometimes) international sites where legitimated institutions are expected to generate news events. For instance, even small papers have a police and criminal justice beat and assign a specific reporter to attend to the activities of local government.

Spreading a news net accomplishes several things. First, the arrangement ensures that events generated by the covered institutions will be caught by the net's grid. Second, because beat reporters consider their task to be filing a daily story, reporters will promote some occurrences as events in order to have a story to write. To be sure, not all such stories will be disseminated. But generating and writing them provide fodder with which to fill a newspaper's columns or a television station's air time. Furthermore, the stories are an economic investment. A news editor may be loath to discard a suitable story for which the news organization has essentially prepaid (by paying the reporter's salary or investing in film), when the alternative is searching for an occurrence that might not pan out as recognizable news. Each inch of space (or second of time) occupied by news of an event located at an institutional beat represents an inch or second that will not be allocated to news happenings at an uncovered location. Because the news net uses a finite number of reporters, its mesh necessarily contains gaps. Some occurrences, particularly those generated by social movements and grass-roots organizations, will escape through these gaps and thus will not be defined as news.

The news net also has temporal gaps. Just as definable news events are expected to occur at some institutional locations, but not at other sites, so too, news events are expected to cluster during normal business hours, 9 A.M. to 6 P.M. weekdays. During these hours, news organizations have the bulk of their reporters and photographers available to cover stories. An occurrence happening before or after these hours must present a clear claim to characterization as a news event in order to justify allocating a reporter to cover it. Sending a reporter to an occurrence whose definition as news is marginal may seriously deplete the supply of reporters on hand should a more readily identifiable news event emerge from the glut of occurrences. The consequences of temporal scheduling are similar to those generated by the news organization's use of space. Some occurrences cannot become news.

However, concentrating reporters' working hours cannot ensure a temporal anchoring of the news net. A comparison makes this clearer. Providing more doctors than usual in a hospital's emergency room on weekend and holiday nights does not guarantee that the seriously ill or wounded will receive adequate medical treatment. To facilitate such treatment, hospitals institute special routines. For instance, they may schedule all elective surgery(12) before 5 P.M. on weekdays. Schedules also take into account the amount of time customarily required by the expected surgical procedures. What appears to be a personal medical emergency to a patient is thus rendered as routine by the hospital so that it may plan the use of both personnel and physical resources and so control the flow of work. When allocating resources each week, some hospitals even check the list of critical patients to estimate the kind and amount of work to be expected by the morgue's personnel.(13)

Just as hospital personnel differentiate among diseases according to their demands for organizational resources, news personnel must anticipate the claims events may make of their resources. To control work, news organizations have developed typifications of events as news stories. Their most important distinction is between hard and soft news.(14)

Most hard news stories concern prescheduled events (a debate on a legislative bill) or unscheduled events (a fire). Reporters and editors do not decide when stories about prescheduled and unscheduled events are to be disseminated. But they do decide when to gather and disseminate information about nonscheduled events. (A nonscheduled event is one whose date of dissemination as news is determined by news personnel.) Most soft news stories concern nonscheduled events. Members of the news enterprise almost always control the timing and flow of work required to process them. For instance, a reporter may be assigned to a story about Valentine's Day several days in advance, and the specific information to be included in the story may be gathered, written, and edited well before its eventual dissemination.

Clearly, decisions to carry items about prescheduled and nonscheduled events facilitate the organization's control of work. Knowing that a reporter will be attending a trial on next Tuesday helps both reporter and editors to plan what next Wednesday's news coverage will be. The ability to predict also has personal and professional components for the reporter: He or she may plan which reportorial techniques to draw upon to cover the story and still accomplish such mundane but necessary tasks as chatting with potential sources. Most important, anticipating what will happen next week — using prediction to control the flow of work — has two important consequences. First, it has a direct influence on the assessment of individual occurrences as news. Second, it influences the mode or tone of the eventual news report.

Scheduling's Impact on the Assessment of Events

One impact of the scheduling of work upon the assessment of routines has already been considered. The anchoring of the news net in time and space prevents some occurrences from being noticed. Having escaped the grid used to predict the flow of work, they cannot become news.

Additionally, events that have defied the predictions of news experts are valued more than those that are expected. Termed "what-a-stories," for the gleeful expressions with which they are greeted, events defying both news predictions and the staff's common stock of taken-for-granted knowledge generate "emergency routines." The term emergency routine appears to be internally contradictory. Yet, when a what-a-story occurs, everyone knows what is to be done. That a what-a-story is routine is forcefully indicated by the reaction of a TV anchorman reporting to work in the midafternoon of the day Robert Kennedy died. (Other staff members were called in at 6 A.M.; the anchorman arrived late so that he would still look fresh on the 11 P.M. newscast.) Entering the newsroom, he asked, "Did we gather the usual reaction?" An apt comparison is the hospital's emergency routine for cases of cardiac arrest.

Scheduling's Impact on Modes of Reporting

Modes of reporting are associated with scheduling. Designated important because it defies prediction, a what-a-story receives larger headlines and more intensive coverage than other news events of comparable historic urgency. Size of headline and extensiveness of coverage may be said to represent the mode in which a what-a-story is routinely handled. Its headline screams. But screams may blur into everyday routines, just as the urgent appeal of a newscaster interrupting an entertainment program to announce a plane crash sounds less urgent every time it is experienced.

Again, a comparison with hospitals helps. Sudnow reports that hospital drivers were instructed to sound their ambulance sirens when approaching the emergency room with an expected "dead-on-arrival."(15) Supposedly, medical staff would scurry to revive the technically dead and near-dead. Instead, recognizing the driver's skill at assigning death, doctors lingered over coffee, requiring a particularly long siren before they would meet the ambulance's patient. Modes of reacting to the expected and unexpected become routine; they decrease any individual's or event's claim to idiosyncratic processing.

The tendency to discount claims to idiosyncratic treatment is even clearer in the case of hard news and soft news. Although both kinds of accounts may be factual (in the sense that observers could agree that a certain phenomenon did happen in a certain way at a certain time in a certain place), both need not be treated with reportorial conventions associated with objectivity. Rather, reporters and editors use one set of reportorial techniques on hard news stories and routinely abandon those conventions when processing soft news. For instance, writing a hard news story, the reporter will lead with the most important "facts"; writing a soft news story, he or she may not do this.(16) Filming a hard news story(17) a TV cameraman will avoid tampering with the time-rhythm of the phenomenon being filmed.(18) At least he will not film in slow motion.(19) But slow motion and fast motion are frequently used to achieve special effects when filming soft news stories.

Ultimately, knowledge of routine modes of processing different kinds of news stories enables reporters to work more efficiently. Significantly, reporters and editors identify this knowledge with professionalism. For them, professionalism — a method of controlling work — consists of mastering techniques of writing appropriate to hard and soft news stories. Mastery also includes knowing what questions must be asked of what sources to elicit "facts" that should appear in the eventual story. In so doing, professionalism also limits the occurrences that may come to be defined as news events.

Knowing what questions to ask promotes trained incapacity. Assuming that certain facts will be associated with certain kinds of stories means other "facts" delineating a different or even contradictory reality will be ignored. What are held to be the "facts" differentiate this occurrence from all other occurrences inasmuch as "facts" are associated with definitions of reality. By training reporters to search for some "facts," news organizations and the news profession may make reporters incapable of seeing what's really going on.

Two contrasting examples may help to clarify this point. Mastery of techniques used to cover occurrences in political institutions may hamper reporters faced with occurrences promoted by social movements. Political institutions generate scheduled events whose actors are frequently familiars of reporters. When reporters witness or learn of such events, they can assess their eventual ramifications and attribute a "plot" to the events as stories. Sometimes the same plot will be given to seemingly different events. For instance, New York City Hall reporters commented that the "story" of New York's fiscal crisis remained the same as it marched from City Hall to Albany and eventually to Washington, D.C. In each case, it was the story of impending disaster, like the threat of an earthquake or tornado. A City Hall bureau chief told me that the day New York City was expected to default, reporters were scattered in the pattern used for natural disasters.

Another example of the attribution of a plot was provided by a New York Times reporter's discussion of political coverage. She felt that male political reporters cover the conventions of the National Women's Political Caucus the same way they cover men's conventions, "only they talk about the women in front [on the podium] instead of talking about men." By applying this plot rather than exploring the other possibilities, the reporters force the story into a possible inapplicable mold.(20)

Concentrating on familiar stories in new forms makes it difficult for reporters, and possibly readers, to deal with issues. As Phillips puts it:

Craft-related habits of mind, such as dependence upon (professional) "instinct," the logic of the concrete, a present time orientation, and an emphasis on contingent events rather than structural necessities, serve to bias(21) the presentation of news. Externally imposed constraints (e.g., regularly scheduled telecasts) and organizational pressures to routinize work combine with the journalist's tendency to view the day's events as discrete, unrelated facts to produce the news mosaic of surface reality. . . Linkages between events are not suggested . . . the news gives the feeling that there is novelty without change.(22)

Covering an issue, such as the emergence of the Women's Political Caucus and the interaction among problem-oriented factions, requires more digging for information by a reporter and goes against the grain of externally imposed constraints and organizational pressures. It also relegates issues to soft news.

Equally important, proponents of an issue may make their case by offering a world view alien to reporters' event orientation. Halloren et al. report that London peace marchers protesting British support of the American-Vietnamese War carried signs about inflation and higher taxes, problems they associated with British foreign policy.(23) Rather than understanding those pickets as components of a sophisticated analysis, reporters read them as indications of a haphazard (nonevent-oriented) approach.

A New York Times reporter provided another example of this trained incapacity. She was assigned to keep track of the women's movement during the early 1970s — a period of turmoil involving squabbles about such issues as lesbianism, broadening minority participation, methods of converging consciousness raising into political action, and defining the movement's next arena of assault on sexism. Speaking of this period, the reporter said, "There were a lot of interesting things going on, but I couldn't nail them down. There was formless kind of talk. I could see things changing, but it was hard to put my finger on it and say to the metropolitan desk, 'This is what's happening.'"(24)

In both cases, the event orientation implicit in routine reportorial techniques blinded reporters to issues.(25) In the second case, professionalism prevented the reporter from realizing that an amorphous happening may be viewed as a defined event and so may yield a viable news story.

In sum, routines intended to control work help define what may be seen as news. Through the anchoring of the news net, through typifications associated with modes of reporting, and through professional techniques, routines enable some occurrences to emerge as news, but banish others from public consideration.

EXCEPTIONS AND POWER

In the previous discussion, I have had to refer to some exceptions to routine in order to clarify news practices. For each instance, I spoke of occurrences that escape the news net, those that challenge the reporter's understanding of previous events and those promoted by agents with world views alien to those of newsworkers, such as the British march against the American-Vietnamese War. In and of themselves, such references indicate that learning of exceptions of customary practices elucidates the rules of newswork: By temporarily suspending agreements about how work is done, exceptions may reveal the taken-for-granted basis of decision making as the researcher observes everyday practices.(26)

Technical Skills and Understandings of Power

Informants' discussions of exceptions and mistakes in techniques used to gather and write stories may reveal aspects of power within the news organization and simultaneously demonstrate ways that the news organization, as a societal force, is allied with other powerful institutions. The following three examples illustrate how accepted professional techniques also serve to mask understanding of organizational and political power. Each example involves the same basic technical skill, the choice of a lead or first sentence for a story. Leads are central to the definition of an occurrence as an event. In the first two examples, an ambitious young black reporter with weak alliances within his news organization bucks authority. In the third, a powerful senior reporter goes against dominant inter-pretations of an occurrence.

A City Hall reporter, assigned to tour a city prison with a committee of the city council, chose not to write a story about the prisoners' complaints.(27) As he tortured over his typewriter to produce a lead before abandoning the attempt, he explained that the event he witnessed violated his editors' preconceptions of the story. He wished to write about the prisoners' view that judicial practices of setting bail violate the Bill of Rights. The reporter stressed that city council members and other reporters could not "even hear" the constitutional complaints skillfully articulated by the prisoners.(28) Furthermore, he reasoned, his editors would demand an article about prison conditions, because a powerful reporter, popular with the editors, had previously penned and published a lengthy news analysis blaming conditions at the prison for a recent riot there. Once a police reporter, this powerful reporter had drawn upon his contact with those institutional sources to gather his information and so turn a riot from an occurrence into a news event.(29) Turning in the story he wished to write would also be problematic, the City Hall reporter reasoned, because another article he had written recently, on violations of teachers' civil rights, had prompted an editorial dispute. The editor who opposed it has since received a promotion.

The reporter decided it was more judicious for him not to file the story he wished to write than to buck authority once more; he could not bring himself to file the expected story.

It is possible that this refusal to file contributed to the following dispute about a lead sentence in which the same reporter's technical skill was questioned. The reporter was assigned to rewrite a press release into a short news item. (Such a task is frequently reserved for inexperienced reporters, not those who, like this man, could boast several years' experience.) Editing the copy, the bureau chief instructed the reporter to convert his lead into a second-day lead, a generalizing sentence that frames an occurrence in terms of an ongoing event.(30) Lead sentences of experienced reporters are rarely challenged, yet the reporter made the change without voicing his objection. When the city editor received the revised copy, he telephoned the reporter to request a first-day lead. At this point, the reporter explained he had originally written a first-day lead and the bureau chief had challenged his judgment. After learning of the city editor's phone call (the copy boy gossiped about it), the bureau chief apologized to his reporter for getting him in dutch with the city editor.

The apparently felt need for an apology suggests that the attribution of basic technical skills depends upon status in the organizational hierarchy. To be sure, to equate reputation for technical skills with status in an organization seems tautological. Yet the reporter claimed he had not been subject to such basic critiques before filing his story on teachers' civil rights and bucking the hierarchy. Apparently he felt that the critique arose from the melding of office politics with disputes about civil liberties.(31)

An incident about a lead sentence involving the top political reporter at a different newspaper affirms that framing a lead depends upon taken-for-granted professional views, such views drawing upon news personnel's ongoing familiarity with official sources.(32) Covering the 1968 New Hampshire primary, the top political reporter had led a story with the statement that President Johnson "is running scared" in his contest with Eugene McCarthy. Despite this reporter's reputation as a specialist, editors challenged and changed the lead. They argued that a president not even officially on the ballot could not "run scared" because of the institutional resources at his command. In this instance, professional news judgment seemed also to reinforce the interests of the more powerful.

That the lead sentence of a high-status reporter was changed enables tentative but more specific formulations about connections between news routines and societal power. It suggests, as Molotch and Lester put it, that professional practices defining occurrences are practices permitted to survive by those with societal power.(33) Historical proof of this assessment is difficult, if not impossible, to locate. However, exceptions to the rule provide evidence of a derivative generalization: Organizational and professional practices entail the stratification of access to the news as a social resource. Those with the most economic and political power in the society have the most access to news processes and the most power over reporters. Those with the least economic and political power in the society are subject to the power of reporters. Although implied and captured by the distinction between event orientation of institutions and reporters and the issue orientation of social movements and reformers, this generalization is directly experienced when exceptions to news practices are uncovered.

Exceptions and Access to News

Reporters are themselves quick to point to several kinds of exceptions to professional practices. Foremost among these is the business-office or front-office "must." Such stories must be carried because they have been requested by an advertiser or a friend of someone well placed in the news organization's managerial hierarchy.

Critics of news practices cite the obverse phenomenon.(34) News organizations are more apt to report about public institutions than powerful private ones. For instance, the New York City media criticize spending at units of the City University, but not at Columbia University or New York University. They discuss waste at the municipal hospitals, but not at Columbia University's Presbyterian Hospital or Cornell's New York Medical Center. This practice is pertinent, because the media's distinction between public and private institutions is at best weak and at worst fallacious. The private institutions receive federal grants; the private hospitals are heavily financed by Medicaid and Medicare funds. A portion of New York State's budget for higher education is earmarked for the so-called private institutions.(35) By maintaining the distinction between private and public, the news media mask the actual economic organization of significant services. They enable so-called private institutions not to make news, much as in an earlier day, members of the upper class sought to keep their names out of the papers except for birth, marriage, and death announcements.

standards may be taken for granted as absolute, as being as clear as day.

Other researchers have departed somewhat from the idea that "newsworthiness" is an absolute, as measurable as the frequencies of discernible light. Roscho put it this way: Definitions of what is newsworthy depend upon people's attitudes; those attitudes in turn are formed by a society's institutional arrangements.(45) Although this theoretical rendition specifies that standards of newsworthiness are socially determined and may change, it too is blind to the way identifications of newsworthiness are themselves a function of reportorial and editorial routines incorporating allegiances to the powerful. Roscho's rendition deflects criticisms of the media. Rather than seeking to introduce social change by studying the activities of media organizations and so locating the media as potential loci of social change, he turns to individual and collective attitudes.

The following passage places the responsibility for changing the media upon the consumers of news:

> The American daily press has a constant potential for social subversion. Its institutional bias as a merchant of the novel and unexpected makes it an instrument for popularizing new attitudes and behaviors. If these deviant ways of thinking and acting are taken up by sizeable segments of the mass-media audience, the consequences are institutional change, revised social values, the restructuring of newsmen's frame of references, and redefinition of who and what is newsworthy.(46)

In this quotation, those seeking to introduce change are "deviant." Identified as unusual (like that old reportorial hacksaw, the man who bit the dog, and who or what is the stuff and substance of soft news), they may sneak into the news. But genuine social change is not to be dismissed as the results of novelty. Pushed by human actors, social change runs its inexorable course as conflicts are introduced by contradictions in social institutions. Identifying seekers of change as novelties and thus relegating them to occasional soft news stories is therefore problematic. It is an extension of newsworkers' professional ideology inasmuch as it directs newsworkers to identify important happenings with established institutions and unusual happenings with deviants.

To be sure, that this statement is an extension of newsworkers' professional ideology is implied, not stated. But it is an uncritical adoption of newsworkers' evaluations, including their refusal to draw connections between events.(47)

Without reflecting upon the use of such important distinctions as hard and soft news to simplify the everyday world for organizational processing, it incorporates them in communications theory. Also, like newsworkers, it locates ultimate responsibility for the nature of newswork with institutions other than the news media. Under the Nixon administration, the news media certainly needed to be defended against coordinated government assault.(48) But there is a difference between defending the First Amendment and launching an apologia, especially if theorists are to understand the role of the media in contemporary society.

It is not sufficient to cite the much-validated theory that the communications media of any society support those in power. To implement changes, one must understand how that support is accomplished by specifying the workings of the media. To this end, I have suggested that exceptions to the rule uncovered through participant observation facilitate an understanding of how news routines make news. Identification of organizational and professional routines and exceptions reveals that an occurrence is not necessarily newsworthy, for there is no objective standard of newsworthiness against which events may be assessed. Instead, the anchoring of the news net, typifications, and professionally sanctioned skills merge to make news.

EXCEPTIONS AND THE RULE

Although observational studies of the media are becoming increasingly common,(49) much communication research is still based upon content analysis. A research method may be used to explore and test different theories, but historically one assumption often accompanies content analysis: The content of the media reflects social values and changing social structures.

This discussion poses several problems for the use of content analysis. First, one may only code material that has been disseminated. Cardinal Cushing's complete remarks on King's death are not available to the coder (although the importance of its omission depends on the research topic). Second, each item is coded by the same standards and according to the same set of categories. Any datum is not and cannot be considered in and of itself. Third, if one wished to comment on kinds of content that are either omitted or underrepresented, one must have some standard against which to compare the published (or televised) material, such as earlier content analyses or some set of independent "facts" about the present.

A variety of solutions have been offered to the problem of finding a standard of comparison. Janowitz commends the use of trend data, particularly when coupled with economic indices.(50) Together, he suggests, a cultural index and an economic index enable substantive statements about emerging social problems.

Gerbner and Gross view content analyses as "cultural indicators" when teamed with survey data about audience response to televised content.(51)   Both sets of data enable comments about social values. Molotch and Lester locate a standard internal to the media,(52) comparing local news reports and national reports to discuss the dispersion of information.(53)   Yet, despite the ingenuity used to find a standard, most researchers still agree that jumping from content analyses to statements about either the structure or the effects of the media is a very tricky business.(54)   That trickiness is clarified by the problem of omission and the problem of standardization.   Whether these are serious issues is, of course, dependent upon the research topic and the theories being tested.

The Problem of Omission

    If one uses the content of the mass media to document the path of social movements, this problem is severe.   Access to the mass media is stratified and least open to those often involved in the early stages of a social movement — the powerless.(55) If a social movement increasingly recruits middle-class and upper-class participants, access will increase.(56)   Furthermore, when the activities of wealthy individuals run counter to the interests of corporations, corporations are better equipped politically to promote their events as news.(57)
    Does the alteration in the pattern of media reports about a social movement indicate change in the quantity of movement activities or in the characteristics of participants, or is it anchored in news practices?   Are all three of these factors compounded?   If so, how?   The last and most likely alternative clearly indicates the dangers of using content analysis alone to study past and present events.

The Problem cf Standardization

    Kraus, et al. have argued that studying key events, such as the John Kennedy assassination, a presidential election, or the Watergate scandal, reveals more about media coverage and American values than content analysis of usual events.(58) Paralleling the psychological theory that key events may foster change (by helping individuals in some new way), they suggest that certain public events prompt new public behaviors and activities.   Unfortunately, standardized content analysis may obscure key events by submerging them in the pattern of qualitatively dissimilar coverage.   Standardization obscures exceptions to the rule, whether or not they would have been recognized as exceptions by newsworkers or observers. And exceptions to the rule may ultimately reveal how the rule operates.

Identifying problems associated with content analysis does not mean that the technique should be abandoned. But it does call for increased sophistication in the use of that method as well as increased awareness of the dangers of generalization. It also suggests the wisdom of using additional methods to validate statements based upon content analysis.

Both theoretically and methodologically, the story that does not get disseminated or that requires special handling may tell more about news processes and American society than published and broadcast stories can. The event that prompts emergency routines may elucidate everyday routines more than other happenings do. Exceptions are a necessary tool in the collection and analysis of observational data. They prove the rule.

These exceptions prove too that the suppression of information is not necessarily deliberate or even conscious, although the exceptions cited here are sufficiently conscious to enable articulation. Rather, the very processes of newswork contain procedures for framing the world that uphold the offices of those in power and the groups that hold power, even if they challenge the competence or integrity of individuals. The news media, any news medium, serve the political, social, and economic interests that dominate a society. Sometimes such service is guaranteed by explicit government interference, by censorship. But in the United States, at least, service of the status quo is built into the very procedures used to define and to process the news.

NOTES

1. S.M. Lipset, M. Trow and J.A. Coleman, Union Democracy (Glencoe, Illinois: Free Press, 1956).

2. See E.C. Hughes, Men and Their Work (Glencoe, Illinois: Free Press, 1964); D. Light Jr., "Psychiatry and Suicide: The Management of a Mistake," American Journal of Sociology 77 (5) (1972): 821-38; and J. Stelling and R. Bucher, "Vocabularies of Realism in Professional Socialization," Social Science and Medicine 7 (1973): 661-73.

3. H. Molotch and M. Lester, "News as Purposive Behavior: On the Strategic Use of Routine Events, Accidents and Scandals," American Sociological Review 39 (1974): 101-12.

4. "Accidents are unplanned occurrences which are promoted by a party other than the agent who inadvertently caused the underlying occurrences. . . . A scandal involves a deliberately planned occurrence which is promoted by a party different than the occurrence's agent." Ibid., pp. 109-10.

5. H. Molotch and M. Lester, "Accidental News: The Great Oil Spill," American Journal of Sociology 81 (1975): 235–60.

6. H. Garfinkel, Studies in Ethnomethodology (Englewood Cliffs, New Jersey: Prentice-Hall, 1967).

7. G. Tuchman, "Objectivity as Strategic Ritual: An Examination of Newsmen's Notions of Objectivity," American Journal of Sociology 77: (4) (1972): 660–79.

8. The collection of data at the City Hall press room and the analysis of data from the City Hall press room and from interviews with the women's movement reporters were funded by the Russell Sage Foundation. Some of the data presented here have been published elsewhere, as indicated where appropriate. Their present use represents a conceptual extension and integration of my previous work.

9. H. Molotch and M. Lester, "News as Purposive Behavior."

10. See J. March and H. Simon, Organizations (New York: John Wiley, 1958).

11. See G. Tuchman, "Telling Stories," Journal of Communication 26 (4) (1976): 93–97; and M. Fishman, News of the World: What Happened and Why, Ph.D. Dissertation, University of California, Santa Barbara, 1975.

12. An important empirical question is how medical personnel distinguish between elective and non-elective surgery.

13. D. Sudnow, Passing On: The Social Organization of Death and Dying (Englewood Cliffs, New Jersey: Prentice-Hall, 1967).

14. G. Tuchman, "Making News by Doing Work: Routinizing the Unexpected," American Journal of Sociology 79 (1) (1973): 110–31.

15. D. Sudnow, Passing On.

16. G. Tuchman, "Objectivity as Strategic Ritual."

17. G. Tuchman, "The Technology of Objectivity: Doing Objective Television News," Urban Life and Culture 2 (1973): 3–26.

18. The term cameraman is used because occupants of this job are overwhelmingly male. The supposed justification is the weight of sound cameras; however, appreciably more men than women are being trained to use the new lightweight portable minipack cameras.

19. Some exceptions that prove the rule are cited in G. Tuchman, "The Technology of Objectivity."

20. This example is discussed further in G. Tuchman, "The Newspaper as a Social Movement's Resource," in Hearth and Home: Images of Women in the Mass Media, G. Tuchman, A.K. Daniels, and J. Benet, eds. (New York: Oxford University Press, 1978).

21. The term bias must be understood in the loosest possible sense. See G. Tuchman, "Objectivity as Strategic Ritual."

22. E.B. Phillips, "Novelty Without Change," Journal of Communication 26 (4) (1976): 87-92.

23. H. Halloren, P. Elliott and J. Murdoch, Demonstrations and Communication: A Case Study (London: Penguin, 1970).

24. Another possible interpretation is that reportorial professionalism could only view this story as either soft news requiring digging or as non-news. To quote Phillips, "ambiguities, developments in flux, and contradictions tend to be non-news." ("Novelty Without Change," p. 92.) I use this example to argue that professionalism prevents reporters from viewing "developments in flux" as news because such developments do not fit into reportorial frames designed to convert occurrences into stories.

25. See G. Tuchman, "The Newspaper as a Social Movement's Resource."

26. Theoretically, the term decision making is inappropriate. My data suggest that routines are so emcompassing that formal decisions are not made. Newsworkers "merely" do what is "natural." By refusing to reflect upon their practical activities, (cf. Phillips, "Novelty Without Change" and Tuchman, "Objectivity as Strategic Ritual") they eschew formal decisions between alternative outcomes. An analogy makes this clearer. The newsworkers are in the position of a man in a shoe store deciding among extra pairs of black shoes and brown shoes. He may not question why he needs to buy extra shoes at all.

27. See G. Tuchman, "Telling Stories."

28. Those complaints were in the last paragraphs of stories written for two other daily newspapers.

29. The reporter transforms a riot into the riot; a happening is publicly defined as the or this riot having specific particulars or characteristics.

30. The reporter was told to speak of a possible hike in taxi fares in terms of added expenses for citizens already beset by New York's fiscal crisis.

31. The reporter's close colleagues tended to affirm his view.

32. I am using the term familiarity in two senses. Reporters and editors have knowledge of institutions through their experiences on beats. Also, institutional sources are their "familiars"; because of ongoing contracts, reporters may trust sources' evaluation of occurrences if the sources have a record of success at predicting shifts of power within institutions. Thus, the police sources used to write the original story about prison conditions as the cause of the riot were known to that reporter.

33. H. Molotch and M. Lester, "Accidental News: The Great Oil Spill."

34. Fred Goldner reminded me of this phenomenon.

35. In the mid-1970s , their share of monies increased, while the funding of City University decreased.

36. See W. Porter, The Assault on the Media: The Nixon Years (Ann Arbor: University of Michigan Press, 1976).

37. W. Breed, "Mass Communication and Social-Cultural Integration," Social Force 37 (1958): 109-16.

38. Everett C. Hughes pointed this out to me in 1968. See also H. Molotch and M. Lester, "News as Purposive Behavior" and "Accidental News: The Great Oil Spill."

39. C. Bernstein and B. Woodward, All the President's Men (New York: Simon & Schuster, 1974), cited by B. Wise, The Politics of Lying (New York: Vintage Press, 1973).

40. G. Tuchman, "Objectivity as Strategic Ritual."

41. This beat is also discussed in Tuchman, "Ridicule, Advocacy and Professionalism: A Newspaper's Reporting of a Social Movement," delivered at the meetings of the American Sociological Association, 1976. Phillips' observation that developments in flux tend to be non-news may also apply here. See Phillips, "Novelty Without Change."

42. See also G. Tuchman, "Objectivity as Strategic Ritual."

43. Nonetheless, the news repertoire includes stories like this one would have been. They are frequently run on Sundays when the large number of advertisements and Saturday's lack of hard news require stories to be fillers. Phillips points out that newsworkers are committed to "facts," not "truth." ("Novelty Without Change.")

44. G. Tuchman, "Objectivity as Strategic Ritual."

45. B. Roshco, Newsmaking (Chicago: University of Chicago Press, 1975).

46. Ibid.

47. E.B. Phillips, "Novelty Without Change."

48. W. Porter, The Assault on the Media.

49. See D. Altheide, Creating Reality: How TV News Distorts Events (Beverly Hill, Calif.: Sage, 1976); M. Fishman, News of the World: What Happened and Why, Ph.D. Dissertation, University of California, Santa Barbara, 1975; M. Lester, News as a Practical Accomplishment: A Conceptual and Empirical Analysis of Newswork, Unpublished Ph.D. Dissertation, University of California, Santa Barbara, 1975; L. Engwall, Travels in Newspaper Country, Unpublished manuscript, Uppsala, Sweden: University of Uppsala, Department of Business Administration, 1976; R. Geles and R. Faulkner, Time and Television Newswork, Unpublished manuscript, 1976; and H. Halloran et al., Demonstrations and Communication: A Case Study (London: Penguin, 1976).

50. M. Janowitz, "Content Analysis and the Study of Sociopolitical Change," Journal of Communication 26 (4) 1976: 10-21.

51. G. Gerbner and L. Gross, "The Scary World of TV's Heavy Viewer," Psychology Today, April 1976: 41-45, 89.

52. Analyses comparing the content of one medium (magazine or newspaper) to another are relatively common. Generally, the contrasts are based upon the demographic characteristics of each medium's audience.

53. See H. Molotch and M. Lester, "Accidental News: The Great Oil Spill."

54. See M. Janowitz, "Harold Lasswell's Contribution to Content Analysis," Public Opinion Quarterly 32 (1968-69): 643-53; and "Content Analysis and the Study of Sociopolitical Change," Journal of Communication 26 (4) 1976: 10-21.

55. Of course, many social movements have their own media. But these may develop after the movement has gained many recruits.

56. See G. Tuchman, "Beating Around City Hall: Professionalism, Flexibility and the Professional Prerogatives of Reporters." Delivered at the meetings of the American Association of Public Opinion Research, and "The Newspaper as a Social Movement's Resource"; E. Goldenberg, Making the Papers (Lexington, Mass.: D.C. Heath, 1975); and C. Jenkins and C. Perrow, "Insurgency of the Powerless: Farm Worker's Movement," American Sociological Review, 1977.

57. H. Molotch and M. Lester, "Accidental News: The Great Oil Spill."

58. S. Krause, D. Davis, G.E. Lang, and K. Lang, "Critical Events and Analysis," in Political Communication: Issues and Strategies for Research, S. Chaffee, ed. (Beverly Hill, Calif.: Sage, 1976).

CHAPTER 2

Princes' Gate, 1980: The
Media Politics of Siege
Management in Britain

BY PHILIP SCHLESINGER

Now that the euphoria following the Iranian Embassy
siege has abated, the doubters step in. But where you
ask? In letter columns of the Guardian, we answer.
Yesterday that newspaper published a fascinating array
of letters which pose some very proper questions. One
complains his televised snooker was interrupted by the
coup de grâce of the siege, and we sympathise;
another grumbles about the role of television in the
affair, and here there must be at least one embryonic
thesis.(1)

The siege at the Iranian Embassy in Princes' Gate,
Kensington, between April 30 and May 5, 1980 was a media event
par excellence, covered from the outset by a veritable circus of
newsmen. It had a bloody conclusion: For the first time the
elite Special Air Services regiment (SAS) was used in an overt
police action on the British mainland and killed five of the six
hostage-taking gunmen. Millions of British television viewers
watched the dénouement live. For many media professionals, such
as Alan Protheroe, the BBC's Editor of Television News, it was
one of television's "finest hours"(2) and a "definitive example of
just how high standards of broadcast journalism really are in this
country."(3) Others were less enchanted and had serious doubts
about the value of the television reporting. The novelist John
Le Carré, eschewing Protheroe's sub-Churchillian rhetoric,
pointed out that both television channels actually failed to

Originally published in Screen Education, Winter 1980/1981,
no. 37. We are grateful to Philip Schlesinger and to the editor
of Screen Education for permission to republish this article.

interpret correctly what was going on during the busting of the siege, and that

> the ITN commentator risked a most perilous theory about what was going on: a disaster theory, a theory of total ignominious failure on the part of the authorities. Assuming — as many of us benighted viewers did assume — that the explosions had been set off by the captors, he floated the idea that the captors had been panicked by the sight of masked men on the outside of the building.(4)

The BBC's commentary was even less informative. Indeed, the moment of the siege-busting made the limitations of television actuality programming plain for all to see. In the excitement of seeing it "for real," one is apt to forget how important was the absence of interpretation.

John Le Carré puts television's communication failure down to the confusion of the reporters, a fact which needs some explanation. The available evidence suggests that the broadcasters were actually in a position to know broadly what was going on at the time it was happening. It also seems that they — at least senior editors, particularly in the BBC — had received briefings on government policy and were aware of the likely outcome of the siege. These contentions are documented below. Commenting on the television coverage, Broadcast (the television and radio industries' journal) observed how both ITN and BBC news "went live from the scene only after SAS men stormed the building, amidst fire and explosions." The moment of entry was videotaped, and ITN's report began four and half minutes after this, and the BBC's only after eight minutes. Broadcast speculated:

> Given the close links between the broadcasters and the security forces during the siege, and bearing in mind that the hostages' captors may have had access to a television set inside the embassy, it is likely that the broadcasting organisations were actually warned off going live during this period for fear of giving the game away.(5)

The suggestion that the transmission time was subject to consultation seems well founded. But I am doubtful that the authorities were worried at this stage of the siege about television coverage "giving the game away." There is no evidence from any of the accounts of the siege that television played any significant role in the hostage-takers' monitoring of the responses to their demands. All references to their concern with broadcasting mention radio coverage exclusively. Given the sophisticated monitoring devices being used by the security forces, it would have been known if the captors and their captives had also been watching television. Neither reports so far nor the reconstruction based on hostages' accounts have mentioned this possibility. It is therefore reasonable to assume that control of television coverage of the siege-busting was as much concerned with the information available to the mass audience as to those inside the embassy. (Had they been watching television, they would have known about activities on the roof and the presence of monitoring equipment from the start, as these were disclosed by ITN on "News at Ten" on the first night of the siege.)(6)

These introductory points raise crucial questions about the extent of state control over the media during the siege. They also raise the question of what role was played by the media, and by broadcasting in particular. I shall try to answer these questions, insofar as published sources permit. My aim is not to chart in detail the media coverage of the siege but to bring out the process of control and set this in the context of the British state's strategies for the control of "news about terrorism"(7) during the past decade.

USING THE MEDIA

In the siege at the Iranian Embassy, both the state and the hostage-takers had conscious strategies for making use of the media. The six gunmen who held 26 persons as prisoners in the embassy were members of an autonomist guerrilla movement from the predominantly ethnically Arab area of Iran. This region is called Khuzistan by the Iranian central government and Arabistan by the autonomists. The group's central goal was to draw attention to the oppression and exploitation of their area — the principal source of Iran's oil wealth — by the Khomeini regime. As it is frequently argued that acts of terrorism are inherently irrational, it is worth pointing out that the seizure of the embassy had a clear political rationale.(8) This was explained by "Oan," the leader of the hostage-takers, in an interview conducted by the journalists Moustafa Karkouti and Mohammed Hashir Faruqi, who were also among the hostages:

Question: What is the immediate goal you think you will achieve by carrying out this operation here and now?

Oan: It will be publicity, propaganda and information outside. I realise that this operation or any similar operation which might happen in the future will not achieve our legitimate rights and might not force the Iranian government to grant Arabistan its autonomy, but what we can achieve from this kind of operation is to make our voice heard by world public opinion, especially in the light of the information blockade which the central government in Teheran is encircling us with, in addition to most of the Arab countries as well as the world media.(9)

Apart from this conscious and evidently rational intention to communicate a grievance by using extreme means, the guerrilla group also held certain assumptions about the British media: apparently not realising that "information blockades" are not the sole prerogative of the Iranian government. Moustafa Karkouti, interviewed after the siege, recalled one of his conversations with the gunmen:

They talked about the freedom of speech and said they thought it was more respected in Britain than in the rest of the world. They made it clear that they thought the media here are stronger than anywhere else in the Western world — they believed the British media and the British population would give their cause a fair hearing.(10)

But their conception of the media, in particular during the exceptional circumstances of siege coverage, was naive in the extreme — hardly surprising as they appear to have had virtually no real knowledge of British politics and society. As the British media were, in effect, absorbed into the siege-breaking operations of the state, the Arabistan autonomists did not find it easy to get their message across. For the control of communications is one of the key weapons in the struggle between the security forces and those who challenge the authority of the state by actions of this kind. The account which follows, therefore, necessarily has psychological warfare as one of its central themes. Aside from these two contradictory communicative strategies, there is another way in which the siege is especially illuminating about points of connection between the media and the state. The capture of two BBC Television newsmen, Chris Cramer, a news organiser, and Sim Harris, a sound technician, meant that the BBC was not just a reporter of the action at Princes' Gate, but also an actor of some significance, as I show below. With its own men on the inside, the Corporation's existing special significance to the state was enhanced. The presence of British journalists inside the embassy probably also had a more general effect on the media, encouraging the already considerable co-operation which had been built up in previous years.

The press and broadcasting were subject to general guidelines issued by the police on the second day of the siege. The request for self-censorship by the press went thus:

> During the course of the current hostage situation at the Iranian Embassy, the Commissioner seeks your co-operation in refraining from publishing or broadcasting details of the deployment of personnel in the immediate vicinity of the Embassy or the use of specialist equipment. The publication or broadcast of such information can provide valuable intelligence to the hostage-takers and by so alerting them could seriously jeopardise the safety of the hostages and the success of the operation. The memo will be cancelled as soon as operational circumstances permit.(11)

The insistence that newspapers should not publish such details seems odd, given that the police were not going to allow them into the embassy. It could presumably be justified on the ground that the police wished to control all publicity in case foreign radios picked up information which could assist the gunmen, or alternatively, to prevent press stories from being developed which the British broadcasting media would feel compelled to follow. Broadcasting seems to have been controlled more precisely than the press: "'We worked more than closely with the authorities throughout the siege,' an ITN spokesman said. And the BBC's involvement with the security forces became inevitable as soon as it became clear that two BBC men were actually among the hostages at the beginning."(12)

After the siege, William Whitelaw, the Home Secretary, expressed his satisfaction at the broadcasting media's self-censorship: "Inevitably events such as these are a matter of major public concern. They are bound to be covered by TV and radio. Had there been a moment when it was necessary to ask the authorities to exercise restraint then that restraint would have been asked for. But . . . such an occasion did not in the final event arise."(13) Such co-operativeness did not emerge out of the blue. There has been a long build-up.

THE STATE SECURITY BACKGROUND

The handling of the Iranian Embassy siege cannot be understood in isolation. As the journal State Research has pointed out, it reflects the state's current rethinking of "administrative, policing and military aspects of internal security. Considerations of terrorism and those of demonstrations and strikes have both influenced the outcome."(14) We should therefore look briefly at some recent observations on the emergence of a "strong state" in Britain.

The development of what Nicos Poulantzas has termed an "authoritarian statist" form of rule derives from at least two key intractable problems.(15) First, there is the continuing economic crisis, with its concomitant industrial relations struggles. The current "monetarist experiment" of the Thatcher government involves the restructuring of capital by following the path of mass unemployment. Given this policy, as Andrew Gamble has observed, "if the economy is to remain free, the state has to become strong; and nowhere stronger than in its dealings with organised labour."(16) But although it is under the present administration that the armed forces and the police have been given a more overtly prominent role in countering "subversion," their strengthening began in the not-too-distant Keynesian days, when other economic policies were being pursued. The second key problem is the persistent failure to achieve a solution to the socio-political problems of Northern Ireland.

Against this backdrop, the outlines of Britain's "secret state" (in E. P. Thompson's telling phrase) have become clearer during the past decade. Its significant features include:

- The refurbishing of a "parallel" emergency state apparatus for use against external attack and internal disorder;
- Major shifts in the practice of policing including the emergence of a para-military "third force" and the strengthening of the political police;
- The increased use of high technology surveillance against loosely-defined "subversives" involving, for instance, uncontrolled data-banks and bugging devices;
- The use of official secrecy legislation against journalists;
- Jury-vetting in political trials;
- Restrictions upon, and aggressive policing of, demonstrations and picketing; and
- The trial use of repressive technology and special forces in Northern Ireland and the gradual application of the lessons learned in Britain itself.(17)

Although I cannot survey all the relevant material here, it is worth mentioning in passing that such evidently accelerating repressive tendencies within the liberal-democratic state-form should not be assumed necessarily to be irreversible.(18) But it is certain that without an effort to defend against such encroachments of existing political space, democratic freedoms eventually will be seriously imperilled.

Most relevant for my argument here are some of the changes in the state's emergency apparatus, the increased role of "military aid to the civil power," and the unceasing efforts to control the media, especially broadcasting, in the reporting of political violence. Control of the Iranian Embassy siege was vested in the Civil Contingencies Committee (CCC). This body, called the National Security Committee (NSC) until 1975, was created in 1972 after the government's failure to break the miners' strike. The NSC drew together military, intelligence, police, Home Office, and Department of Trade and Industry personnel and was serviced by a full-time staff. Its tasks were two-fold: "to prepare short-term contingency plans for emergency situations, and to redraw the standing 'War Plan' to meet a possible internal threat to the security of the state."(19) From 1972 to 1975 a National Security Plan was worked out, involving the military, in which preparations for intervention were made for situations ranging from limited strikes to civil war or invasion. As Tony Bunyan points out, this plan is actually "directed at an internal rather than an external enemy" and it basically concerned with effective counter-revolution.(20) The NSC/CCC drew up new guidelines about the occasions on which the Ministry of Defence could assist the police and the civil power. During the Iranian siege the SAS were brought in under the rubric of "military aid to the civil power" (MACP), an arrangement which had been used on previous occasions against armed terrorists.

Although the SAS action at Princes' Gate may have been unprecedented, the use of an elite military unit in an urban action represents no more than the latest stage in the growing co-operation between police and army. The police have become increasingly prominent and vociferous over recent years as they have become involved in confrontations with political demonstrators, trade unionists, and racial minorities, and as various forms of political violence have been encountered and have required suppression. The political imperative to control such "law-and-order" problems has led to the construction of the "third force" which has lately emerged to take up the para-military ground between the army and the more traditional functions of civil policing. Most controversial, probably, has been the activity of the Special Patrol Groups; despite official denials, these are armed para-military units, highly mobile and trained in riot control. But the SPGs are only the most visible part of the new "third force." According to State Research, there are now over 12,000 riot-trained police organised as Police Support Units and there has also been a growth in specialist units such as the anti-terrorism squad and the diplomatic protection group:

The police's answer to providing a "third force" in the UK has been double edged. The anti-terrorist role is carried out by SPGs, newly formed Tactical Firearms Units . . . and, as a last resort, by the army's Special Air Service (SAS). The public order role of a "third force" is undertaken by the Police Support Units and the SPG. Taken together this means that a qualitative change in the role of the police . . . occurred.(21)

It is clear from this analysis that the use of the SAS in extremis should be seen in the context of a drift toward tougher policing in the era of the "technological cop." The higher profile largely forced on the police by social change has created an atmosphere in which the deployment of troops becomes acceptable.

During the past decade, both Labour and Conservative governments have brought the SAS into operations, first in Northern Ireland and now on the British mainland. The SAS's post-war role was primarily in the field of counter-insurgency actions during the gradual dissolution of the empire. It became a bogeyman in Northern Ireland, where it was important both in combat against the IRA and in intelligence work.(22) The SAS's specific anti-terrorist role on the home front dates back to 1972, when the British government, like other Western European administrations, became concerned about the growth of political violence in the aftermath of the Munich Olympics. A special "counter-revolutionary warfare" (CRW) team was developed within the SAS. This was first deployed in Britain during the hijack of an aeroplane from Manchester in January 1975.(23) In December 1975, the SAS were present during the Balcombe Street siege; the mere announcement of their presence was apparently sufficient to make the cornered IRA surrender. In that same month, the "Europeanisation" of the anti-terrorist campaign gathered steam when, at a European Council meeting in Paris, it was decided that the European interior ministers should discuss how to combat terrorism. Meetings were held in June 1976 and in May 1977, and agreement was reached on the exchange of information about terrorism and techniques for dealing with terrorist incidents. The exchange of information and personnel between national security forces was also agreed. The first occasion on which this arrangement came into operation was in October 1977, when an SAS liaison team assisted the West German anti-terrorist unit GSG-9 to bring an end to the Lufthansa aircraft hijack at Mogadishu. Joint military co-operation of this kind would seem to be well-established now. A further instance was the SAS's involvement in the hunt for Aldo Moro, the kidnapped Italian Christian Democratic leader; the West German police also assisted in this.(24) Although it went unreported by the British media, the head of GSG-9, Ulrich Wegener, came to London during the Iranian Embassy siege.(25)

The full-scale commitment of the SAS to a domestic policing role resulted from a decision by the Callaghan government, after the successful military action at Mogadishu, to increase the CRW force substantially:

> From now on, each squadron was committed in turn to the CRW role on rotation, between tours in Northern Ireland and training sessions abroad. The implication of the decision was that Britain was now a potential SAS operational zone in a way not previously contemplated.(26)

The commitment of resources has been significant, with the SAS receiving sophisticated weaponry, more training facilities (such as the "Killing House" where close-quarter battle is practised), and the specialisation of CRW units in "assault" and "perimeter containment."(27) These developments lie behind the dramatic 11-minute SAS action which took place on May 5, 1980.

"LAW-AND-ORDER" NEWS AND THE STATE

State security actions such as the breaking of the Iranian Embassy siege are reported within a specific ideological framework, that of "law-and-order" news. Stuart Hall and his colleagues have pointed out how this form of news has developed during the past decade within the context of a growing "crisis of hegemony" in the British state. The continuing inability of governments to discipline labour and restore adequate profitability to capital has lead towards a more authoritarian structure of rule, aspects of which were outlined earlier. The role of the media in winning consent for this shift from the social democratic consensus to the "exceptional" law-and-order state has been crucial.(28) In a convergent analysis, Steve Chibnall has demonstrated the especial significance of the focus upon "violence" in media discourse — in particular, the way in which it is used to police the boundaries of legitimate dissent. Within the media-created artifact of "the violent society" wildly differing activities, with quite distinct causes, have come to be classified as fundamentally the same, as "violent." This "mugging," the Angry Brigade bombings, IRA terror campaigns, criminal shootings of the police, football hooliganism, picketing, and political demonstrations are represented within the dominant media discourse as the symptoms of an underlying social malaise — one for which the big stick of coercion becomes an increasingly attractive policy option.(29)

Winning consent for actions like those taken by the SAS at Princes' Gate involves an exceedingly complex process which is by no means just a cognitive one. Hijacks, assassinations, sieges, and bombings — especially where they are directed against important people like Lord Mountbatten or Airey Neave — can provoke a sense that the entire society is under threat, and, as Philip Elliott has pointed out, they evoke ritualised responses from the media. For instance, where IRA activities have taken place on the British mainland, Elliott argues, the press and broadcasting have carried out "affirmatory rituals" which emphasize the integrity of the social order. In Britain itself, it has been possible to presume adherence to a common symbolic order articulated by those in authority, whereas in Northern Ireland given the social divisions there, such a mobilisation of common sentiment has proven impossible.(30) Similarly, Yves Lavoinne has argued that in cases of hostage-taking the dominant discourse emanating from the state and reproduced by the media stresses social consensus. Like Elliott, he points to the utilisation of a discourse which is quasi-religious, through which assaults on hostages are taken as affronts to the social collectivity, requiring terrorism to be evaluated as inhuman and irrational, as the very embodiment of chaos.(31)

All these analyses either conceptualise media coverage of violence in terms of its ideological effects, or alternatively as ritual performances that are simultaneously ideological practices. Although knowledge of how audiences perceive such accounts of violence and terrorism remains fragmentary, the evidence is stronger when it comes to the efforts made by state agencies to control media coverage. This suggests the background to the strategems adopted during the course of the Princes' Gate siege: the long-term efforts to control the flow of information and to secure a privileged place in media representations for the agent of the state. Two instances are briefly covered here: Sir Robert Mark's media strategy and the de facto partial censorship of broadcast news and current affairs coverage of Northern Ireland.

The Mark Strategy

The degree of compliance shown by the British media during the Iranian Embassy siege derives in part from an initiative taken in 1972 by Sir Robert Mark, then Commissioner of the Metropolitan Police. Mark decided that his force should be more accessible to journalists, keeping back information "subject only to judicial restrictions, the right to individual privacy, and the security of the state."(32) The Metropolitan Police and the national media agreed upon the new terms of reference, and the Home Office ratified them. Mark's objective, as he later said in a General Memorandum issued on May 24, 1973 was to improve the police's relationship with the news media and "consequently a better understanding on their part and that of the public of the force's problems and policies."(33) But the new "openness" was coupled with a determined effort to secure a measure of control over journalists. The General Memorandum made reference to a new press identity card. This enabled the police to sift the accredited journalists who hold the card from among the nonaccredited, and so to those they deemed unhelpful, in particular members of the radical press. Efforts by the National Union of Journalists to ensure that its card alone should constitute acceptable accreditation have so far been unsuccessful.(34) In September 1975, Mark organised a conference at Scotland Yard for the editors of the national media aiming to work out agreed procedures for "mutual aid in dealing with kidnapping." It was stressed that the lives of victims should be the principal concern and that "any self-denying measures adopted by the press should apply to all."(35) A distinction was made between "commercial" and "political" kidnappings and hijackings, "political" offences being excluded from the agreement.(36) Hardly had this initiative been taken when Sir Robert's media policy was tested on three occasions with results that evidently satisfied him greatly. Two of the incidents were sieges and the third involved the news blackout of a kidnapping.

The sieges are obviously of greater interest here: What were their continuities with, and differences from, Princes' Gate? Unlike the latter, both the 1975 sieges were under the sole operational control of the Metropolitan Police. At the Spaghetti House in Knightsbridge, a group of three black gunmen held up the managers of a restaurant chain as they were about to bank the day's takings. The gunmen and their hostages were cooped up in the basement for the duration of the siege. The police put into operation a plan devised over the previous two years. The area was sealed off: The Home Office supplied liaison officers and psychiatrists to assist in the bargaining. The liaison officers were present in case troops were required and because some Italian nationals had been taken hostage. The police refused to bargain over the gunmen's demands, but provided them with a radio to help "make clear to them, not only in shouted conversation, but through the news broadcasts, that they were going nowhere except to a cell, or by implication, to a mortuary, if they preferred that."(37) The police were able to monitor activities inside the basement, first through sound recordings and later through a television picture supplied by surveillance devices developed by C7, Scotland Yard's technical support branch. The police found the media exceedingly co-operative. The editor of the Daily Mail, David English, agreed to kill a scoop about the arrest of one of the gunmen's accomplices. Mark sought the suppression of this information as he did not want it broadcast over the radio. Although Scotland Yard thanked the Mail and the rest of the press, this was not published, provoking from Mark the disingenuous comment that "It was almost as if they felt there was something wrong in suppression of news in the interest of saving human life."(38)

The Balcombe Street siege in December 1975 was a more clearly political event. The successful conclusion at the Spaghetti House—where no one was killed—gave the police added confidence in dealing with it. This siege was the climax to a bombing and shooting campaign by the IRA in Britain. The police had set an ambush for the Provisional IRA active service unit involved, and after a chase from Mayfair four of its members were cornered in a private flat in Balcombe Street. The siege was handled according to the principles established a mere two months earlier. Once again, the Home Office sent a liaison officer; this time the SAS were moved in, and a team of psychiatrists was organised. The police controlled communications by cutting off the telephone and sending in a field telephone. The police strategy was, again, to play a waiting game, using time to wear down the resistance of the gunmen. Sir Robert Mark noted the important role played by the media:

> They asked, at our prompting, loaded questions such as "What about the safety of the hostages?" which enabled me to reply, "The best guarantee of their safety is the swift and ruthless retribution that will follow any harm that befalls them."(39)

As the siege wore on, and the likelihood of sending in the SAS to shoot things out increased, the ambiguities of the media presence became obvious. On the one hand the police did not want any "gory end to the siege" shown on the screen, and so they blocked off the view of the cameras. On the other hand, the media were again open to manipulation. As the flat was blocked off from the cameras coincidentally, both the Daily Express and the BBC disclosed that the SAS were there. This was, of course, broadcast on radio for the encouragement of the terrorists. Thereafter they could hardly surrender fast enough.(40) In another account Mark says quite bluntly that the presence of the SAS was "leaked" to the media — so there was little that was "coincidental" about the disclosure.(41)

The police scored a further success in their relations with the media over the kidnapping for ransom of a Greek Cypriot girl, Aloi Kaloghirou, in November 1975, when Mark described their behaviour as "opening a new era in police-press relations."(42) Editors were requested not to publish the story in the public interest. In order to maintain the media's compliance, the police gave daily conferences at Scotland Yard to inform journalists of progress. This news blackout was sustained for ten days until the girl was released unharmed. Chibnall has noted that many journalists were disenchanted by their end of the bargain. He also makes the point that such "stops" are common practice in Britain, the only unusual feature being the extent of co-operation on this occasion.(43) After the Met's success with "voluntary co-operation," the Home Office extended the London model of "guidelines" to editors of the provincial press. However, these guidelines make no distinctions between "political" and "commercial" terrorism, and had in some cases been very widely interpreted by chief constables to mean that they can ask for a news blackout whenever publicity might endanger life.(44) Clearly, the establishment of such common procedures helped the authorities in their eventual handling of the Princes' Gate siege.

Northern Ireland

The prime focus of "news about terrorism" in recent years has been Northern Ireland.(45) Coverage in the British media, as Philip Elliott has pointed out, has tended to simplify violent incidents, to avoid historical backgrounds, to concentrate upon human interest stories, and to rely upon official sources. Even during periods of intense political activity, the story has been pre-eminently one of violence — and irrational, inexplicable violence at that.(46) Apart from weakness in the journalistic practice of the British media, there can be little doubt that the one-dimensional coverage reflects, at least in part, the effective long-term strategy of attrition waged by the state in its psychological warfare campaign. Most critical attention has been focused upon the British state's repeated efforts to control broadcast news and current affairs coverage without stepping over that fatefully delegitimising line into overt censorship. It is a struggle which has been waged patiently and with skill, despite an orchestrated series of apparently intemperate rows. On the other hand, there are indications that the pitch of intimidatory rhetoric has risen of late, and overt intervention looks more likely than ever.

The immediate relevance of this Northern Ireland coverage to the Iranian Embassy siege is that it had led to strained relations between the BBC and the Thatcher government. Two incidents involving the television reporting of political violence were the cause. The first was a "Tonight" interview in July 1979 with a representative of the Irish National Liberation Army, the group which assassinated the Tory Northern Ireland spokesman, Airey Neave. This resulted in representations to the BBC from the Northern Ireland Secretary, Humphrey Atkins, questions in the House of Commons, shocked reaction from Neave's widow, criticism from the Opposition Northern Ireland spokesman Merlyn Rees, and Mrs. Thatcher's comment that she was "appalled." The BBC defended its action as responsible, in part by arguing that "We believed that this was an exercise in exposing the enemies of democracy, not condoning them" and by pointing out that this was only the fourth member of a proscribed organisation to be interviewed in ten years.(47)   Mrs. Thatcher asked the Attorney-General to consider taking legal action.   Later, reference was made to Section 11 of the Prevention of Terrorism Act (PTA) — a new departure in English jurisprudence.(48) Under Section 11 it is a criminal act not to disclose information to the police about suspected terrorism, with the attendant possibility of five years' imprisonment or an unlimited fine, or both.

The reverberations had hardly died away before the second incident in which the BBC disgraced itself in the government's eyes, this time by filming an IRA roadblock in Carrickmore. Again, this led to frenzied declamations in Parliament against the BBC, which had not even transmitted the film, and which invariably gives painstaking attention to any decision to screen manifestations of IRA strength. On this occasion, after saying that it was time the BBC "put its house in order," Mrs. Thatcher said that the film would not be shown. The police — for the first time — seized an untransmitted copy of the film under the Prevention of Terrorism Act. The threat of a prosecution under the PTA hung over the BBC until July 1980. One immediate response was to tighten up further guidelines on Northern Ireland reporting: There is little doubt that the exemplary intimidation of the BBC raised widespread anxiety among journalists about the legality of contacts with para-military organisations. The government's views became clear in August 1980, when, in a letter to BBC's Chairman, Sir Michael Swann, the Attorney-General, Sir Michael Havers, said that he thought both incidents constituted offences under Section 11 of the Prevention of Terrorism Act (1976). While denying any intent to censor, Havers accused the BBC of aiding terrorist propaganda and decried the fact that BBC personnel had not attempted to "contact the appropriate authorities to pass on the information required" to apprehend or prosecute terrorists.(49) As the government has not chosen to test its arguments in the courts, the legal standing of its view remains obscure. Nevertheless, this pressure on the BBC to "behave" forms part of the background to the period of the Iranian Embassy siege, and may have influenced the BBC in its eventual interpretation of its proper role as that of a model corporate citizen.(50)

THE ROLE OF THE MEDIA DURING THE SIEGE

It is perhaps unreasonable to expect the police to think first of the press, though in this case they thought very carefully about the press because . . . they realised . . . that they were part of the game.(51)

How, in detail, did the state authorities and the gunmen pursue their respective communicative strategies? In what ways was publicity a crucial factor in the management of the siege? My analysis is provisional; I merely seek to clarify the role of news broadcasting and of BBC personnel. It is also restricted by being based largely upon the accounts provided by the Observer and Sunday Times "instant" books,(52) which are obviously incomplete. A good deal more of the "story" of the siege has yet to come out. Nonetheless, the books do provide a great deal of material which illuminates, in particular, the importance attached to broadcasting. As I pointed out in the introduction, radio reporting seems to have been of paramount significance, as the gunmen and the hostages had receivers. There is no clear evidence whether any television viewing went on, but it seems reasonable to suppose that it did not. Newspapers were not allowed into the embassy (ST. p. 115).

The growth of the Civil Contingencies Committee (CCC) as part of the emergent "strong state" which I noted earlier is of especial importance here, since, unlike the Spaghetti House and Balcombe Street sieges, operational control was vested in the Civil Contingencies Committee rather than in the police. It is also worth recalling that since the early 1970s the British government has refused to countenance the escape of hijackers and hostage-takers — a policy in keeping with the emergent European position on anti-terrorism — and has increasingly made the SAS a part of domestic policing under the formula of "military aid to the civil power." In the present case, the unit used was the Special Air Services' Special Operations Group, SAS-SOG.(53) The deployment required the formal request of the Metropolitan Police Commissioner, Sir David McNee. The police decision eventually to call on these crack troops, however, can only be understood by recognising the guiding framework of constraints which emanated from the Civil Contingencies Committee, or COBRA, as it was labelled by the media. From the start the siege was correctly perceived to be political in character. It was a calculated gesture aimed at the Iranian government, and, given the complex international ramifications, this meant that direct British government involvement was inevitable. The CCC was chaired by William Whitelaw, the Home Secretary, and had 15 staff members drawn from relevant departments of state, the Civil Service, and the security and intelligence forces. The Foreign and Commonwealth Office was represented by Douglas Hurd, and the Ministry of Defence by Barney Heyhoe (Obs. p. 23; ST. p. 43).

DAY 1: WEDNESDAY 30 APRIL. The embassy was seized at 11:32 AM. At noon, the commercial radio's IRN broadcast a report about the seizure; shortly afterwards, they indicated in an eye-witness report from the scene that the police were on the embassy roof (ST. p. 20). The gunmen's leader, Oan, was evidently upset by a BBC report early in the afternoon which suggested that he and his group were Iraqis (ST. p. 30). He wished to correct this view. At this point, the Guardian made contact through the embassy's telex and managed to establish that the group were Arabistan autonomists before Oan terminated the interview (ST. p. 31; Obs. p. 25). It was the journalists among the hostages who suggested that their captors make contact with the media. At 2:45 PM the Syrian journalist Moustafa Karkouti managed to get in touch with the BBC's External Services at Bush House, and explained that "he was a hostage acting under orders to pass on a message. The men holding him wanted ninety-one prisoners in Arabistan to be released. And the BBC should also note that the hostage-takers were from Iran — not Iraq" (ST. p. 31; Obs. p. 32).

This was the first time this demand was transmitted. The Metropolitan Police received details of the demands at 3:15 PM according to their log. Either they were already tapping the line, or alternatively the BBC made them available (ST. p. 32). At 3:45 PM Karkouti spoke to the BBC's External Services again, and Oan relayed his demand that the 91 prisoners be released the next day of the embassy and the hostages would be blown up. Some 15 minutes earlier, Chris Cramer, the captured BBC news organiser, had telephoned or telexed BBC Television Centre listing the gunmen's demands. Apart from the threat to blow up the embassy, there was a request for Arab ambassadors to mediate between the gunmen and the British government and a promise that the non-Iranian hostages would not be harmed. The request for mediation was suppressed, at the request of the police, for three days (ST. p. 33; Obs. pp. 26-27, 137-38). Before the first day ended, the telephone links had been used to make several personal calls, and in addition the gunmen had spoken to the Iranian foreign minister, Sadeq Ghotzbadeh, who had refused any compromise (ST. p. 33).

Although the gunmen were able to make use of their access to the media to put across their aims during this first day, these were not relayed in full detail at the request of the police. According to the editor of BBC Television News, the telex from

Cramer was immediately made available to the police.(54)   The
contacts with Bush House probably were as well.   Given the
position of its two men inside the embassy, the BBC has assumed
a crucial role.   Even without this chance the Corporation was
apparently considered important by the gunmen.   In his account
of the siege, Chris Cramer notes:

> Barely a matter of minutes after the firing and the
> shouting had stopped, I chose to identify myself to the
> gunmen as a BBC journalist . . . . On reflection, I was
> taking a stupid risk by singling myself out as
> representing what, to many worldwide, is a less than
> perfect organisation.   The crazy thing was that it
> actually worked.   The BBC's credibility rating is
> obviously high with terrorists. . . . They seemed to
> know the time of every bulletin in English, Persian and
> Arabic.   Without that kind of worldwide publicity
> things might have got very nasty.(55)

DAY 2:   THURSDAY 1 MAY.   Only some of the press acceded
to the police request not to mention the noon deadline for the
release of the prisoners in Iran — namely the Times, the
Guardian and the Daily Telegraph (Obs. p. 44).   But this was of
little note;   once again, the BBC was of paramount importance.
At 6:20 AM, at Oan's request, Karkouti again telephoned Bush
House to remind the British public that the noon deadline stood,
but that the non-Iranian hostages would not be harmed in the
meantime.   The duty editor of Radio Newsreel managed to
engage Oan in a lengthy interview which was subsequently
broadcast on early morning domestic bulletins (ST. pp. 35-39;
Obs. pp. 45-47, 138).   Alan Protheroe has surmised, presumably
on an informed basis, that this recording was made available to
the police before it was broadcast.(56)   The gunmen evidently
kept listening to the radio, because they heard Karkouti's voice
on the BBC, and also mentioned that Tehran radio had broadcast
the rejection of their demands (Obs. p. 48).   Chris Cramer, who
had been taken ill overnight, was released by the gunmen at
11:20 AM.   He was evidently an important source of information
for the police;   for instance, he told them that P. C. Lock, the
Diplomatic Protection Squad Officer held captive, still had his
gun (Obs. p. 52;   ST. p. 41).   Cramer says nothing about what he
told the police.   He had promised the gunmen, obviously under
duress, not to reveal anything.(57)   However, his unconstrained
attitude is revealed in this comment:

> After my release, lying in a hospital bed, I mentally
> pleaded with all the broadcasters to do exactly what
> the gunmen wanted, to co-operate fully with the Police

and the Home Office . . . if necessary to broadcast complete lies. Anything to get the remaining hostages out and to safety. That thought process is completely alien to all my professional beliefs. But, as one of my close BBC friends said last week, professional beliefs don't save lives.(58)

By the afternoon of the second day, the gunmen had modified their position. They dropped the demand for the release of the prisoners, and asked instead that their demands be broadcast and that three Arab ambassadors arrange for a plan to fly them out. Such a solution was closed off by the security policy of the British state. The government, operating through the CCC, did not want any Arab mediators it could not control. It was worried about the requested use of the Iraqi ambassador, given Iran-Iraq tensions. And it did not want to seem to be endorsing the seizure by taking a soft line (Obs. pp. 58-59; ST. pp. 43, 45). Karkouti, an astute observer, is quoted as noting retro-spectively that "from the second evening, I felt it was being treated by those outside the embassy as a security problem and it was going to end in a critical situation. It was no longer a political situation and that was very frightening" (Obs. p. 57).

In truth, it had been defined as a security situation from the very beginning, in line with the developments in anti-terrorist policy since the early 1970s. During the second day the police cut off the telex and telephone links, and the gunmen were entirely dependent upon the police field telephone or conver-sations through the window from communications (Obs. p. 50; ST. p. 46). By the end of the day, therefore, the media had no direct access to informants inside the embassy, and could reveal nothing of the changing intentions of the gunmen.

DAY 3: FRIDAY 2 MAY. It was on this day that the BBC became directly involved as an intermediary between the gunmen and the police, although much is not yet known about the precise role of its personnel. Cutting off communications caused the gunmen intense frustration, and led to the first death threat against a particular hostage. However, despite the plea of P. C. Lock that there was "a man about to be killed" unless Oan was allowed to talk to the media by telephone or telex, again this request was refused. Oan modified his demand, and asked to speak to someone at the BBC known to Sim Harris. Apparently, this idea originated with Sim Harris, the BBC sound recordist, who had suggested the previous night that his captors speak to a senior BBC executive to find out why their demands had not been broadcast.(59) The police had then said no one was avail-able, which was false.

After the death threat, however, the police did contact the BBC, asking for the Television Home News Editor, John Exelby. As it turned out, the Managing Editor of Television News, Tony Crabb, took his place and departed for the embassy at 9 AM (Obs. pp. 73-74; ST. p. 47). By 9:30 Crabb was talking to Harris at the embassy (Obs. p. 74; ST. p. 51, differs, and presumably wrongly says this conversation did not take place until the afternoon).(60) Harris asked why the gunmen's demands had not been broadcast. Crabb asked "What demands?"; this seems odd, as Cramer had telexed them through to Television Centre on the first day. Although the Observer team comments that "it was never clear why the police had decided to keep from the press the fact that gunmen had demanded the presence of Arab ambassadors to act as mediators" (Obs. p. 74), their own evidence indicates that the BBC did have this information (Obs. pp. 27, 131). So the BBC alone of all the media colluded with the police in keeping this crucial demand secret.(61)

Crabb had been told by the police that he could offer nothing, and that he should keep the content of the conversation to himself. At the centre of this request was the suppression of the key demand for the intervention of the Arab ambassadors; this apparently "neither surprised nor particularly upset" Crabb (Obs. pp. 74-75). He took notes of the gunmen's demands:

Oan said he wanted:
1) A coach to take gunmen, hostages, and one Arab ambassador — unnamed — to Heathrow;
2) The non-Iranian hostages to be released at Heathrow;
3) An aircraft to take the remaining hostages, gunmen, and Ambassador to a Middle East country — again unspecified — and there released. (ST. p. 52)

It appears that the communication of their aims now obsessed the gunmen, who did not doubt that they would be allowed a safe passage. It was only 11:30 that night that a BBC bulletin referred to the new demands.

But, to Oan's fury, the BBC not only truncated his statement, but got it wrong. The broadcast said that the gunmen wanted the three Arab ambassadors to negotiate not with the British government, which was the fact, but with Iran. (ST. p. 52)

This error seems quite extraordinary, unless, of course, it was an intentional one. But the two books differ about this incident. The Observer account contains no reference to a BBC bulletin late on Day 3, but reports that at the beginning of Day 4 Oan

was listening, as ever, to what the radio had to say
about the siege, preoccupied with the demand for three
ambassadors which the police had not yet made public.
He heard Radio Tehran say that the ambassadors were
needed to negotiate with the Iranian government, not
the British. (Obs. p. 81)(62)

This indicates that, rather than getting the demands wrong, the
BBC did not report them at all — a point which merits further
inquiry.

DAY 4: SATURDAY 3 MAY. By the late morning, the gunmen
were evidently getting edgy about the non-broadcasting of their
demands, as well as the non-appearance of any ambassadors.
They demanded to see Crabb once more. As tension mounted, the
police realised that something had to be done about a public
statement, and made urgent efforts to find Crabb, who was
unavailable until the afternoon (Obs. pp. 82-83). The bugging of
the embassy was obviously important in providing intelligence, not
least in allowing the police to monitor the gunmen's reactions to
the radio reporting. The police apparently knew "how disastrous
the previous night's inaccuracies had been" (ST. p. 56), whether
these are attributed to the BBC or Tehran radio.

Tony Crabb reappeared at the embassy just before 2 PM. He
was clearly an intermediary for police demands, and, during the
hour before he again spoke to the gunmen, seems to have
received a briefing: "The police asked me to stress that
anything they did for the gunmen had to be reciprocated by an
act of goodwill from them. I was asked to emphasise that my
own presence at the embassy was a concession from the police."

To Harris's question about why the statement had not been
broadcast, Crabb replied that there had been a "misunder-
standing." Given the evident anger of the gunmen's leader, the
police negotiator on the spot said that the statement would be
taken down correctly. Either the police officer or Crabb took
down the statement (ST. p. 56;   Obs. p. 84). The accounts
conflict. The gunmen demanded that the statement be broadcast
accurately. Crabb hesitated, but the police agreed to the terms
provided that two hostages be released (Obs. p. 84; ST. p. 56).
There were delays before the statement was broadcast, caused by
the time taken by the CCC in evaluating its consequences. Oan
threatened to kill a hostage unless the statement was published,
but was prevailed upon to release one instead. "Almost
immediately, the police rang back to say thank you and told Oan
that the statement would be released in full on the BBC World
Service at 9:00" (Obs. pp. 84-85;   ST. pp. 56-57). This
formulation suggests very close co-operation.

Adie, the reporter who covered the SAS's taking of the embassy. Another participant was Deputy Assistant Commissioner John Dellow, the officer in charge of operations during the siege. According to the report by State Research:

> One of the case studies in which those present participated concerned the seizure of hostages in a Western capital by a dissident movement from the Middle East. The dénouement of this case study was a shoot-out, organised by the Government, which, although it had carried on talking had throughout never intended to allow the hostage-takers to escape. Discussion centred on whether a newspaper, which had been told that the hostage-takers were in the end to ambushed and shot rather than any deal being struck, should release the information.(73)

Knowledge of such scenarios, coupled with Protheroe's "certain briefings" and "hints," suggest that top broadcasters could hardly have been unaware of the government's intentions on the occasion of the Princes' Gate siege, and that some of these expectations must have been transmitted, via briefings, to the reporting teams.

But if this is so, then why was the actual live coverage so incoherent? The trade magazine Broadcast has noted that it was

> obvious for at least half an hour before the assault took place that a turning-point had been reached in the siege. Both ITN and BBC News had broadcast news flashes at 19:14 and 19:11 respectively, announcing that the body of a man, probably a hostage, had been pushed out of the embassy. Newspaper reports speak of increased police activity toward 19:18.(74)

On the face of it, well-briefed reporters familiar with previous anti-hijack and anti-siege actions should have been able to interpret the event more adequately than they did. Admittedly, the "frame charges" used by the SAS to blow out the windows were a new element, but the "stun grenades" were familiar from the Mogadishu hijack rescue in 1977. Also unclear is the significance of ITN's camera at the rear of the embassy, ingeniously smuggled in on the last day of the siege in defiance of the police, who had wanted the preparations round the back to be unobserved. Oddly enough, no reports of police or Home Office displeasure at this have emerged. The ITN director in the field was aware of the immediate build-up to the SAS attack three minutes before it happened (ST. p. 116).

A final point about the television coverage is that the most complete programme available is undoubtedly that in the hands of the security forces. Throughout the siege, events at Princes' Gate were continuously monitored by police cameras. Television viewers who knew what to look for could see them, and in the aftermath coverage there was film of the cameras being dismantled. A police helicopter was flying overhead throughout the ending of the siege. Such helicopters are generally fitted out with television cameras, and six months after the siege viewers of the BBC's "Nine O'Clock News" saw some of the pictures taken from this vantage point. A further source of televised material is the BBC. It is reliably reported that videotapes of the SAS action have been made available to the regiment. On previous occasions, the BBC has been rather sensitive about such co-operation. For instance, there was concern in top editorial circles about the Royal Ulster Constabulary having "pirated" a videotaped recording of a controversial programme about "The Republicans" shown in December 1977, as this could give the appearance of collusion with the security forces. The BBC's minutes noted that the

> BBC must respond to any formal legal requests for access to transmitted material but in all other cases it always considered most carefully the consequences of making it available, both in relation to the BBC's own position and to that of individual members of staff.(75)

During the same meeting Alan Protheroe said that the BBC had given film for "instructional purposes" to the Ministry of Defence and the Metropolitan Police.

It is unclear at present whether ITN also co-operated by releasing film of the siege, but it is known that they would not have raised objections had they been asked. Such requests are largely a matter of form as television coverage can be monitored and taped by the police anyway. Evidently the SAS had their own videotape of the rescue. Mrs. Thatcher, who was visiting their tactical headquarters for a celebration party on the night of the action, was invited to watch a recording.(76) Of special interest to the authorities would be the pictures not being transmitted, especially those from ITN, which switched between cameras at the front and the rear of the embassy. Somewhere there must exist a fascinatingly detailed compilation tape of the way the SAS stormed the Princes' Gate Embassy — one which will never receive a public showing.

CONCLUSIONS

Sieges, hijacks, and hostage-takings raise major problems for the media. There is strong pressure on them from the state, supported by public opinion, to act "responsibly" in order to save life. Such pressure is perhaps most intense on radio and television, whose transmissions may be directly monitored by the gunmen. In the Iranian Embassy siege, radio news was of unquestionable importance as the gunmen were aiming to obtain airtime for their views: The broadcasting of their demands undoubtedly saved several lives. The BBC became particularly involved in the bargaining process on two days of the siege, and although its representatives have played down their contradictory position, the Corporation seems to have put the demands of safeguarding law and order before any journalistic imperatives. The presence of two BBC men among the hostages gave them good institutional reasons for this; less clear is whether there will be any future consequences of such close compliance with the security forces' aims. Alan Protheroe's plea for greater "trust" from the authorities could surely result in an even greater absorption into the crisis-management apparatus of the state. A somewhat different position has been taken by the editor of the Observer, Donald Trelford, who suggested in "The Editors" on BBC TV that "better communication" was needed between the police and journalists, but reserved the right of editors to decide what to use. Such a position is plainly more tenable for newspapers which are not so proximate to the state as broadcasting.

It would be dangerous to accept too readily the public rhetoric of state officials about the need to save life. Without being too cynical — such humanitarian concerns are certainly not totally absent — they do have other priorities. Foremost among them are state security and the maintenance of political credibility by stamping firmly on any manifestation of "terrorism." The duality of official attitudes is well-illustrated by some remarks from Sir Robert Mark. When agreeing on procedures for covering kidnapping with editors in 1975, he "emphasized at the outset that the safety of the victims should be the primary concern of the police and, hopefully, of the Press."(77) Compare this with his reflections on the Balcombe Street siege:

> Though we were deeply concerned about the safety of the hostages I did not consider for one moment that they were not expendable. I felt heartfelt sympathy for Mr. and Mrs. Matthews but felt that human life was of little importance when balanced against the principle that violence must not be allowed to succeed.(78)

Raison d'etat thus guides the actions of state agencies; it would therefore seem appropriate to evaluate carefully all requests for total co-operation. Otherwise the media are apt to become tools of a given "psywar operation," and this would foreclose any basis for criticism of the deficiencies in the state's conduct.

Although it is not my purpose in this article to raise detailed questions about the conduct of the Iranian Embassy siege, it is worth noting that it was not an unmitigated success. Most obviously, there was loss of life — five gunmen killed by the SAS and two hostages killed by the gunmen. The eventual shoot-out stemmed from the British government's determination not to allow the gunmen to go free. As the Sunday Times team comment: "in the final analysis, the Government was prepared to sacrifice the lives of the hostages if necessary rather than give in" (ST. p. 71). The deaths were politically acceptable, because, to be blunt, they did not involve any of the British hostages. Indeed, this "invisibility" of the non-British hostages charac- terised the handling of the story, coupled with the adulation for the undoubted bravery of P. C. Lock.

To their credit, several newspapers — the Observer, the Sunday Times, and the Guardian — did raise questions about the circumstances in which the SAS killed the gunmen, and about the wisdom of the government's policy in not bringing in the ambassadors earlier. On the first question, using hostages' accounts, both the Observer and the Sunday Times revealed that after killing a second hostage, and attempting to kill two more, three of the gunmen threw away their arms and surrendered (Obs. pp. 119-20; ST. pp. 124-28). Two of these gunmen, having been identified by the hostages, were shot by the SAS. Both the Sunday Times and Observer writers expressed unease about the circumstances in which this took place, but both papers argued that there was little else the SAS could have done, given the uncertainty about whether the men were still armed or whether they could blow up the embassy. Tony Geraghty, the Sunday Times's defence correspondent (and historian of the SAS), had no reservations: "The only ways of saving the hostages' lives. . . . was to kill the terrorists unless it was unequivocally clear that they were identifying themselves for what they were and were very plainly surrendering. This was far from clear at the time. . . ."(79) Nevertheless, questions do remain. The Observer team asked, "Did the SAS team have orders to take no prisoners — and if so who issued them?" (Obs. p. 119). This question obviously runs across the purely situational explanation offered for the SAS's action — that in the battleground which was the embassy they had no choice but to eliminate the enemy. The Sunday Times investigators were at odds with their defence correspondent: "The crucial question is, had the gunmen dropped all of their weapons and genuinely surrendered before they were shot? And if so, can their killings possibly be justified on any legal and moral basis?" (ST. p. 127).

Tony Geraghty has, in fact, suggested that there certainly was a strong legal basis for the action:

> the SAS is stringently subject to the rule of law, for which the police are responsible. The Army's CRW (counter-revolutionary warfare) teams are reminded of this by a litany of ground rules, more elaborate even than the "Yellow Card" governing the rules of engagement for soldiers in Northern Ireland. It travels with the team for display in their tactical operations room near the scene of the siege.(80)

This observation adds to our knowledge; when State Research tried to find out more about these regulations, the Ministry of Defence would not even comment on their existence. To know that they exist, however, is not to know what they detail. Nor does it reveal whether they were observed — it seems that they have not on occasions in Northern Ireland.(81) At the time of writing, some six months after the siege, these questions have not been pursued by the British media; at any rate, nothing has been published.

What of the FCO's refusal (at the behest of the CCC) to let the ambassadors mediate? Obviously, this was a matter of high-level political calculation, in which the possibility of a negotiated solution that allowed the gunmen to escape was rejected. The deterrent effect of a hard line seems a plausible enough argument if hostages' lives are not the top priority. It is surely a matter of public interest, though, that the BBC, which, alone of the British media was privy to the demand for diplomatic intervention, aligned itself uncritically with government anti-terrorist policy. By keeping quiet about the Arab ambassadors, the Corporation played a crucial role in facilitating the pursuit of the government's strategy for three days. It is extraordinary that this has occasioned no comment — indeed, has evidently gone unnoticed. Did the Corporation have no doubts about the wisdom of the government's approach? Its unique status in the affair was also reinforced by the way in which the BBC's personnel — Tony Crabb on the outside and Sim Harris on the inside — assisted in the exchange of publicity for hostages, and in contributing to the attrition of the gunmen's will. The BBC was certainly in a difficult position: it had to co-operate extensively with the security operation and was rightly concerned for the safety of its personnel. At the same time, the siege undoubtedly represented a further milestone in the peacetime exercise of the state control over broadcasting in a moment of crises. Perhaps the configuration of circumstances was unique; equally, it could have enduring consequences.

No doubt from the siege-managers' point of view a partial censorship is better than none at all. But although successful in practice, the present British model has a paradoxical long-term consequence. The very absence of total censorship makes it possible for interested parties to reconstruct the details of siege operations, including the role of communication media — as I have done here. This means that the security forces have to think out a new "game plan," at least on the most pessimistic assumption that future hostage-takers will be literate and will understand how things work in Britain. At the extensive debriefing of all those involved in the security side a week after the conclusion of the siege, the question of whether it would be "necessary to change contingency plans to counter terrorist incidents because of the extensive television coverage of the siege including 'blacked up' SAS men storming the building" was considered.(82) Although total censorship remains unlikely and would anyway be utterly unacceptable to both media and public, a clear code of practice governing media-state relations on such occasions is needed. Fudging the reality of existing ad hoc agreements (as with the BBC in this case) is of course the preferred British way out. But it is hardly the most democratic: We have a right to know just how compliant the media propose to be at given moments, and why they choose (or are constrained) to be so.

Finally, the overall coverage of the siege does give cause for serious concern. The episode was generally treated in patriotic, even chauvinistic, terms. A violent solution was favoured, even glorified. From the point of view of civil liberties, this is worrying indeed. The operation seems to have given the use of the SAS in Britain's cities some legitimacy at a time when social turbulence is likely to increase. Will this mean that strong-arm tactics for dealing with political problems will become an accepted part of our political culture? Not a single politician, and most especially not one of those usually most vociferous in defence of civil liberties, dared to raise a voice in criticism of the SAS action. As we go forward into the Eighties, we may come to consider this silence an index of the drift toward authoritarianism.

NOTES

1. Leader in Daily Telegraph, May 10, 1980.
2. An observation made on BBC television's "The Editors," broadcast on June 16, 1980. Quotations are taken from the BFI Education Department's transcript of this programme.

3. Alan Protheroe, "The Authorities Were Reluctant to Trust the Media: The Iranian Embassy Siege," The Listener, May 22, 1980, p. 641.

4. John Le Carré, "Introduction," Siege: Six Days at the Iranian Embassy (London: MacMillan, 1980), p. 2. This book was written by the Observer's reporting team and published on May 30. Extensive use is made of this account below, hence referred to as Obs.

5. "After the Siege: How TV Covered the Kensington Gore," Broadcast, May 12, 1980.

6. "News at Ten," April 30, 1980.

7. The term terrorism is inevitably value-laden. In the official discourse of the West, largely reproduced by the media, it refers to violent anti-state activities, but is never (or hardly ever) used of the repressive activities of states themselves, except those in the Communist bloc. For a more detailed account, see my essay "Terrorism, the Media, and the Liberal-Democratic State: A Critique of the Orthodoxy," Social Research, special issue, forthcoming.

8. See Conor Cruise O'Brien, "Liberty and Terror: Illusions of Violence, Delusions of Liberation," Encounter, October 1977, for a cogent presentation of the orthodox liberal view.

9. An interview quoted in Siege! Insight on the Great Embassy Rescue, (London: Hamlyn, 1980), pp. 61-62. This is the Sunday Times reporting team's account, which is also extensively used later; hence referred to as ST.

10. Obs, pp. 76-77.

11. ST. p. 42.

12. Broadcast, op. cit. "Newsnight" (May 6, 1980) revealed that the police had asked the television organisations not to show the plans of the embassy.

13. Ibid.

14. State Research Bulletin, "How SAS Ended the Princes' Gate Siege," no. 18, June-July 1980, p. 117.

15. State, Power, Socialism, (London: New Left Books, 1978), see especially part 4.

16. "The Free Economy and the Strong State," the Socialist Register, 1979, p. 15.

17. Restricting oneself to books alone, information on all of these issues may be found in the following: Carol Ackroyd, Karen Margolis, Jonathan Rosenhead, and Tom Shallice, The Technology of Political Control, 2nd ed. (London: Pluto Press, 1980); Tony Bunyan, The History and Practice of the Political Police in Britain (London: Quartet Books, 1977); Tom Bowden, Beyond the Limits of the Law (Harmondsworth: Penguin, 1978); Peter Hain, ed., Policing the Police, vols. 1, 2 (London: John Calder, 1979 and 1980); E. P. Thompson, Writing by Candlelight (London: Merlin Press, 1980). The State Research Bulletins are

an indispensable source.

18. See the interesting essay by Alan Wolfe, "Political Repression and the Liberal Democratic State," Monthly Review, December 1971, pp. 18-37, where this is argued more fully. Martin Kettle has argued for a cautious assessment of current trends in Britain in "The Drift to Law and Order," Marxism Today, October 1980, pp. 20-27.

19. Bunyan, op. cit., p. 293.

20. Ibid., p. 277.

21. State Research Bulletin, August-September 1980, p. 152; emphasis added. This issue provides a searching analysis of these developments under the title "Policing the Eighties: The Iron Fist."

22. For a circumspect account, see Tony Geraghty, Who Dares Wins: The Story of the Special Air Service (London: Arms and Armour Press, 1980), Ch. 6.

23. Ibid., pp. 168-69.

24. State Research Bulletin, no. 5, April-May 1978, pp. 83-84; Bulletin no. 11, April-May 1979, pp. 84-85. The convergence over policing has a legal dimension too. The United Kingdom has extended the grounds for political extradition by its Suppression of Terrorism Act which ratifies the Council of Europe's Convention on the Suppression of Terrorism. State Research Bulletin, nos. 4 and 8, February-March 1978, pp. 63-64; October-November 1978, pp. 6-7.

25. Reported by ABC network news, May 2, 1980.

26. Geraghty, op. cit. p. 173; emphasis added.

27. Ibid., pp. 174-75.

28. Stuart Hall et al., Policing the Crisis: Mugging, the State and Law and Order (London: MacMillan, 1978), especially Ch. 8 and 9. Also Stuart Hall, Drifting into a Law and Order Society, Cobden Trust Human Rights Day Lecture, 1978.

29. Steve Chibnall, Law-and-Order News: An Analysis of Crime Reporting in the British Press (London: Tavestock, 1977). A splendidly succinct account.

30. Philip Elliott, "Press Performance as Political Rituals," in The Sociology of the Press and Journalism, ed. H. Christian, Sociological Review Monograph, (Keele University, forthcoming).

31. Yves Lavoinne, "Presse et cohésion sociale: Le case des prises d'otages" Revue Française de Communication, no. 2 (Winter 1979): 35-41.

32. Robert Mark, "The Case of Great Britain," Terrorism and the Media (International Press Institute, 1980), unpaged; his emphasis.

33. Robert Mark, Policing a Perplexed Society (London: Allen and Unwin, 1977), pp. 123-29.

34. State Research Bulletin no. 9, December 1978–January 1979, pp. 29–30; and Bulletin no. 12, June–July 1979, pp. 106–07.

35. Mark, "The Case of Great Britain."

36. Peter Harland, "Terror and the Press, Politics and Greed: When Lives Are at Stake Where Is the Difference?" IPI Report 26, no. 10 (November 1977): 5–7.

37. Robert Mark, In the Office of Constable (Fontana/ Collins, 1979), p. 199.

38. Ibid., p. 201.

39. Ibid., p. 193.

40. Ibid., p. 194.

41. Mark, "The Case of Great Britain."

42. Ibid.

43. Chibnall, op. cit., pp. 186–87.

44. Harland, op. cit., p. 7. It is worth noting that the Met's pressure on the media has continued. An important instance occurred when the Met tried to obtain censorship rights over programmes about the police after the controversy following the BBC programme "Law and Order." For details, see The Leveller, no. 28, July 1979.

45. See Philip Schlesinger, Putting "Reality" Together: BBC News (London: Constable, 1978), especially Ch. 8; Anthony Smith, "Television Coverage of Northern Ireland," in Index on Censorship, no. 2, 1972; John Howkins, "Censorship 1977–78," and Chris Dunkley, "Programmes on Northern Ireland," in Official Programme of the Edinburgh International Television Festival 1978; and Media Misreport N. Ireland, Belfast Workers' Research Unit, 1979.

46. Philip Elliott, "Reporting Northern Ireland," in Ethnicity and the Media (Paris: UNESCO, 1977).

47. Ian Trethowan, Director–General of the BBC, in a letter to the Editor of the Daily Telegraph, July 14, 1979.

48. See Dorothy Connell, "Reporting Northern Ireland, 1979–80," in Index on Censorship, vol. 9, no. 3, June 1980.

49. Guardian, August 2, 1980.

50. Perhaps the BBC's final expiation came when, on October 6, 1980, it broadcast a eulogistic drama–documentary entitled "Airey Neave: A Will of Steel." The title picked up a phrase of Mrs. Thatcher's, who, suitably enough, had the last word too.

51. Professor John Gunn, psychiatric advisor to the police during the siege, speaking on "The Editors," op. cit.

52. In the development of the argument which follows I have tied particular statements to accounts given in the two "siege" books. I have read them with particular questions in mind concerning the role of the media, whereas the books have been written with that as an important, but subordinate issue. The critical reading offered below points up some crucial moments

which were left rather implicit in the books and as it traverses controversial ground, especially concerning the relationship between broadcasting and the state, it is crucial to provide evidence for each turn in the argument.

53. State Research Bulletin, no. 18, op. cit., p. 118.

54. "In the case of the telex that was sent to us from Chris Cramer on the first day, the contents of that were, in fact, made immediately available to the police. The police had copies of the telex. They talked to the people who had received the telex at this end." Alan Protheroe, in "The Editors," op. cit.

55. "Inside the Embassy," Broadcast, May 19, 1980.

56. "The Editors," op. cit.

57. A point he made during an interview on the BBC television programme "Newsnight," May 5, 1980.

58. Broadcast, op. cit.

59. According to his diary printed in The Day of the SAS: The Inside Story of How Britain Ended the Siege of Princes' Gate. This war comic is the Daily Express's siege special. On the whole its interest is iconographic rather than factual.

60. Harris's diary supports the Observer version.

61. Given the importance of this point the evidence for it should be quoted in full: "At 5:30 Karkouti and Cramer were allowed to use the telephone again. Karkouti called the BBC World Service at Bush House and Cramer BBC Television at Shepherd's Bush, dictating the statement of the gunmen's demands, the threat to blow up the embassy if they were not met, a request for Arab ambassadors to mediate, and a promise that the non-Iranian hostages would not be harmed . . . the demand for Arab ambassadors to mediate was concealed for three long days" (Obs, p. 27). Astonishingly, even media pundits like Simon Jenkins of the Economist, who chaired "The Editors" discussion, seem not to have grasped the point: Jenkins said on the programme: " . . . there was an occasion when the police failed to communicate . . . with the media that the gunmen were demanding that their ambassadors act as liaison officers. Now, why didn't the police communicate that to the broadcasting authorities, even though they didn't want it to be broadcast?" Well, in one case at least they didn't need to.

62. This account accords with Harris's diary, Daily Express, p. 56.

63. The Listener, op. cit.

64. Ibid.

65. "The Editors," op. cit.

66. According to Harris, Daily Express, p. 60.

67. Broadcast, op. cit.

68. The Listener, op. cit.

69. "The Editors," op. cit.

70. The Listener, op. cit.;   my emphasis.

71. "The Editors," op. cit.

72. Ibid.

73. State Research Bulletin, no. 18, op. cit., p. 119. The two other scenarios discussed at the conference concerned the reporting of extreme Left and Right politics and the question of how to handle torture allegations against the security forces in Northern Ireland.

74. Broadcast, op. cit.

75. "News and Current Affairs," minutes, March 7, 1978, n. 115.

76. Geraghty, op. cit., p. 181.

77. Mark, "The Case of Great Britain," emphasis added.

78. Mark, In the Office of Constable, p. 193;   emphasis added.

79. Geraghty, op. cit., p. 180.

80. Ibid., p. 169.

81. Bulletin, op. cit., p. 118, n. 18.

82. Daily Telegraph, May 11, 1980.

CHAPTER 3

Press Freedom in France:
Private Ownership and
State Controls

BY C. R. EISENDRATH

Fear is the basis of all limitations on free expression — fear that words will defeat some cause, embarrass some person. Words are highly subjective ammunition. Unlike bullets, they leave no visible wound; unlike bankruptcy, there are no accountable marks on a ledger. Only the person hurt by words knows precisely how he has been offended, or how badly, and even he may change his mind as time passes and mood varies. Because everyone fears in his own way and because the effect of fearsome words is so difficult for others to judge, the amount of free expression encouraged, or tolerated, or risked in any society always depends on intensely personal variables.

"How can I let them get away with this?" the politician fumes about "muckrakers" who cost him votes. "How can I not answer my enemies through my newspaper?" asks the publisher. "How much can I risk saying?" wonders the reporter, or his editor. These everyday journalistic questions are interdependent. Government officials balance toleration against outrage when criticism stings. Publishers weigh self-interest against retribution. Reporters and editors in the West, of course, do not hold public office or benefit directly from advertising and newsstand revenues. But they do have consciences and careers that thrive or wither according to their choice of what to say, when to say it, in which way, and about whom.

Answers to those questions arise in some form in every society no matter what its political structure. They are "the rules of the game" in journalism. In great measure, they depend less on laws than on a broad range of social, cultural, and economic incentives. Together, they determine whether saying something — or permitting it to be said — is a worthwhile

enterprise. With the game itself depending on personal variables, it is not surprising that there are often considerable
discrepancies between codified regulations governing free
expression and what actually appears on the street.

This gap is illustrated by three societies that attach great
importance to what can and cannot be said by their citizens
about one another. The constitutional fabric of the United
States encourages the world's freest exchange of words in a
single sentence. The First Amendment simply commands Congress
to "make no law" in abridgment of free expression. Article 50
of the constitution of the Soviet Union, a system with one of the
world's most restricted ranges of expression, is much more
positive:

> In accordance with the interests of the people and in
> order to strengthen and develop the socialist system,
> citizens of the USSR are guaranteed freedom of speech
> (and) of the press.(1)

The French example is far more complex than either of these two
extremes. Article XI of the Declaration of Rights of Man and
of Citizen, the ancestor of both the U.S. First Amendment and
the Soviet Article 50, gives every French person the right, in
principle, to be "free to speak or publish" but then adds "except
as prohibited by the law."

The French model is particularly interesting because its
approach to free expression puts it squarely between the
philosophies of Watergate and the Gulag. Ownership of the print
press is private (broadcasting is a government monopoly),
bringing with it the multiplicity of viewpoints, and controls,
characteristic of capitalist societies. Yet, the state also
exercises irresistible restraints by using both the carrot and the
stick.

In France, the tension between these principles of freedom
and the varying prohibitions of the law has made the regulation
of public criticism and discussion highly unpredictable. In
October 1980, for example, the French government provoked a
coup de théâtre that would be unthinkable in either the United
States or the Soviet Union. It brought criminal suit against the
nation's leading journal, Le Monde, and its top news executive,
Jacques Fauvet, for criticizing court decisions including one
involving then-President Valéry Giscard d'Estaing's acceptance of
gift diamonds from an African emperor. Officially, the charge
did not concern either the truth of the reports or their effect
on the president. Instead, Le Monde was held answerable for
"bringing discredit"(2) to the judicial system. A few weeks later
Giscard admitted having accepted the jewels, which he donated
to charity. A few months after that he lost his bid for

reelection. The verdict on freedom of expression, however, went his way. Merely by remaining pending, the lawsuit silenced Le Monde on a sensitive subject and, with it, the rest of the French press. (One of Socialist François Mitterand's first acts as president was to give amnesty to all suits pending against the press.) In the United States, presidents and other public officials simply lack the prosecutorial machinery to do anything like this, as Watergate dramatically demonstrated. Soviet censorship resolves political differences long before the collective decision appears in Pravda.

DICTATES OF LAW

On August 24, 1789, France was the first country in the world to adopt formally freedom of the press as a fundamental tenet of government. The National Assembly that day approved Article XI of the Declaration of the Rights of Man and Citizen:

The free communication of thoughts and opinions is one of the most precious rights of mankind. Each citizen may therefore speak, write, print cases set forth by the law.(3)

It has been this final clause that has bedeviled press freedom in France since then. Far more than the First Amendment of the U.S. Constitution, Article XI has been blunted by a host of "cases set forth by the law."

French free speech laws are scattered in the Penal Code, Code of Penal Procedure, the Code of Military Justice, the Law of July 29, 1881, and a host of special edicts.(4) Together, they form a web of remarkable hold and breadth, one capable of entrapping an extremely wide variety of free–flying comment.

Some of the important restrictions involve categories for punishment. For instance, criminal sanctions for "offenses-by-writing," unknown in the current American precedent, are common in France. Libel is merely one of the several causes of this action. It involves fines and imprisonment of up to one year. It might be argued that, from a monetary standpoint, there is little difference between damages and fines. But one dimension looms so large in free speech issues that it blots out all seeming similarities. Criminal actions involve the full power of the state, with its investigative, policy, and punitive resources as an intimidating factor. This is an awesome opponent to even the most powerful publisher. Civil actions allow a more manageable equation as well as the freedom from the potential stigma of a criminal record. The state in civil cases merely provides an unbiased tribunal to resolve disputes between journalists and their subjects.

Other procedural aspects of French law make its reliance on criminal law in press cases even more intimidating. For instance, in defamation cases, the usual presumption of innocence is reversed. The burden of proof is shifted from the accuser to the accused. In addition, four tests of good faith must be established for an alleged libel to be judged unintentional. Writers, for instance, stand third in a ranking of those legally responsible in criminal cases. That ranking extends down to street vendors. The prime target, however, is the director, who, by inclination and responsibility, is usually far less willing to risk jail for what employees write than are journalists themselves.(5)

In Western societies, most legal limitations on free speech stem from the basic concept of _defamation_, the harming of some person, institution, or interest by things said publicly without consent. By French classification, _diffamation_ refers to damage involving some verifiable evidence. _Injure_, however, covers epithets and insults with no particular factual content. The separate crimes of _offense_ and _outrage_ are even more broadly construed.(6) Although both relate to expression that damages the well-being of society, offense basically refers to journalistic comment on public officials; outrage, some more general transgression, such as pornography or interference in the course of justice.(7) These are highly refined doctrines, full of niceties and ambiguity.

Many differences in French and American libel law are basically of degree, although the differences are dramatic. French law designates a significant field of "no fault" libel. Publications may be fined or their personnel imprisoned for expressing true facts. In three basic areas, the test is merely whether the statements were made and damaging:

● Personal privacy restrictions involving virtually anything potentially diminishing a person's honor that is said without permission. To strengthen further the stringent provisions of the Penal Code, the National Assembly in the laws of July 17, 1970, made it a crime to publish any "word or image" from a private place without consent.(8) The same law amended the Penal Code to allow steps ranging up to seizure of any publication that, for instance, ran classified documents or pictures of a starlet behind a garden wall.
● Facts more than ten years old. These may not be mentioned without risk of libel, if they can be shown to damage an individual's reputation.
● Crimes specifically pardoned or that took place in a period officially amnestied. These are also totally off limits. This provision takes on particular importance be-

cause incoming national leaders, borrowing from loyal tradition, routinely amnesty ordinary crimes and, frequently, those involved in particularly troublesome historical episodes such as the Dreyfus case, World War II, and the Algerian crisis. The law formally seals them off from further discussion in the press by making all references to them targets for civil or criminal action.(9)

Beyond libel laws lie other imposing barriers to free speech. In their volume The Law of Information, authorities Jean Marie Auby and Robert Ducos-Ader relate these additional regulations to general "public interest" and the repression of reports deemed harmful to it. Four areas are clearly stamped "no trespassing" by French law:

1. Provocation to commit crimes. Journalists may be held accountable not only if they knowingly assist criminal action but also for a host of far more ambiguous actions. Provocation can be direct, indirect, or one of nine categories of "special provocations." All carry criminal sanctions with journalists treated as accomplices. In punishing for direct incitement (for example, the urging of opponents of nuclear power to join an illegal demonstration), French law does distinguish between "provocations followed by the effect" and those that are not. Direct provocation, of course, implies editorialization rather than straight reporting.

When an article is accused of having indirectly encouraged theft, murder, pillage, arson, grievous bodily injury, harm to or destruction of property, or crimes and misdemeanors against state security, the press finds itself on more subjective, less defensible ground. The law calls for punishment of what a court finds to be an "apology" for lawbreaking. In this, an apology is defined as presenting lawbreaking in a "praiseworthy, meritorious or legitimate light," whether in a civil, an administrative, or a military context.(10)

2. Offenses against public authorities, official bodies, and protected persons. The more powerful a person is, the more protection is granted by law. At the top is the president of the republic. The doctrine of "offense" for these cases is defined by Auby and Ducos-Ader as being

much broader than the notion of injury or defamation it encompasses. Thus, it does not require (even) a precise imputation against honor, nor the presence of profanity, but simply an assault on the dignity or the authority of the president of the republic.(11)

French law extends the president's "red-carpet" insulations to members of foreign governments and their diplomats. The aggrieved need not lower themselves to actually bringing suit. That may be left to the prosecutor's office.

Lesser institutions must rely on ordinary libel law. But they, nonetheless, can force publications to prove the truth of articles written about them. The rationale is "to grant special protection to institutions playing an important role in public life." These the law defines as including chambers of commerce, les Grandes Écoles, academic councils, and the Legion of Honor, as well as the courts and branches of the armed services.

Although institutional safeguards also shield the people who run the offices, the doctrine of "protected persons" grants another layer of armor to virtually anyone doing anything, permanently or temporarily, for the state. To be sure, members of the Council of State, the Senate, and National Assembly get special consideration in disputes with the press. But the same is accorded regional, municipal, and local authorities whose legal status also rubs off on their part-time employees (including court judges and witnesses). All receive partial immunity as a perquisite of the job. Nor is the designation necessarily as concrete as a living person performing a public task. Members of religious or ethnic groups may be "protected persons." So are all the deceased of France. The dead take their honor to the grave. Heirs may sue in response to aspersions cast by the press on the good name of their predecessors or on their own reputations through reference to alleged ancestral antics.(12)

3. Outrage. "Any scornful expression that diminishes respect for the moral authority of a public function, or the purpose for which it is exercised" falls under the mantle of legal outrage. Even broader than injure, outrage can involve anything from the use of actual facts to "ironic or insolent" statements or mere gestures. In the eyes of French law, these are the most serious of press offenses. They draw the most stringent penalties from what Auby and Ducos-Ader call the "most supple" procedures.

The French judiciary has adopted outrage as its chief bulwark against press scrutiny of its work. Article 226 of the Penal Code specifically bans anything that "throws discredit on a judicial act or decision . . ," or which "aims to strip judicial acts or their authors of the consideration inherent in their function." Nor does this interpretation leave much room for maneuver: "It is not necessary in terms of recent jurisprudence," write Auby and Ducos-Ader, "that the accused intend to attack the authority of justice; it suffices that the act could have had this result."

Media comment before court decisions are handed down is regulated by the Forbidden Disclosures doctrine contained in the press laws of July 27, 1849, July 29, 1881, and October 30, 1935, which, collectively, provide that:

- Before trial, nothing may be said or shown on the "circumstances of a crime of blood" or anything that could pressure witnesses or reveal court procedures before the official announcement of a verdict.
- During litigation, personal privacy for all participants is maintained. The mere fact that statements are made in open court does not give French reporters the privilege to make them public. This includes, of course, all references to private life, facts more than ten years old, and previous crimes amnestied or pardoned.(13)

4. Exempted Subjects. In addition to defamation, privacy, and protected public authority provisions, French law simply bans certain subjects outright. The following list, while by no means complete, suggests the size and tone of the dossier of unmentionables. Without previous authorization, periodicals may not report:

- Anything concerning the military that may damage its "effectiveness or morale."
- Anything that might "attack the credit of the nation, whether undermining confidence in its currency or the value of public funds."
- Anything relating to parliamentary investigations or commissions.
- Anything that might "outrage public morals" or attract "undue attention to debauchery."(14)

PUNISHMENT BY PRINT

One of the most imaginative features of French press law is a sanction quite independent of fines, imprisonment, or civil damages — the requirement that certain material be inserted in the press as a result of a court judgment. This requirement is not simply because of journalists making mistakes, nor is the insertion simply in the one paper involved. Rather, French law awards persons dissatisfied with coverage involving them the right to force retraction. The press, in other words, can be forced to run specific editorial material against its will. The "right of rectification" grants "any embodiment of public authority" accused in the press of misperformance the right to demand a free insertion. The only restrictions on the correction the periodical must run in a prominent position in its next issue is that it be no longer than twice the length of the original article.

By contrast, the "right of reply" gives any person or organization, public or private, the ability to force insertion whether or not the piece written about them was correct. The only requirements are that the plaintiff be identified and discussed. That alone guarantees the right of "reply." The reply itself can be anything from a denial to simple amplification. The publication must print it within three days of receiving the complaint in precisely the same position as the original and in the same typeface. Frequently, judges extend the requirement of publishing the reply to other periodicals. In doing this, they require editors to pay for insertions 50 to 250 lines long in competing papers as well as in their own. Placing the replies does not mitigate the damages. It simply allows the publication to escape the fine that might otherwise be levied.(15)

A miniscule incident in the recent history of French-American interaction sheds light on differences in journalistic expectations and legal exigencies between the two countries. In 1978, the International Herald Tribune ran two Associated Press articles on the U.S. Church of Scientology. Editor Murray M. Weiss received a call from the church's French representative demanding the "right to reply" to criticism. Politely but firmly, Weiss explained that nobody but the Trib's editors decided that sort of thing. He was wrong. Although wholly owned by American parent companies, the Trib is a French corporation. The paper's lawyers advised the astonished editors that, if they refused the Scientologists' demands, the case would go against them. Such a decision would carry with it possible penalties of fines and jail sentences. Negotiations awarded the church 50 lines in the Trib.(16)

When confronted by these French press laws, American journalists are simply stupified by the restraints. A brief recitation of events in recent American history about which coverage would be illegal in France provides a vivid illustration of the legal restrictions for the French press:

- All reporting on Watergate would constitute "outrage" to the chief of state, who also could have prosecuted the press on grounds of protecting national security, precisely the argument that Richard Nixon unsuccessfully tried to make.
- The Pentagon Papers were unreleased products of a government commission and, therefore, would have been an "exempted subject."
- All unauthorized reporting from Vietnam (the sort that won Pulitzer prizes for David Halbertstam and Seymour Hersh) might have been prosecuted for "damaging military morale." The same would have been true for sympathetic

treatment of draft "refusniks" living in Sweden and Canada.

● Anything more than the barest police–blotter facts concerning Senator Edward Kennedy's misfortune at Chappaquidick, Massachusetts, on July 18, 1969, would fall in the area of his personal life. Therefore it would have been private and protected. He would have received further shielding as a national legislator, one of several classes of "protected persons." As of midnight July 18, 1979, the law covering facts more than ten years old would draw a third curtain of legal shrouding across the incident, making any mention of it in the press actionable per se.

The mere possibility of prosecution, of course, does not mean that every incident becomes a case. French experience with the law governing "offense to the chief of state" shows the highly personal nature of the decision to prosecute. President Charles de Gaulle invoked it 350 times. Once he even invoked it to punish a reporter who broke the law by shouting "Hou, hou"(17) at him during a parade. Giscard d'Estaing entered office pledging never to use it, and did not. He left it on the books, however, and found other provisions to accomplish the same ends. One such action was in the Le Monde case discussed earlier. François Mitterand's amnesty of pending press litigation made no special mention of that celebrated incident, nor did it commit him to any course other than that already provided for by French law.

Such formidable weaponry deployable at such wide personal discretion has a powerful effect on the French press. It makes much serious reporting very risky. But, like the atomic bomb, laws capable of destroying much of free expression deter most effectively by not being used. In fact, the French press is in daily operation a good deal freer than the law would allow. Yet, although the best French journals take risks every day, the knowledge that there may be a preemptive attack at any time can add sufficient insecurity to give them pause.

STATE ASSISTANCE

If the French state sets harsh limits on what newspapers and magazines may print without fear of legal retribution, it positively showers benefits on those — publishers and journalists alike — who play by the rules. Nothing in the elaborate web of state–press interaction encourages challenging the system. In fact, protective administrative planking and a cargo of tax breaks and financial aid make "rocking the boat" self–defeating for either those who own publications or their employees. The boat they rock is, after all, their own.

Every autumn the 491 deputies of the National Assembly take one of their few scarcely contested votes of the legislative year to authorize the expenditure of hundreds of millions of dollars in public funds ($533 million in 1978) to the profit-making enterprises of the press.(18) Everyone, politically speaking, gets aid, from the crypto-fascist weekly Minute to Humanitée, the Communist Party daily. French politicians identify strongly with publications that support their causes. So they do not oppose aid to them, even though their enemies also benefit. To do so would be "political suicide," as the Assembly's press subcommittee chairman once put it.(19)

Another reason why public subsidization of private enterprise remains popular is that it is not considered aid to publishers. Officially, newspaper aid is reader aid. Without it, goes the theory, there would be fewer, weaker newspapers. This would then mean a narrowed range of opinion and a lowered reportorial quality in French journalism. Only once since the Second World War has this reasoning been challenged. The challenge drew a scholarly squelch from the prime minister's office: "If the objective of subsidization is the reader of the paper," wrote Jean Serise, who formulated a government white paper in 1972, "the immediate assignee is necessarily the newspaper enterprise, which must reflect back to the reader, whether through expanded or improved content, the benefit provided."(20) Whatever the assumption of the law, it does not regulate the actual use of the money. Publishers may do as they please with the additional resources, plowing them back into the business or harvesting them as profit.

About 90 percent of this state assistance to the press is indirect and avoids outright cash payments from the public to the private sector that might offend voters. Credits and exonerations render it "not aid which is given, but rather resources which are not taken away."(21) The most interesting provision — attacked as "shocking financial heresy" by critics and staunchly defended by publishers as "our" Section 39-b — concerns the taxation of reinvested profits. Eighty percent of any amount spent on improving productive capacity of a press enterprise within five years of its accrual is free of all taxation.(22) Other indirect aid categories range from cut-rate postage and telegraphic service to exemption from professional taxes.

Indirect Government Press Subsidies
for 1978 (in francs)(23)

Press telegrams	70,000
Other telegraphic services	2,800,000
Preferential postage	1,402,000,000
TVA exoneration	203,000,000
Profit reinvestment (39-b)	46,000,000
Professional tax exoneration	180,000,000

In addition to this indirect aid, calculated in terms of the amount treasury receipts are diminished by exemptions, there is extensive direct underwriting. This includes provisions that illustrate the sometimes "Alice-in-Wonderland" complexity of state assistance. The Fiscal Reform Act of 1976, for example, gave publications a choice. They could either pay less TVA (value-added tax) or be reimbursed for the tax they were paying on newsprint, printing processes, and other news production costs. In 1978, all but 414 of the 9,900 publications eligible for a tax cut found it more lucrative to pay higher taxes. State subsidies of $47 million more than offset them and actually produced additional revenues for those companies.(24)

For some, this has not been enough. Deputy Roger Vivien scolded less generous colleagues for their performance in an official comment on the 1978 figures: "One has every right to ask the powers that be to explain their reasons (for niggardliness). If they accept the aid policy, it is indispensable that they support it with funds sufficient for proper execution."(25)

Mercantilist aspects of the French economic system also benefit the press. Because the state owns the nation's railroads, for example, it can facilitate newspaper distribution while protecting itself from competition by reimbursing its customers for a portion of their freight costs. In other contexts, this sort of payment is frowned upon as a kickback. At the same time, the state makes no such help available for privately controlled transit — trucks, for example. International distribution of French publications is also deemed a matter of legitimate state interest, as a means of strengthening national prestige. Accordingly, $2 million in public funds was spent in one year to put Le Monde, L'Express, and other journals on the newsstands of the world.

Direct Government Press Subsidies
for 1978 (in francs)(26)

Telephone calls	9,978,000
Subsidized printing	6,000,000
Railroad reimbursement	38,160,000
International distribution	10,000,000
TVA reimbursement for publications electing to pay increased taxes	235,000,000
	299,138,000

Surprisingly, the provision with the greatest impact on both domestic and international news is not considered aid in official terms, nor is it carried as such on the National Assembly books. Yet the large-scale subsidization (161,215,000F or about $37.5 million in 1978)(27) of Agence France Presse (AFP) is of fundamental importance. Part of it goes to offset the expense of furnishing AFP to publications within French borders. This cut-rate service effectively locks competition out of the country. Only with state underwriting can AFP afford the 850 journalists and elaborate bureau system it uses to provide most nonlocal news to French publication and broadcast outlets. Without the financial assistance, AFP would be hard-put to battle the extensive competition among Associated Press and United Press International (US), Reuters (UK), and Tass (USSR).

The state treats France's 14,000 journalists no less handsomely than their employers, beginning with a 30 percent reduction in their income tax liability.(28) No less wondrous, at least to American eyes, are some of the provisions of the National Collective Bargaining Agreement for journalists that is negotiated biennially by journalists and publishers with active participation by and enforcement from the state.(29)

Pay. Bonuses are left neither to chance nor to merit. By law, every French journalists receives a "treizième," or thirteenth-month compensation at the end of the year. This is 30 days' salary at the highest level earned in that year. At some large publications, contract provisions extend the payment year to 16 months. Night work requires a 15 percent premium. No circumstance is overlooked in the guarantees of benefits. Hazardous assignment (defined as anything from domestic riots and foreign wars to epidemics, spelunking, and "underwater reporting") guarantees journalists of additional life insurance coverage that must be not less than ten times the reporter's salary and not more than ten times the editor in chief's. Anyone disabled in the line of duty receives full salary for a year. If permanently maimed, journalists receive full retirement benefits. If a media employee is killed on the job, his or her family receives generous cash payments. The publisher is also required to pay the cost of returning the body to its residence or anywhere else "an equivalent distance away" from the scene of misfortune.

Vacations and Leaves. The French national contract awards everyone one month paid time off in summer and another 12 days in winter. In addition, official holidays commemorating religious sanctity and political tumult ring the calendar so there is at least one in every month except in February. Family life is encouraged. Journalists get a week's leave when they marry, three days if they become parents, and two days when they move or become parents-in-law. Death merits equal reverence, requiring publishers to grant one day off for the death of an employee's brothers- or sisters-in-law; two days for brothers, sisters, or grandchildren; and four days for a spouse, parent, grandparent, or parent-in-law. Maternity adjustments are also guaranteed.

The "call or recall to the flag," as military conscription is colorfully described in the journalists' contracts, constitutes a break in employment but the management must find work acceptable to the journalist upon his return. If it fails to do so, a full year's pay is due complete with the treizième provision. Special provisions grant journalists protection from being required to do promotion work and from being refused permission to free-lance for other publications if it would not render the employer "professional or moral prejudice." Continuing education comes free of charge to journalists. A 1974 law designed to upgrade the profession required publishers to set aside 1 percent of their profits (tax-free) to support studies pursued by their employees at Paris's Center for the Perfection of Journalists (Centre de Perfectionnement des Journalistes) for up to one year. "It doesn't matter if the fellow who covers railroads decides to study Mandarin," said the president of France's largest journalists' union, "the paper is obliged to let him do it."(30)

Job Security. The national contract for journalists balances opportunity for the young against protection of senior employees. In the frequently hectic world of meeting deadlines, management often finds it convenient to shift junior employees into jobs of greater responsibility on a temporary basis. Americans consider these stints primarily as chances for advancement. Additional salary is neither paid nor expected. In France it is mandatory. And, while protecting beginners from exploitation, the law also seeks to prevent management from using tryouts to humiliate senior people (perhaps into resigning) by stipulating that someone coming into a job cannot make more than his predecessor.

Being fired or even quitting can also be a highly remunerative affair in France. The national contract says flatly that "If an employer dismisses an employee, indemnity is due." Should the cause for firing be "grave or repeated" faults on the part of the journalist, a special commission may reduce severance pay. Otherwise, it is fixed by law: one month's pay for each year (or fraction) employed. For those with 15 years' seniority, special boards decide how much more than the legal formula must be paid. Costs to employers can be considerable. Firing a $12,000-a-year reporter with ten years on the job, for instance, would mean paying him $120,000.

Personal Integrity. A special "conscience clause" extends full severance benefits to journalists who quit or who are forced to resign because a change in their publication's political orientation affronts their "honor, reputation, or general integrity." Its use is commonplace. Journalists fleeing papers taken over by press baron Robert Hersant to escape his strident, right-wing politics have made legendary claims. So many left Paris-Normandie that their enforced severance pay enabled them to set up a (short-lived) competing paper.(31) Another wave abandoned Paris's staid Figaro when Hersant bought control. Celebrated journalistic donnybrooks in 1979 contrasted the French and American approaches. Faced with insubordination by two editors who refused his orders to run highly political pieces, the Panax newspaper chain's John McGoff fired one and forced out the other on his own terms.(32) In France, on the other hand, Philippe Grumbach applied conscience clause terms to his situation at the newsweekly L'Express when it had been sold by liberal Jean-Jacques Servan-Scheiber to Sir James Goldsborough, the conservative Anglo-French financier. Grumbach won $500,000.(33)

ADMINISTRATIVE SYSTEM

The seductive terms of state aid to publishers and journalists are not extended without strings attached. A network of considerable suppleness and subtlety brings state representation to the innermost councils of French journalism. There, its influence is often hidden. The system is designed to permit the maximum play of personality, politics, and reciprocally owed favors.

Students of French history such as the Sorbonne's Pierre Deyon called this system Colbertisme, in honor of Jean-Baptiste Colbert, the inventive finance minister who found ways for Louis

XIV to pay for the world's most expensive palace at the same time he was fighting history's costliest wars. As Deyon puts it:

> the idea was simple. Louis needed all sorts of equipment for his projects, but lacked funds to buy it outright, or the administrative structure which would be necessary for running industries directly. So Colbert created an in-direct way of funneling private capital and entrepreneurial energy into investments and behavior favored by the crown.(34)

The key mechanism is state _representation_ in everything important and state _ownership_ of very little. This gives enough flexibility to make Colbertisme particularly useful in state relations with the modern press because, in all but a few instances, disputes are resolved and controls exercised before they come to open, public test. This is also what critics find insidious about it.

One of the first steps in the production of periodicals provides an apt example of Colbertisme in action. It is the so-called obtaining of a _numero paritaire_. As is typical of the system's guiding ambiguities, this registration is neither legally mandatory nor issued directly by the state. Instead, approval must come from the _Commission Paritaire des Publications et Agences de Press_ composed of seven government officials and seven publishers.(35) Together they verify that the periodical will appear at least monthly and will devote no more than one-third of its space to advertising. These preconditions augment 11 other stipulations, including the requirement that owners be French nationals of legal age without police records. Why would publishers go through this theoretically optional process? Because, as a practical matter, they could not hope to compete without it. The numero paritaire is the precondition for receiving all state aid. And this, in 1978, amounted to 12 percent of the total financial turnover in the newspaper industry.(36) Without such aid, all but the strongest Paris dailies would quickly go under, and very few of France's 84 newspaper companies would remain profitable.

Other points of state-press contact involve legal deposition requirements and a host of special commissions for services ranging from newsprint price setting through newspaper delivery and the guarantee of the independence of Agence France Presse. Newspaper publishers are reminded daily of the state's interest in what they print: Two copies of every issue, bearing their signatures, must be left with the district attorney.(37) Nor can they forget who decides which publications will receive advertising from Air France, Renault, and other nationalized companies. Ranking among the nation's largest advertising accounts, their advertisements are distributed by Havas, the state-controlled advertising agency.(38) The state is even represented, although indirectly, in the cooperative that distributes all but a few of the 3.7 million newspapers read in metropolitan Paris, Nouvelles Messageries de la Presse Parisienne.

The French publishing world fizzes with rumored government interventions — that one newspaper publisher has been blocked, another invited, to take over a daily by discretionary loans from nationalized banks or that antitrust legislation is mysteriously held in abeyance for a publisher whose papers back the current leadership. May 29, 1978, however, brought a rare chance to watch Colbertisme out in the open. By statute and in structure, Agence France Presse seems elaborately protected from interference. Its constitution states that it

> will in no circumstances take account of influences capable of compromising the exactness or the objectivity of its information; nor must it, in any circumstances, pass under the control in law or in fact of any ideological, political or economic group.(39)

Unions and management and print and broadcast journalists are elected to AFP's Superior Council. Of its eight members, only three represent the government. Even on the Administrative Council, AFP's supreme body, the state accounts for only 5 of 15 members. Yet that neatly stacks the deck when the game is Colbertisme.

Just as Claude Roussel was about to begin the traditional second term as AFP's chief operating officer, the minister of culture intervened and forced him out. In came Roger Bousinac, whose journalistic credentials, some argued, did not match Roussel's but who was undeniably politically useful to the administration of Valéry Giscard de Estaing, at a time when it had been faring poorly at the polls. Bousinac was director-general of France's most powerful publisher's group, the Syndicat National de la Presse Quotidienne. Its members largely determine which political candidates get how much coverage, and of what kind.

The coup was as unambiguous as AFP's statutory independence, and France's preeminent journalist would have none of it: Hubert Beuve-Méry, a founder of both AFP and Le Monde, angrily resigned from the wireservice. He thundered against "the grave attack on the spirit, if not the letter, of the agency's statute."(40) To students of press freedom a-la-française, however, the most significant aspect of the encounter was its aftermath. There was none: no screaming headlines, no reporters sent to question the minister, let alone the president. Even Le Monde buried its founder's remarks in the "Presse" section deep inside the paper. To the French, Colbertisme is an old story; it is not for the front page.

Colbertisme embraces journalists as thoroughly as publishers. No benefit is received without screening by quasi-official bodies. As publishers find numero paritaire registry a necessity, journalists cannot function without a **carte professionelle d'identitée**. Only holders of the official press card, for example, receive the 30 percent income tax break or the generous protections of the national labor contract. These assume particular importance against the background of French journalism's traditionally high (about 15 percent) unemployment rate.

In essence, this theoretically optional document is as much a license to practice as the numero paritaire is to publish. Striking similarities appear in the processes of obtaining both forms of state sanction. The **Commission de la Carte d'Identitée Professionalle** (CCIP) is composed of seven working journalists and seven government officials. It determines each applicant's "high moral standards," financial arrangements, and standing within the profession. Disputes on entry qualifications, any change in the mandatory annual renewal, or changes in working status (all of which must be registered with the CCIP) are referred to a Superior Council. There, state representation is more decisive. It includes two judges and one journalist. Denials are not uncommon on grounds that somebody does not meet the definition of "journalist" stipulated in Article 761-2 of the National Labor Code.(41)

CONCLUSIONS

Indirect controls on free expression in the newsrooms of France involve both carrot and stick, but, more important, they carry the promise of reward or the threat of punishment, contingent upon future behavior. This imposes pressure for self-censorship. With the cards that could be dealt known but not their order and with the possibilities of gain and loss known, much depends on the needs, predelictions, and integrity of the dealers who represent the state. When French journalists and publishers weigh their options, they do so within the context of Colbertisme. At this particular time, would this official prosecute? Might that quasi-public board cause trouble if we go to print? Will taking this step jeopardize my eligibility for aid?

This is not to suggest that there is more of a personal element in each interaction between the press and the state in France than elsewhere. There are simply many more points of contact than in the United States and far more state-established institutions to guide them. The cumulative effect is not lost on those who live in this system. Quoted in the government-published Cahiers Francais, Le Monde's Claude Durieux described widespread self-censorship as the "prudent conformity, the silence of complicity to which journalists are often given on certain subjects."(42) There is little of the American expectation that truth, openly expressed, will somehow "make us free." Quite the contrary. Robert Escarpit, a distinguished columnist and founder of the University of Bordeaux journalism school, questions the wisdom of regarding ventilation as an absolute value:

> Why should we bring out all the facts? This is an ancient country, with a past full of feuding. Some of us make mistakes; we all live in glass houses. For instance, I'm from the Resistance. I could walk down the street in Paris and point out those who collaborated . . . who was responsible for deaths. What if I did that? What if we all did it? How could we live together afterward as a nation? What would be the point?(43)

Jean-François Lemoine, whose Sud-Quest newspapers dominate southwestern France, sat in his elegant office and compared French and American journalism; a wry smile crossed his fact. He summed up the French position: "Freedom of the press?" he mused, "here, we have freedom from the press."(44)

NOTES

1. Europa Yearbook 1981, vol.1 (London: Europa Publications), p. 1243.
2. J. M. Auby and R. Ducos-Ader, Droit de l'information (Paris: Dalloz, 1976), p. 301.
3. Ibid., p. 249.
4. L. Solal, Guide du Droit de la presse (Paris: Centre de Formation et de Perfectionnement des Journalistes, 1976), p. 57.
5. "Article 42, Loi du 29 Juillet 1881," Journal Officiel de la Republique Francaise (Paris: Direction des Journaux Officiels, 1881).
6. Auby and Ducos-Ader, op. cit., pp. 299-300.
7. Ibid., pp. 285-315 passim.
8. "Loi du 17 Juillet 1970," Journal Officiel de la Republique Française (Paris: Direction des Journaux Officiels, 1970).
9. Solal, op. cit., p. 72.
10. Auby and Ducos-Ader, op. cit., pp. 278-84 passim.
11. Ibid., p. 286.

12. Ibid., pp. 286-89 passim.

13. Ibid., pp. 299-310 passim.

14. Ibid., pp. 310-17 passim.

15. "Loi du 29 Juillet 1881," op. cit., Article 13.

16. Interview with Murray M. Weiss, Paris, 1978.

17. S. de Gramont, The French (London: Hodder Stoughton, 1969), p. 230.

18. M. Papon, Rapport fai tau nom de la commission des finances, de l'economie generale et du plan (1) sur le projet de loi de finances pour 1978 (No. 3120) (Paris: Assemblee Nationale, 1977), pp. 7-10 passim.

19. Interview with Robert-Andre Vivien, chairman of the National Assembly subcommittee on aid to the press, Paris, 1978.

20. J. Serise, "Pourquoi l'Etat droit-il aider la Presse?" Rapport du groupe de travail sur les aides publiques aux entreprises de presse (Paris: Les Cahiers de la Presse Francaise, 1972), p. 28.

21. Interview with Nadine Toussaint, Paris, 1978.

22. A. Smith, Subsidies and the Press in Europe (London: Policy Studies Institute, 1977), p. 7.

23. Papon, op. cit., p. 10.

24. Ibid., p. 8.

25. Ibid., p. 9.

26. Ibid., p. 8.

27. Ibid., p. 6.

28. Solal, op. cit., p. 52.

29. "Convention Collective Nationale de Travail des Journalistes," Journaliste (Paris: Syndicat National des Journalistes, 1976), pp. 9-15 passim.

30. Interview with Daniel Gentot, president of the Syndicat National des Journalistes, Paris, 1978.

31. N. Brimo, Le Dossier Hersant (Paris: François Maspero, 1977), p. 77.

32. Interview with Robert Skuggen, editor, The Marquett Mining Journal, Ann Arbor, Michigan, 1979.

33. "The Right to Edit," Time, February 26, 1979.

34. Interview with Pierre Deyon, Paris, 1978.

35. N. Toussaint, "Les Organismes de 'Controle' de la Presse," Supplement aux Cahier Francaise, No. 178, Octobre-Novembre 1976 (Paris: La Documentional Francaise, 1976), p. 1.

36. Interview with Jacques Sauvageot, general manager, Le Monde, Paris, 1978.

37. Solal, op. cit., p. 32.

38. J. Fitchett, "Hersant: The Press Baron of France," International Herald Tribune, January 27-28, 1979, p. 6.

39. "L'Agence France-Presse," <u>Notes et Etudes Documentaires,</u> Nos. 4:336-4:337, 23 Novembre 1976 (Paris: La Documentation Francaise, 1976), p. 17.

40. "M. Bousinac est elu President de l'Afp," <u>Le Monde,</u> May 31, 1978, p. 20.

41. Solal, op. cit., p. 77.

42. N. Toussaint, "Le Metier de Journaliste," <u>Le Presse Quoitidienne,</u> Les Cahiers Français, No. 178, Octobre-Decembre 1976, Paris, p. 16.

43. Interview with Robert Escarpit, Bordeaux, 1978.

44. Interview with Jean-François Lemoine, Bordeaux, 1978.

PART II
CONTROLLING THE
COMMUNIST PRESS

CHAPTER 4

Media Direction and
Control in the USSR

BY LILITA DZIRKALS

In diversity of genre and format, the Soviet media mirror those of the West. There is an abundance of books and periodicals for the general reader and for different age and interest groups as well. The reader can choose among local and central newspapers, and specialized newspapers that, in addition to current events, cover developments in a particular profession or industry. The reader can keep informed with magazines that offer both words and pictures or rely on cultural and scholarly journals that examine current events and issues in broader perspective. The broadcasting media similarly offer programs for varied audiences, whether it be information, education, or entertainment.

Distinct from the media of Western and other modern, non-Communist states, the variety of forms and topics offered by the Soviet media is firmly anchored in a common purpose and philosophy. On the grounds that it has developed the ideology and policies that enable the Soviet people to build a Communist society, the Communist Party of the Soviet Union (CPSU) appropriates the leading role in the Soviet "state of the entire people." The CPSU controls all Soviet media, whether officially identified as Party-managed or not. The raison d'être of the Soviet media is to propagate the directives of the Party and to indoctrinate the populace to carry out Party policies.

This chapter is a condensation and revision of the Section, "External Controls," in Lilita Dzirkals, Thane Gustafson, and A. Ross Johnson, The Media and Intra-Elite Communication in the USSR, Report R-2869 (Santa Monica, Calif.: 1982).

The very diversity of Soviet media offerings attests to the importance that the Communist regime attaches to media as a policy instrument. The more audiences the media effectively reach, the more successfully they carry out their assigned role in the system of political controls. The Party's constant concern is twofold: to expand, specialize, and modernize the media so that they meet the communications requirements of an increasingly modern and complex society, and to ensure that in the process of doing so, the media do not come to promote any concepts that undermine the CPSU's leading role in Soviet society. In political reality, the latter concern translates into ensuring the perpetuation in power of the present leadership grouping.

This chapter focuses on the mechanisms through which the Soviet political leadership directs and controls the media, ensuring that they serve its purposes. The internal controls by which the Soviet media monitor their own performance are touched on only briefly, as their role in defining the limits of media operation is secondary.(1) The reader should keep in mind that this is a brief and technical outline of the devices (or what we know about them) that the Soviet system uses to place the media potential totally at the service of Party-state interests. The creative talent and vitality of the media profession in the USSR is as strong as anywhere in the world and as aware of its audiences' true desires. It frequently challenges the bounds that authorities impose on its striving to communicate meaning-fully with its audiences. In many small ways, journalists and broadcasters have succeeded in bending and reshaping the official limits, and editors and producers have braved recrimin-ations to present controversial works. The human dynamics that fuel a never-ending struggle between the creative masters of the media arts and those who define the interests of the state are outside the scope of this chapter.

Most of the information presented here derives from published Western sources. The rest stems largely from the accounts of former Soviet journalists and others who worked in the Soviet media. The recent emigration of Soviet Jews brought out many media professionals. Interviewed for a Rand Corporation study, they significantly updated and enlarged the existing knowledge of controls operating in Soviet media.(2) Highlights of this new information are also presented here. The Soviets themselves have published several studies on their journalistic practice, as well as collections of Party directives dealing with the media. The latter have been utilized here for the evidence they offer of the Party's comprehensive involvement in the media.

PARTY SUPERVISION OF MEDIA

The USSR's political and economic system determines the Soviet system of media control. The Party disposes over all resources of society and mobilizes them for tasks set in Party directives. In media, as in all other spheres of Soviet life, the Party allocates the resources, sets the tasks, and appoints the managers to carry them out. Party approval is required to found any media organ, including those formally subordinated to governmental bodies or small economic or scientific organizations:

Decisions on founding new republic, territorial, province, city, district, state agency, and branch newspapers, as well as on changes in size, frequency of papers' publication, honoraria, staffs, and editors' rates of pay come into force after their confirmation by the CC CPSU [Central Committee of the Communist Party of the Soviet Union] . . .
The present CC CPSU resolution establishes that radio broadcasting at plants and construction sites and in kolkhozes and sovkhozes is set up by decision of Party city and district committees . . .(3)

Although formal authority for media belongs to the specialized State Committees for the printing trade, television, radio, and cinema, actual control and supervision are the job of the Party apparatus. The Central Committee Propaganda Department oversees the central media, the city Party committee oversees the local media, and so on down to the plant Party committee that oversees the factory newspaper. Party organizations decide the extent of coverage offered by media organs, appoint key personnel, and control the content. They set tasks: themes to be handled, viewpoints to be promoted, even authors to be published. Designed to ensure that the public word promotes only the policies of the Communist state, the web of Party controls governs all aspects of Soviet media: administration and financing, information and entertainment, ideology and moral teaching.

The Party explicitly obligates the media to observe the principle of Party loyalty, or **partiinost'**. The legacy of the founder of the Soviet state, V. I. Lenin, the principle of press partiinost' remains immutable and to this day legitimizes Party domination of all media: "Party leadership of press, television, and radio is the chief factor determining that the partiinost' principle is adhered to and implemented." In the Soviet view, Party leadership of the information media guarantees steadfast political orientation, purposeful effort, and task fulfillment. Party documents state frankly that the Party sees to it that editorial staffs are made up of people who are both professionally competent and "unreservedly devoted to the cause of the Communist Party."(4)

At the highest level of Party leadership, the Politburo decides overall media policy, including organizational questions and top personnel appointments. An illustration of Politburo involvement is its appointment of a special commission in 1978 to prepare recommendations for improving ideological work and media performance.(5) The Politburo appoints the top media officials in the Party supervisory structure as well as in the media themselves. Former Soviet journalists maintain that the chief editors of Pravda, Kommunist, Mezhdunarodnaia zhizn' (International Affairs), and the international Communist journal World Marxist Review are Politburo appointments. They also believe that individual Politburo members or Party Secretaries are involved in the final confirmation of editorial appointments in the journals published by the leading international affairs institutes of the USSR Academy of Sciences.

The Central Committee Secretariat, which partly overlaps in membership with the Politburo, supervises the media for the top leadership.(6) Senior Politburo member and Secretary M. A. Suslov, who died recently, had long held top responsibility for the ideological integrity of the media. Below him, a Central Committee Secretary supervised propaganda and ideological affairs. Former Pravda chief editor M. V. Zimianin has held this post since March 1976. Politburo member P. N. Demichev supervises the cultural media within his general responsibility as the USSR Minister of Culture. According to Soviet emigres, it was generally believed in Soviet media circles that Suslov approved media statements originating in the Politburo. Together with Central Committee Secretaries B. Ponomarev and K. Rusakov he directly supervised the editors of Kommunist, the Party's leading periodical.

Each Secretary is responsible for a particular area of Soviet economic or political affairs and usually heads the corresponding Central Committee department or supervises several related departments. It remains unclear how the media responsibilities inherent in the Secretariat were distributed among Suslov's office and those of the Secretary directly responsible for propaganda and ideology and the Secretaries in charge of other policy areas. Emigre interviewees indicate that the Propaganda Secretary's responsibilities include supervising Glavlit, the censorship agency. Secretary Zimianin and his predecessor, L. F. Il'ichev both had prior experience as chief editors of Pravda and deputy foreign ministers. But in managing media coverage of international affairs, Secretary Ponomarev has had an active role as head of the International Department, responsible for relations with nonruling Communist parties and leftist movements. Since the founding of the International Information Department in 1978, its chief officials also have had prominent roles in handling major international issues in both foreign and domestic media.(7) Konstantin Chernenko, head of the General Department and a longtime associate of Brezhnev, has had the main editorial responsibility for publishing Party documents, including a volume of Brezhnev's speeches on ideological indoctrination.

Several of the 23 specialized Central Committee departments participate regularly in decisions concerning the media. But the Propaganda Department has the overall administrative responsibility for directly supervising all central press organs and broadcasting media. The propaganda departments of Party committees from republic to district (raikom) level extends this control to media throughout the country.

The Propaganda Department is one of the largest of the Central Committee departments and the only one that has special sections for publishing houses, journals, and newspapers. Appointments of central press chief editors and top management of publishing houses require approval by the Propaganda Department before they are confirmed at the Secretariat level. The Department approves editorial board appointments in the central press. Chief editors of republic press must receive a Department recommendation before they can be confirmed by the leadership of the republican Party. In many cases, the Department has firsthand knowledge of the appointees' qualifications, having previously dealt with them as its staff members or practicing journalists.

Together with the censorship agency Glavlit (see below), the chief editors constitute the critical control factors at the operational level of Soviet media. In the case of a local paper, the chief editor serves on the executive board of the Party committee, under whose jurisdiction his newspaper operates, and in the case on central newspapers usually he becomes a member of the Central Committee. His interest in career advancement (and the generous material rewards associated with it) ensures that he will faithfully implement Party policy in his publication, knowing that he can be summarily fired for even seemingly minor infractions. When that happens, his career is over, and he is likely to be relegated to a minor position somewhere in the media industry.

Serving as liaison between the leadership and media editors, the Propaganda Department holds regular biweekly instructional conferences for senior editors of the central press, informing them of current policy and providing guidelines for media coverage.(8) At these meetings, Department representatives also critique press performance during the preceding period. Former Soviet journalists report that the Department also issues specific directives to individual media organs to present certain material. Department staff members regularly monitor assigned publications and provide feedback to editors. On potentially sensitive articles, editors can consult the monitor, or kurator, who either resolves the question or refers it to other Central Committee departments.

In the early and Stalin periods of the Soviet regime, when it was known as Agitprop, the Propaganda Department exercised a vaster and more exclusive control over press and broadcasting than today and enforced a uniformly rigid propaganda policy throughout. As political terror eased in the post-Stalin era and as Soviet society modernized and expanded its international contacts, Soviet propaganda and information policy was compelled to develop a more differentiated and sophisticated media approach in order to reach important audiences effectively. Consequently, other Central Committee departments besides the Propaganda Department have become increasingly involved in determining media content bearing on their areas of concern.

Addressing current issues in foreign policy, economics, or science, in the specialized media in particular, but also in the mass media, requires a level of competence in such diverse fields that the Propaganda Department alone cannot provide guidance in all of them. Moreover, these and other policy areas are the well-defined spheres of authority of departments other than the Propaganda Department. Thus, responsibility for implementing important aspects of the Party's foreign policy resides in the International Department and for science policy in the Science Department, and these departments, as all others, must also ensure that the media properly serve their particular policy concerns. They accomplish this not only by interacting with the Propaganda Department but also by advising central and specialized media editors directly. The Propaganda Department has the important task of reconciling these diverse interests in the media and preventing any open contention between sometimes conflicting interests that could damage the Party's image of "monolithic unity" and commanding influence.

A special arrangement governs the direction and control of the military press, which is supervised by the Main Political Administration (MPA) of the Soviet Army and Navy. Organizationally, the MPA is intimately intertwined with the regular military establishment run by the Ministry of Defense. Distinct from the regular military, the MPA functions with the status and prerogatives of a CPSU Central Committee department ("rabotaet na pravakh otdela TsK KPSS"). The MPA has its own propaganda and agitation board.

The MPA is in charge of (rukovodit) the central military newspapers, journals, and the publishing houses, which are within its purview; it controls the content and ideological direction of the entire military press; it publishes political and literary-artistic journals, authorizes the publication of educational-methodological handbooks, manuals and posters on political and military education questions, and participates in the work of creating training and art films on military themes.(9)

ROLE OF MINISTRIES

Ministries control information on their activities by the "visa" procedure.(10) To publish specialized material, the media must obtain a "visa" from the ministry in whose province the material falls. Glavlit requires the visa before it accepts such material for final publication clearance. A deputy minister's office normally handles media requests for visas, but increasingly ministry press departments have taken over this function.

The visa procedure recognizes both ministerial expertise and authority. Consulted to ensure that no sensitive or secret information appears in published material, ministries also have the discretion to veto material they find objectionable. However, in the infrequent event that the Central Committee wants a ministry criticized in the press, such an article needs no visa from the ministry involved. According to emigre reports, the Central Committee department concerned will call the Propaganda Department, which then orders the chief editor of the appropriate paper to print a critical story; Glavlit is so informed. In the city and district level media, local Party committee staffs rather than ministry subordinates regularly decide which activities and problems receive coverage.

Former foreign affairs journalists testify that Foreign Ministry clearance or visa is necessary for major journal articles and books on international affairs. The Ministry's press bureau, said to be very conservative, reviews articles, while its different departments clear book manuscripts in their area of specialty. The government news agency, TASS, has close ties with the Foreign Ministry. TASS directors have come from the ranks of Foreign Ministry officials. At the same time, they are also Party Central Committee members, and this ensures that TASS operates in full accordance with the policies pursued by the Party leadership. TASS essentially monopolizes international news coverage in the Soviet media.(11) It controls the availability of foreign news by maintaining several wire services. Besides regular TASS news service distributed to the open media, there are several others restricted to different levels of officialdom, with only the top layer of Party functionaries having access to complete coverage of foreign developments.

In the mid-1960s, several ministries established press centers. Staffed with professional journalists and filmmakers, these press centers generate media material on ministry activities, thus, in effect, lobbying for their interests in mass as well as in specialized media. Sometimes a press center journalist is simultaneously a newspaper's correspondent and uses this access to place articles favorable to his ministry in that paper.

CENSORSHIP

While most stories and articles originate in response to official directives to feature particular topics, much media material is initiated by journalists and authors themselves. In all cases, the censorship process starts with the author, who knows from experience what is not permissable to publish. Editors constitute the next censorship control: first, the department editor, then the managing editor, and, finally, the chief editor. Any questions about the prepared material are usually resolved at this stage. Editors consult the appropriate Party offices when in doubt and, in case of material relating to ministries or other agencies, direct the authors to obtain the necessary visas. Material dealing with the military or with defense-related scientific subjects additionally requires clearance from specialized censorship agencies. Then the material is placed in the final layout and goes to the chief editor for his approval. Finally, galley proofs are submitted to the censor, whose stamp and sign off culminate the censorship process and release the material for publication.

Glavlit

Officially attached to the USSR Council of Ministers, Glavlit — or Main Administration for Safeguarding State Secrets in the Press — maintains a countrywide network of censors, estimated to number at least 70,000. Although the agency's title invokes only the press, its actual responsibilities also include radio and television. Located at printing plants, editorial offices, and broadcasting studios, Glavlit censors scrutinize all media material before stamping it for public release.(12) Preventing the unauthorized use of printing equipment is also their duty, enforced so exactingly that not even wedding announcements can be printed without first receiving the censor's stamp.

Glavlit's mission is to ensure that no information affecting the security of the Soviet state appears in public communications. The Committee for State Security (KGB) and Glavlit jointly prepare the censor's Index (Perechen'), a classified handbook on "state secrets," which may not be disclosed in the media. The Index also incorporates Defense Ministry instructions. Variously described as being 300 to 1,000 pages thick, the volume is updated regularly and lists military, technical, statistical, and other data, such as names of persons, not to be mentioned in the media.(13)   Its standards of what is considered sensitive from the standpoint of military and state security are extreme. The censor once rejected an article on the draining of a Lithuanian swamp as "revealing geographic and topographic subtleties which might be useful to an invading military." Every censor and chief editor has a copy of the Index in his safe, but the censor is the one held ultimately responsible for enforcing the Index's myriad prohibitions, thus ensuring against editorial oversight.

The secrecy in which Glavlit operates and the almost total absence of any mention of it in Soviet publications preclude determination of the precise extent of its authority.   During Stalin's reign and before, Glavlit was empowered to approve political content of media material, but its prerogative in this area since then remains ambiguous. Since the end of the Stalin era, Soviet commentators have emphasized the editors' deciding role in what is published, claiming that Glavlit's authority extends only to material in certain "scientific spheres."(14) Former journalists among Soviet emigres of the late 1970s as well as those of the 1960s describe Glavlit's mission as primarily a technical one.(15)   They confirm that, starting in the early 1960s, editors have assumed the primary responsibility for political soundness of material.   Chief editors of Pravda and Izvestiia, who are Central Committee members, have the right of "second signature," whereby they can sign off alongside the censor and print material on their own responsibility, if they choose to disregard the censor's objections.(16)   At TASS, senior officials can override the instructions contained in the censor's Index, presumably with the concurrence of higher authorities, because TASS censors stay in contact with the Propaganda Department (and likely with the International Information Department as well).   In 1965, Glavlit readily reversed its refusal, based on its instructions in force, to allow Stalin's photo in a publication, after the editor cleared this with the Central Committee Secretary in charge of propaganda and ideology. These accounts indicates that Glavlit censors defer to editors, who as political insiders may anticipate forthcoming revisions in Glavlit's instructions.

Dismissing as mere formality Glavlit's subordination to the USSR Council of Ministers, former Soviet journalists are certain that in practice the KGB and the Central Committee Propaganda Department supervise Glavlit. The Propaganda Department provides its ideological and political guidelines. Glavlit's longtime head (since 1957), Pavel Romanov, worked on press affairs as a Central Committee staff member following World War II. The KGB is involved in defining classified information and handles Glavlit's funding and staffing matters. Many censors are former KGB employees. During 1963-66, when Glavlit was absorbed by the newly created but transient State Press Committee of the USSR Council of Ministers as one of its departments, KGB General I. Agayants served as its deputy director. Glavlit chief Romanov became the chairman of the new Press Committee, which was empowered to control the content of all published material in the country. In 1966, with the demise of the Press Committee, Glavlit recovered its status as a separate agency attached to the Council of Ministers. But its official title no longer referred to military censorship, as it had until 1963, when it was known as the Main Administration for Safeguarding Military and State Secrets in the Press. How this change in Glavlit's title may relate to the development of the military censorship (see below) is not known.(17)

During the Stalin era, Glavlit had formidable enforcement authority, reflecting the power of the secret police with which it was openly associated. The chief of Glavlit was also the official in charge of military censorship. The cases of editors who repeatedly failed to follow censors' directives were referred to the OGPU for further action.(18)

Nowadays, the Glavlit censor may report a presumptuous editor to Central Committee offices, but the editor's fate depends on his political connections and their willingness to support him. The censor has the more vulnerable position when a controversy over published material turns out badly for the paper. In such cases, interviewees note, the censor assigned to the publication gets fired, even if he has expressed initial misgivings, for failure to take adequate steps to prevent the occurrence.

Deterred essentially by self-interest to avoid jeopardizing their careers, editors and writers seldom risk outright violation of the censor's rules. The penalties for doing so can be dismissal and even include being barred from practicing journalism. But those determined to slip controversial material past the censors have found ways to do so. The limits of censors' authority and lapses in censorial thoroughness provide opportunities for evasion to those willing to risk the consequences.

Cultivating the trust of Party officials, who can influence publishing decisions and protect writers and editors in case of subsequent retaliation, is the safest way of defeating censorship and getting new ideas in print.   In the literary field, in particular,   concerted   protests   by   the   editorial   staff   to sympathetic   Central   Committee   functionaries   have   reversed negative decisions by the censor.(19)   The limits of the censor's power in the face of determined defiance are illustrated by a 1965 controversy involving the literary journal Novyi mir.   Know- ledgeable interviewees assert that its chief editor, Tvardovsky, simply bypassed the censor in printing an article that decried the promulgation of fabricated legends as official history, as in honoring the cruiser Aurora for firing the first shots of the 1917 Revolution.

Translations of foreign scientific literature have been used to smuggle in new views in natural and social sciences, which conflict with official ideology.   A former Foreign Literature Publishing House editor reports that during the period 1954-62, censors checked only the preface and notes supplied by Soviet editors, because they could not understand scientific terminology. The   editors   were   responsible   for   censoring   the   translated text.(20)   In the early 1960s, the flowering of Soviet science management studies (naukovedenie) also provided opportunities for natural scientists to publish ostensibly technical writings, which contained controversial social criticism as well.(21)

The censorship system has dealt with the challenges to its competence by upgrading its personnel.   In the last 10 to 15 years, the older Glavlit employees have been retired and replaced by people between the ages of 25 and 35.   Generally, the newcomers have completed higher education, predominantly in the humanities.   Recruited   mainly   from   Party   and   Komsomol memberships, they include former KGB employees and individuals who   have   previously   worked   as   journalists   and   editors. Specialized censors, located at the USSR Academy of Sciences, have assumed the main responsibility for clearing media material in key scientific areas.

Emigre   journalists   note   that   censors'   competence   and sophistication   vary,   depending   on   the   importance   of   the publication to which they are assigned and the locality.   In republic capitals and even in Moscow, local newspaper censors are "nice girls," who perform their task in a routine and unassuming   manner   and   are   regarded   as   mere   clerks.   In publishing   houses,   censors   are   thorough   and   sophisticated   in detecting any attempts to circumvent the rules.   In republic publishing   houses,   in   particular,   censors   have   had   to   be especially alert to compensate for the laxness of editors who are reluctant to order changes in manuscripts submitted by popular local nationality authors.

The competence and assertiveness of censors appear to be a function of their position in the Glavlit structure.   Head- quartered in Moscow, Glavlit extends its control to outlying regions through branch offices, known as Obllit in provinces (oblasts) and Gorlit in cities. Province Party committee (obkom) propaganda departments and the local KGB branch also supervise these offices. A Gorlit office also operates in Moscow, censoring the Moscow city Party committee (gorkom) papers Moskovskaia pravda and Vecherniaia Moskva, and other local papers, as well as Literaturnaia gazeta and Novyi mir. Interviewees depict the regional censors as less sophisticated but stricter than the Glavlit censors they encountered.

Of the estimated 70,000 censors in the USSR, no more than 100 are located at the Glavlit headquarters in Moscow. A former editor who visited the headquarters estimates that some 30 to 40 of the censors housed there are ordinary censors. The rest are chief censors and a more senior group "who exercise what is called 'supercontrol.'"(22) The headquarters censors stay well attuned to the latest political currents in the capital, meeting in almost daily internal seminars. In his encounters with these censors, the editor found them assertive and arbitrary in exercising what was essentially political censorship.(23) He reports that even in Moscow censors at printing plants and editorial offices pass "important" material, having approved it for printing, to "highly placed censors," who are free subsequently to request changes in the copy. This may occur because the on-site censor recognizes that he lacks the latest censorship instructions. But it also suggests that high-level Glavlit officials are in the powerful position to reverse publication approval granted to controversial material by another top-level office. In the absence of information on who these officials are, their power base in the sanctum of the Soviet leadership remains unidentified.

Specialized Censorship Agencies

While responsible for affixing the censor's stamp granting final approval for publication or broadcasting, Glavlit defers to specialized censorship agencies to censor material dealing with the military and with advanced science fields relating to national defense. As in the case on ministry visas, editors and authors know to secure the necessary approvals from the specialized censors on their own initiative and submit them to the Glavlit censor along with the prepared copy. If not, the censor will refer them to the appropriate agency before giving his approval.

Military Censorship

All media material referring to any aspect of military life and affairs, past or present, must be submitted to military censors before forwarding it to Glavlit for final approval. In Moscow, editors take their prepared copy, together with a form letter giving information on the author and the sources used, to the Military Censorship (Voennaia tsenzura) of the General Staff in the General Staff building.(24) They pick up the material, now bearing the stamp of the military censor, several days later at another building. The censors are military officers. If they have questions or desire changes in the material, they notify the editorial offices to send an editor to discuss that matter. An interviewee who dealt with them frequently characterizes the military censors as friendly and straightforward and notes that they explained the reasons for their objections, even though under no obligation to do so.

The military censor's stamp specifies that approval relates only to the military subject matter contained in the article. Glavlit censors subsequently approve the article as a whole, without, it is reported, ever questioning military censors' decisions.

It remains unclear whether Glavlit censors the regional military press, which is distributed only to the military. Those who worked in the regional military press report dealing only with military censors attached to their publications. At a military district newspaper, the chief censor usually holds the rank of colonel. His staff includes no one below the rank of captain. Censorship personnel do not rotate back to line duty or participate in military drills. Many remain with the same military media organ for the duration of their careers.

Military censorship regulations are very tight. District and unit newspapers distributed exclusively to military personnel contain only minimally more information than the open military press. Examples of material in the public media that require military censor's rather than Glavlit's approval include such minutia as a news story about a small-town hero who was a colonel, since this was seen as revealing the presence of a division-level unit there, and an announcement that a stretch of asphalt highway was completed in a particular locality, because this could inform an enemy that airplane landings were possible there. In the case of a TV film, military censors in Moscow declined to approve aerial shots of power installations in Siberia, referring the filmmaker to the Siberian military district censor instead.

Interviewees assume that the Military Political Administration of the Soviet Armed Forces and the military department of the KGB provide guidance to the military censors, despite their official subordination to the General Staff.

Science Censors

Special censors, located at the USSR Academy of Sciences, review material in key science and technology areas related to national defense. As in the case of military censorship, formal Glavlit approval is still required for publication. All publications and broadcasts referring to space activities require prior authorization from an office of the Commission for Research and Exploitation of Cosmic Space, attached to the Presidium of the USSR Academy of Sciences. Established in 1957, the "space" censor is said to be very closely associated with Glavlit.(25) Other known censorship offices specialize in radio electronics, chemistry, geology, and computer science.

Responsibility for censoring material on atomic energy has been assigned to the atomic censorship office, housed in a building of the State Committee for Utilization of Atomic Energy in Moscow. It screens everything that mentions nuclear energy uses, including science-fiction stories. Editors have complained about the slow and bureaucratic work methods of the atomic censorship. Their attempts to pressure or influence the censor's decisions have been easily frustrated by its chief's control over their access to the high-security building.(26)

Well into the 1950s, the KGB and Glavlit controlled the release of scientific and technical information. KGB-run "first departments" in industrial plants and applied research institutes cleared all material for publication. That system apparently failed to ensure satisfactory central control over published information, and the censors' technical competence was not up to the task. A former researcher claims that some institute directors exploited the situation to gain publicity for their institutes. His experience also indicates that technical research institutes in general retain considerable control over published data. A publications commission, made up of five to six institute officials, reviews manuscripts the institute staff has prepared for publication and submits a certification to Glavlit that they contain no classified information. The commission rather than Glavlit then assumed responsibility for any problems that may arise later. Commission members include the deputy director of the institute, the chief of the KGB-connected "special department" responsible for safeguarding classified as well as patentable information, a union representative, and several engineers.

KGB Censors

The KGB functions as a specialized censorship agency for any material that deals with KGB activities. Its approval is obtained by Glavlit, not the media. However, a former magazine editor reports that he himself took stories dealing with the KGB and the militia to a KGB literary group officer at the Lubianka for clearance. In Moscow and Leningrad, KGB representatives have a say in approving stage productions. Interviewees variously describe these individuals as affiliated with a KGB culture and art, literature, or ideological department.

Former Soviet journalists relate that the lines of authority are not always clearly drawn on which specialized agency may issue approval in a particular case. At times, at this juncture, material has been passed for publication by someone who later turns out to lack the proper authority. Conversely, sometimes a specialized censorship agency can kill an article by claiming that it is not within its competence to approve. Looking for the right agency or ministry can be so time consuming that the story becomes obsolete and may never be printed.

CONCLUSIONS

The Soviet media are unique in that they have been at the service of the ruling party in a one-party state for over six decades. Central political control has evolved and consolidated, creating a network of reliable executors of Party policy from chief editor down to the working journalist. All know that advancing their professional careers depends as much on their effectiveness as professionals as on their usefulness to the existing power structure. Moreover, success in the media profession opens the door to participating in wielding power and enjoying prerogatives and comforts available only to a limited segment of the Soviet population. At the higher levels of the Soviet media system, the media specialist and the Party functionary merge into one. In resolving the tensions that arise between the often conflicting goals of modernizing media to meet the needs of a modern society (and meet the competition of foreign media for Soviet audiences) and preserving the political status quo, political concerns have always taken precedence over professional or institutional goals. At the same time, the Party-state leadership seeks to make the best use of the media potential both as mass information and propaganda means and as a means for working communication indispensable in a complex society. As communication needs and services have diversified and expanded, so has the official supervisory establishment. Specialized Central Committee departments and censorship agencies and various state committees operate alongside Agitprop and Glavlit to fine-tune the utilization of media resources.

The principle of central Party control remains constant, but the challenge of preventing specialization from developing into compartmentalization, which could undo the traditional unitary central control, is formidable. The pressure of modern circumstances and Suslov's passing from the scene could lead to divesting final media responsibilities in important areas to Party leaders who possess proven expertise in those fields. Should media leadership at the very top become specialized and segmented, the Soviet media could well find themselves freer from ideological restraints in some areas but likely to become involved in political struggles among contenders for power.

NOTES

1. For a broader discussion of the Soviet media system and process, see The Media and Intra-Elite Communication in the USSR, Report R-2869 (Santa Monica, Calif.: Rand Corporation, 1982). An earlier, valuable description of all aspects of Soviet media can be found in Mark Hopkins, Mass Media in the Soviet Union, (New York: Pegasus, 1970).

2. Between 1978 and 1981, Rand Corporation's Communist Media Study interviewed 56 former Soviet journalists and others connected with the media. See The Media and Intra-Elite Communication in the USSR.

3. O partiinoi i sovetskoi pechati, radioveshcanii i televidenii (On Party and Soviet Press, Radio Broadcasting, and Television), "Mysl'," Moscow, 1972, pp. 362-63.

4. These statements appear in the introduction of a collection of Party documents, KPSS o sredstvakh massovoi informatsii i propagandy (The CPSU on Mass Information and Propaganda Means) (Moscow: Politizdat, 1979), p. 4. A recent Soviet discussion of press partiinost' occurs in the monthly of the USSR Journalists' Union, Zhurnalist, no. 12, December 1980, pp. 3ff, 45 ff.

5. At the November 1978 Central Committee plenum, Brezhnev reported that the Politburo had recently examined letters received in the CC CPSU, criticizing the media for persistent failure to tackle effectively various current economic and social problems. Brezhnev expressed complaints particularly about the state of international affairs reporting and commentary. He announced that the Politburo had formed a special commission to examine all these questions and decide on measures to improve ideological and mass-political work. (KPSS o sredstvakh massovoi informatsii i propagandy, pp. 549-50.) A new Central Committee Department of International Information had just been established in early 1978, and in April 1979 the Central Committee adopted a comprehensive resolution "On Further Improving Ideological and Political-Education Work" (ibid., pp. 344-58.) Inter alia, the directive urged media to expose corruption and mistakes, arrange discussions with reader participation on current domestic and

international issues, and regularly interview government agency leaders on topical problems.

6. Ned Temko, "Soviet Insiders: How Power Flows in Moscow," Christian Science Monitor, February 23, 24, and 25, 1982, reports that the chief editors of Pravda, Izvestiia, and Sovetskaia Rossiia told him they participate in the weekly sessions of the Secretariat. The chief of the State Committee of Television and Radio Broadcasting also attends. The chief editors of Kommunist and Sotsialisticheskaia industriia claimed to have attended Secretariat meetings also.

7. Soviet officials told a U.S. journalist that both Zimianin and International Information Department chief Zamiatin, a former TASS director, prepared the Soviet response to President Reagan's announcement that the United States would start producing neutron weapons (Temko, February 24, 1982).

8. Leonid Vladimirov, The Russians (New York: Praeger, 1968), pp. 86-91.

9. Sovetskaia Voennaia Entsiklopediia (Soviet Military Encyclopedia), vol. 2 (Moscow: Voenizdat, 1976), pp. 562-63.

10. On this, as on all other points discussed, more extensive discussion can be found in the Rand Corporation report on Soviet media, op. cit.

11. The main central press organs have their own correspondents abroad, but still rely mainly on TASS for international events reportage.

12. The censor's code number appears on the printing data page of all Soviet publications, except the volumes of Brezhnev's and other top leaders' collected speeches and writings, official publications of party and government directives and legislation, and publications in foreign languages.

13. Relatively detailed information on the contents of the Soviet censors' "Index of Information Not to Be Published in the Open Press" is given in M. Dewhirst and R. Farrell, eds., The Soviet Censorship (Metuchen N.J.: Scarecrow Press, 1973), pp. 55-56; Leonid Vladimirov, "Glavlit: How the Soviet Censor Works," Index on Censorship, 1, no. 3/4 (Autumn/Winter 1972): 38-39. Boris Gorokhoff, Publishing in the USSR, (Bloomington: Indiana University Press, 1959), pp. 258-60, gives the text of the Secrets Law of 1956, which lists types of information considered state secrets. The 1956 law repealed the 1947 law governing the lists of proscribed information.

14. Boris Kampov-Polevoy and Valentin Berezhkov, U.S. News & World Report, November 11, 1955, pp. 76-92; see also comments by emigre journalist L. Vladimirov/Finkelstein in Dewhirst and Farrell, The Soviet Censorship, p. 64.

15. For emigre journalist comments on the censor's role as a "secondary" and "purely technical one," see "A Conversation with Viktor Perel'man," Radio Liberty Dispatch, July 9, 1973, p. 10;

Nikolai Gavrilov, "Letter from a Soviet Writer," The New Leader, December 9, 1963, p. 16; and Antony Buzek, How the Communist Press Works (London: Praeger, 1964), pp. 140ff, 195.

16. Vladimirov claims that at Pravda censors' enforcement of the Index regulations is very lax, and the paper contains a lot of "errors" in this respect (Dewhirst and Farrell, The Soviet Censorship, p. 67). But the chief editor reviews thoroughly all material with ideological content. A study based on tabulations of the censors' log numbers in Pravda and five other central dailies found that Pravda and four of the other papers were censored by the same team of seven censors. The study speculated that this was evidence of a "top" censorship team (John H. Miller, "The Top Soviet Censorship Team? — A Note," Soviet Studies, October 1977, pp. 590-98). But information from other sources does not corroborate so important an assessment of this particular censorship team. For one, all of the papers scrutinized in the study are printed at the Pravda printing plant, which additionally prints 35 different magazines and journals, including Kommunist (Hopkins, Mass Media, p. 209). Vladimirov, "Glavlit," p. 32, notes the "joint Glavlit pool shared by all journals put out by the Pravda press located on Bumazhny proyezd."

17. In late 1967, Soviet editors in Kiev and Irkutsk told an American journalist that Glavlit censors were checking their copy mainly for military information (Hopkins, Mass Media, pp. 128-29). The 1931 decree defining Glavlit's functions is not known to have been repealed. It ordered Glavlit "to exercise all aspects of politico-ideological, military, and economic control" over all media. Robert Conquest, ed., The Politics of Ideas in the USSR (New York: Praeger, 1967), pp. 43-49, provides much of this decree.

18. Dewhirst and Farrell, The Soviet Censorship, p. 72; Merle Fainsod, Smolensk Under Soviet Rule (Cambridge, Mass.: Harvard University Press, 1958), pp. 155-56, 364-68, 373, and 376. Other informants claim that the secret police had a special unit, "Litkontrol OGPU," which carried out surveillance and supervision of writers and also the officials of Glavlit and the Central Committee's propaganda office (Dewhirst and Farrell, The Soviet Censorship, p. 11, note 21).

19. Dewhirst and Farrell, The Soviet Censorship, p. 132.

20. Ibid., pp. 73-74.

21. Yakov M. Rabkin, "Science Studies as an Area of Scientific Exchange," in Soviet Science and Technology: Domestic and Foreign Perspectives, John R. Thomas and U. M. Kruse-Vaucienne, eds., (Washington, D.C.: George Washington University for the National Science Foundation, 1977), p. 72.

22. Dewhirst and Farrell, The Soviet Censorship, p. 52.

23. Vladimirov, "Glavlit," p. 39.   L. Finkelstein, who uses the pen name L. Vladimirov, supplies this information as well as the estimate of 70,000 Glavlit censors.   For explanation how he derived his estimate, see ibid., p. 65.

24. Ibid., pp. 34-35.

25. Some reports describe the "space" censor as concerned only with the political, ideological, and propaganda aspects of copy.   The ministry building spacecraft had its own censorship department, which clears material for publication.

26. Vladimirov, "Glavlit," pp. 35-36.   He states that the atomic censor clears material dealing with both peaceful and military uses of nuclear energy.   Other reports specify that military censors handle material dealing with military applications, and the atomic censor is concerned with civilian uses only.

CHAPTER 5

Media Control in Eastern Europe:
Holding the Tide on Opposition

BY JANE LEFTWICH CURRY

For the Communist leaderships of Eastern Europe, control of the media's messages is a critical part of rule. For the populations over which they rule, access to that media and to true and comprehensive information is equally central. For the Soviet Union, tolerance of regimes in Eastern Europe requires that they maintain media that do not openly challenge either the primacy of the Soviet Union or the leading role of the Party. As a result, conflicts in these societies always center around access to the mass media. When control by the Communist leaderships has diminished or been lost, the media transform themselves. And, when the media no longer reflect the leadership of the Communist Party, liberalization has been brought to an end.

The irony of all of this, though, is that although the mechanisms of Communist governance were transferred directly from the Soviet Union to the states of Eastern Europe, and the same demands for media freedom crop up repeatedly during periods of liberalization, the mechanisms of media control do not vary dramatically. Each state in Eastern Europe developed its own response to the propaganda needs it had after World War II. From the beginning, the basic media production processes were comparable, but the styles and instruments of direction varied from country to country. Furthermore, as leaderships changed and the relationships between the rulers and the ruled evolved, the processes of media direction and control changed in each Eastern European state.

Throughout Eastern Europe, the strongest controls grow out of the journalism work and media production. Journalists are, after all, privileged members of a society conditioned by 35 years of Communist control to have a sense of the limits of discussion. As a result, most Eastern European systems have, at least since the late 1960s, relied not on the formal, prepublication censorship customarily posited as a key lever of totalitarian rule, (1) but on the inherent rewards for and pressures on journalists and editors to conform to the needs and programs of the Party leadership. Currently, only in Poland and Czechoslovakia, where the inherent controls are the weakest, does an institution of prepublication review exist to check the editors' decisions. For Rumania and Yugoslavia, abolishing institutional censorship was a de-Sovietizing process that in Rumania increased the conformism of the media and, in Yugoslavia, led to greater freedom. But in Hungary, East Germany, and Bulgaria, prepublication censorship outside the editors' offices never existed as a formal institution.(2)

During the past 35 years of Communist control over Eastern Europe, four basic models of media control and direction have existed:

1. The initiation mode in which censorship exists to prevent errors and teach journalists the art of self-censorship since, although fearful of offending their rulers, they have not worked in a Communist media system long enough to have inculcated all of its rules and regulations. Such a situation existed for most Eastern European leaderships after the Communist takeovers. It currently exists in Czechoslovakia and, potentially, in postmartial law Poland — societies where the reassertion of strict control brought with it a transformation of the journalism profession that left it run by relative newcomers unsure of themselves and uncommitted to professional ideals.

2. The directive mode in which party and government directions — given explicitly through the various press committees and agencies to journalists and editors, or implicitly through general Party statements and the overall political atmosphere in which journalists work — are effective enough to allow the media to be produced with no formal, external prepublication censorship. Inherent in this system is an entire system of sanctions and rewards built into the very process of journalism work. Such systems may be run to produce a relatively open media (as in Yugoslavia and Hungary) or a very restricted media (as in Bulgaria, East Germany, and Rumania). The nature of the media product is dependent on the political leadership.

3. The political monitoring mode in which the normal journalistic processes and the Party and government directions are supplemented by an external censorship institution. This Office of Control monitors the media not only for inadvertent mention of "secrets" but also for political errors and for reflections of problems and issues reflected by journalists from their contacts with the population and the administrative process. Such

information is used by the leadership in assessing the tenor of popular opinion over which it has less control and is more dependent than other regimes in Eastern Europe. This system has existed since 1956 in Poland, where the Party leadership has been less secure than elsewhere in the Communist world.

4. The revolutionary mode in which censorship, whether it is journalists' own self-censorship or formal, external censorship, ceases to exist as a result of pressure from the population and the professional community or as a result of disillusionment among the censors themselves. Such conditions existed in Poland and Hungary in 1956, Czechoslovakia in 1968, and Poland in 1980.

"NATURAL" GUIDELINES

Underlying all of the articulated institutions of direction and control in Communist states are the forces of control inherent in the media production process itself. Journalists are, after all, select and privileged members of their own societies. Although lower level journalists and those with special talents who outwardly support the basic ideology of their regime must not always belong to the Communist Party, membership is expected of prominent journalists and their editors. In fact, editorial positions on all but the most marginal journals are a part of the Party's nomenklatura. This means that not only is membership in the Party required for anyone in top journalistic posts (such as foreign correspondents and individual commentators) but individuals must also be well enough known and connected with Party leaders to get their nomination. To lose any but the lowest position in the mass media is to lose a comparatively high salary; far greater access to information than others in the society have; and special privileges for travel, vacation homes, and hard-to-get consumer goods. To lose a media position filled by nomenklatura is essentially to be blocked from any other privileged position of employment.

As it does in the West and in Third World states, the process of producing a story carries with it inherent limitations. Journalists tend, because of their work schedules and pressures, to become their own community. The desire for respect from that community is a defining factor in journalists' work and their lives put them in contact with a limited number of groups in their societies: largely the powerful and politically involved or the weak whom they help. As a result, although they tend to be seen as enemies of the administrators they are supposed to monitor, they have little contact with the general population and have a perception of issues and answers limited by virtue of their personal perspectives.(3)

Journalists also face limits on their access to information. These occur most often on an <u>ad</u> <u>hoc</u> basis with industrial managers or government bureaucrats keeping journalists from information that might make them and their work look bad. Although this occurs at all levels and in all systems, it is done in spite of the formal statements by government and Party officials ordering the media to monitor the governing of society. To surmount this, journalists and editors must either use their personal prestige and contacts to get information from other sources or to force information from these bureaucrats — a costly and time-consuming process. These possibilities do not exist in states like Bulgaria and Rumania, where the use of information in the media requires the approval of the institutions from which it comes.(4)

Time is another limitation on what journalists do and how far they deviate from the norm. It affects the mass media in a different way than time constraints do in the West. There is in the ideology of the Communist press no sense of the necessity of quick, unbiased information. Instead, journalists' work is based on a tradition of the media as forums for discussion and advocacy. But, because the predominant portion of journalists' earnings comes from "piecework" and not from a net salary, there is a clear incentive to make sure that everything is publishable so that time is not wasted on articles "for the drawer."(5) This, even without the threat of sanctions, leads all those who are not in a position to guarantee publication by virtue of their connections or their reputations to avoid complex and controversial issues that are time consuming and potentially unpublishable.

Within an editorial office, these unspoken pressures are repeated at every level. So it is not only the individual journalist who monitors his own work as it is conceived and produced but also his department editor, the assistant editors who oversee a group of departments, and top editors. For those in higher positions, their concerns are not only about their own positions but for a need to protect the journal as a whole from criticism for deviation, unpopularity, or inefficiency. This task is complicated by the fact that these three sins are often mutually exclusive: To appeal to readers, for instance, articles must be critical and special. Editors' sensitivity to the nuances of any article or topic is heightened by their greater contact with political leaders and officials in charge of propaganda. The knowledge that they gain from these contacts is radiated downward to their staff as are the officials' concerns about the performance of the journal as a whole. All of this increases the filters and pressures on the work that journalists do.

For Eastern European journalists and editors, there are also other far more direct incentives and sanctions than those built into basic journalism work. Both Party and government have special agencies organized to deal with the media and the presentation of information. In addition, Party and government officials concern themselves directly with how they are covered in the media. And, because all work is ultimately state-run, these individuals, as well as Party and government press organizations, have far more possibilities of influencing journalists and their lives than do comparable agencies in the West.

The major organ involved in guiding and supervising the mass media in all of these countries is the Central Committee Press Department. It and its regional subdivisions are ultimately responsible for supervising personnel selection, ideological direction, resource distribution, and all prohibitions and regulations for the media. The general pattern is for instructors in the Press Department to supervise journals and radio and television programs by meeting formally and informally with their editors; to call meetings for groups of journalists and editors to give instructions on the coverage of specific issues or events; to participate in the compilation of guidelines for the mass media's coverage; and to review formally the work of various media organs. The press departments are also each responsible for their Party committee's organ (the central Party papers of their districts), although the editors of these organs are customarily members of the Central Committee or the regional organs so that, in fact, they are part of the body for which the Press Department works. In addition, through their guidance over the work of state agencies involved with the media, the press departments are able to determine the funding, the extent of circulation, and the aid any given organ will receive.

How actively any of these media-related activities is performed or what balance is struck between them depends on what the goals of the Press Department and the leadership it is to serve are for the media and for itself, as well as what other structures exist to influence the work of journalists. For instance, in Poland during the Stalinist period, the Press Department kept in touch with editorial offices so that it knew the new, young journalists and their skills. To "test" their capabilities, it did not give them detailed instructions but made them rely on their own caution in the face of the terror that existed throughout the society. At the same time, top editorial positions were filled by individuals who were either members of the Central Committee itself or closely tied to members and got their directions from personal contacts. Under Gomulka, a leader who had very little concern with the media as a political force, the Press Department maintained only a distant presence. It took note of positions taken in the media and reported them upward, but regulation occurred largely through ad hoc demands made by individual leaders and institutions. Gierek, on the other hand, regarded the media as a prime tool in his goal of forming a mobilized population. Under him, the Press Department grew from the 10 instructors' positions it had had since the takeover to 60 instructors' positions. Regional departments under regional Party organizations lost their autonomy in the move toward a total focus on national guidance. The Press Department under Gierek provided detailed instructions as to how things should be covered, what could and could not be said, and how journals would be distributed. As his era progressed, the media served less and less as a measure of public opinion simply because so little was allowed to appear.(6)

Similarly, in states without formal censorship that seek a controlled population, the Press Department is an active initiator, organizer, and controlling force. In others, the Press Department is a far looser central force relying largely on journalists' and editors' own professional socialization and their responsiveness to broad official critiques and instructions on the media and their work.

State institutions also affect the work of the mass media. Newspapers, magazines, and broadcast media are all under government administrative bureaucracies (as their counterparts in the West tend to be under publishing houses and broadcast association bureaucracies),(7) which handle financial and administrative matters. These involve determinations of what journals should be published and in what quantities, who should be hired and for what salary, and what special allocations should be made. In the case of books, the Ministry of Culture approves publishers' book lists. This is presented as a content decision. In other cases, administrative decisions are couched as simple bureaucratic matters but seen as political actions based on the approval or disapproval of a journal's work. Under these conditions, journalists and editors are left reacting to what they imagine state reactions will be.

State institutions in all of these societies also exert "positive guidance" over the information and discussion that appears. Under various names, institutions of all kinds and at all levels have some form of "press liaison office" that puts out packaged press releases for domestic and foreign journalists; intervenes in journalists' contact with their institutions by setting up "tours" and "interviews" for journalists, thereby blocking unsupervised contacts; and surveys the media for references to their institutions so that there can be a quick reaction to positive or negative publicity. Particularly for journalists without their own contacts or established expertise, these offices at least steer coverage under the guise of assistance if not dictating it by providing packaged and approved articles.

In other areas, state institutions exert more direct influence. Individual institutions tend to defy Party directives urging that journalists have access to information and be treated as "colleagues" by simply blocking access to information or actively trying to prevent journalists from publishing damning material. Normally, this includes direct intervention with editors or higher officials to prevent an article from going to press or to sanction a journal or editor for publishing a given critique. Protesting these blocks on information and criticism is both time consuming and personally costly for journalists and editors who are not well enough placed to counteract pressure.

Issues that are considered to affect state security (military, internal security police, and foreign affairs, especially in relation to the Soviet Union) are the most directly censored areas of information. In each of these areas the controls are explicit. Military information, defined by the military itself to include topographical information as well as a broad range of military affairs, is checked by the military itself in Poland(8) and, apparently, in other Soviet bloc countries. Security police matters are also carefully watched by the police. As a result, under normal circumstances, journalists simply are unable to deal in any of these areas. Foreign affairs is generally something about which journalists or editors refer to higher authorities if they have any qualms about their articles, even in the most unrestricted press systems like Yugoslavia. But, in spite of the fact that on critical foreign affairs issues there are most likely to be declared and detailed instructions as to what cannot be covered or implied, on broad issues of foreign reporting, journalists have enough "play" to camouflage critiques of domestic and foreign affairs.(9) In the area of military and foreign relations, the Soviet Union tends to take special notice. According to reports from Poland, in the 1970s the Soviet Embassy read and reacted to a wide range of journals and sent out its own instructions for editors and censors. Earlier, its direct contact with active journalists and editors was less explicit. The Soviet Union influenced coverage related to its perceived interests through the granting of visas, invitations to the Soviet Union, and (in the most dramatic cases) direct intervention with the Polish leadership.(10)

The ultimate impact of these various forces is generally considered to be far broader than the specific directives that they give. Because one's livelihood and position are dependent on not violating the written regulations as well as on the political climate, journalists, their editors, and their sources self-censor themselves. This occurs long before the submission of an article. It is a part of the entire journalistic process. And because the boundaries are never completely articulated, journalists and editors are far more cautious than the regulations themselves would require.

MODELS OF INTENTIONAL CONTROLS

Ironically, journalists in the Eastern European states that have not undergone recent and violent upheavals like those in Czechoslovakia and Poland have had long tenures in the profession — many since the takeover period. Yet, they are not completely trusted in any country to self-censor consciously or unconsciously. In all of these systems, the Party and government have mechanisms by which they make explicit to journalists the specific requirements of what is sought by the leadership and what is appropriate in the specific political climate. They also reward those who follow the line and sanction those who deviate from it. These tend, however, to be system-specific. Ultimately, though, whatever their severity and breadth, they produce media that adhere to the desires of the domestic political leaders.

The Initiation Mode

By the late 1940s and early 1950s, the Communist regimes of Eastern Europe had dropped the charade of co-rule with non-Communist parties. They were securing control through terror and through agitation and propaganda. To do this, they expended the mass media system and brought in new, young journalists to replace less trustworthy prewar journalists and fill the expanding number of slots in the media. Along with this, most of the leadership in Eastern Europe also established a separate, formal layer of professional censors to supplement the Party and state direction that was developing and the terror that guided the population's actions. These professional censors also supplemented the other controls that were initially placed on the mass media: licenses for publication granted only to journals of organizations that the Communist authorities approved; distribution facilities and newsprint supplies controlled by these same authorities; information provided by official sources rather than from individual correspondents; and "cadre safeguards," the need to have staff members approved for work in the media.(11)

Ironically, with the exception of Yugoslavia, which instituted formal, prior censorship in 1946, formal censorship was not a part of the initial years of Communist rule; as one journalist explained about Czechoslovakia during the late 1940s:

> there existed no censorship as a mechanism. You knew
> what you were supposed to write and when you did
> something which was not in line you were fired. Only
> later did the leadership discover it was much easier to
> have a censorship machinery.(12)

In the minds of many participants and observers, the installation
of formal censorship was, actually, the result of the failure of
the other controls.(13) First of all, the growth of the mass
media the regime needed to educate and propagandize its less
than supportive population brought the need to expand rapidly
the number of working journalists. There were simply not
enough ideologically and professionally skilled individuals to fill
these positions. As a result, large numbers of new, unskilled,
young people (largely workers and peasants) had to be quickly
selected and trained. They wanted to keep their new positions,
but they also were not experienced enough to make accurate
judgments about how appropriate their reports or commentaries
were. Second, as the Communist authorities took over the entire
society, there were simply too many complex issues and events to
have everything completely covered by regulations beforehand.
Finally, as the administration grew in size and responsibilities,
the Party leadership felt some need to have an independent
monitor on its activities for both the public and themselves.
Journalists and readers' letters performed this function as long
as there were censors to filter out what was acceptable for
public consumption and what was not.

The mechanism of censorship in this period worked much like
the Soviet mode, as few journalists had enough information or
daring to deviate from the standard line. There was generally
little political censorship. Instead, censors' decisions were based
primarily on the regulations and guidelines that they were given.
Censors concentrated on the details in the few articles written
by the staff that were published and on the general layout of
every journal. Journalists were severely sanctioned for being
censored and thus learned quickly from their errors and those of
their colleagues. Censorship therefore served as a device to
teach journalists the rules of the game. In addition, the
censors' office served to a limited degree to provide the
leadership with information about the state of the country that
it felt would be counterproductive if it was known to the entire
population.

This system existed in Czechoslovakia, Poland, Rumania, and
Yugoslavia in the 1950s and early 1960s. Today it exists only in
post-1968 Czechoslovakia and, potentially, postmartial law Poland.
In East Germany, Soviet military censorship served this purpose
for a short period after the takeover. There was never a formal
office of censorship in Hungary, even during the brutal Stalinist
period. The end to this formal censorship in all but Poland was

a result of deliberate government decisions to codify censorship and to shift responsibility more to editors and writers themselves. In Poland, censorship collapsed under the turmoil of the mid-1950s and was reinstituted to fit Gomulka's needs.

The reemergence of censorship of this mode in 1969 in Czechoslovakia came with the strengthening of all the other kinds of controls that had existed in the Stalinist period. It reflected the fact that

> a hard core of journalists [had to be] identified and deployed simultaneously with the ouster of unreliables. Then new people must be attracted to the profession. . . . And both the old trustees and the tyros must be tempted and rewarded by lucrative salaries and specifically high fees.(14)

The imposition of these controls and the use of salary inducements did not, however, ensure that the quality of journalists' judgments was sufficient for an educated population 30 years after the takeover. The staffs were new (half of the 4,000-member journalist union were removed after the "Prague Spring"); young (28 percent of working journalists in 1974 were under 30 as compared to 8.6 percent in 1967); and untrained (only 41.8 percent had university education and most of those were journalists under 30).(15) As a result, a high percentage of the postinvasion media messages are not written by journalists but by Communist Party functionaries.(16)

Ultimately, the weaknesses of the profession and the leaders' ability to lead dictated that formal censorship had to be reestablished to filter out judgmental errors by novices and pre-1968 journalists who had, in large part, not been leading journalists or outstanding editors knowledgeable about politics from before. As in the Stalinist period, this made censorship allowed for sanctions aimed at both frightening and schooling journalists into submission. In theory, it should have been a temporary measure. In fact, it has continued to be necessary for over ten years in spite of the increased stability and material gains of the profession, a reflection of the failure of the indoctrination to take even among the agents of indoctrination.

The Directive Mode

The directive mode is the most pervasive model of media management in Eastern Europe. In Hungary and East Germany, this model of carefully directed self-censorship by journalists, writers, and editors has been in place since the establishment of the Communist regimes after the war. In Rumania and Yugoslavia, it was part of a deliberate leadership move to increase individual responsibility while at least appearing to liberalize. Wherever it exists, it is predicated on the existence of trustworthy journalism cadres kept within the bounds either by terror or by a broad social consensus in support of the policies of the leadership. In Bulgaria, East Germany, and Rumania, where terror is an essential part of control, the lack of formal censorship leads to media where no risks are taken. In Hungary and Yugoslavia, where a relatively high degree of acceptance of the leadership and its basic policies exists, much is left to the initiative of individual journalists and editors working with an awareness of the acceptable ideological path.

The least controlling of these systems, the Yugoslav and Hungarian ones, allow and encourage criticism on most topics in the media and in the society itself. They do not, however, give free vent to any and all discussion. The media, whatever self-management exists, are ultimately licensed and owned by the state. Offending journals can be and are closed down or hampered in their publication and circulation.(17) Editorial positions are filled in Hungary with the approval of the appropriate party body.(18) Yugoslav journalists and editors owe their positions to their journals' sponsoring organizations and their own self-management groups — both of which are interested in the popularity and acceptability of their journal because these factors determine its profitability.(19) All of these personal and institutional concerns weigh against dramatic deviations from basic ideological tenets.

Beyond these controls inherent in any state-owned media, and normal newsroom controls, the Yugoslav and Hungarian media are subject to government and Party agencies that control information and frequently supply prepared articles that are carefully tailored. They are also continually bombarded by advice and instructions from Party and government sources.(20) And, given their concerns with avoiding problems, editors also contact ministers or Party officials formally and informally to check on what is appropriate coverage. According to Yugoslav sources, this occurs in daily paper offices at least two times a day.(21) Often, too, this direction is neither conscious nor formal: As in any Communist system, editors often hold political positions or are closely connected to political leaders so ideology and politics are integrated in their lives and work.

In Bulgaria, East Germany, and Rumania, media controls are far more exacting and strongly applied. No attempt is made to encourage journalists to explore facets of the society that, although unpublishable, would provide revealing information on the state of the society for the leadership. Instead, all of the "natural" guidance that occurs in these systems is imposed explicitly: Training and hiring are explicitly political, regulations and prohibitions are given directly to journalists as orders, and instructions on what information and criticism are to be public are put out and monitored by the Party Press Department.(22)

For journalists, most of whom have had ideological education and long years of experience, the potential sanctions for dissent are too great and the chance of achieving anything with it too small to even be considered. Ultimately, decisions are reached on the basis of information journalists receive through official channels and precedents they see set by ideologically and politically "mainline," established journals like central Party papers.(23) This is true to a lesser degree in Hungary and Yugoslavia. For instance, the practice in editorial offices in Hungary was said

> to avoid using any really "biting" cartoon unless it deals with a generally admitted social problem. If an editorial has already been written about a certain subject or the television network has already dealt with a matter, then a cartoon is permitted about it. But, if the cartoonist himself discovers certain controversies or abuses and wants to express his disapproval, he finds himself up against the authorities.(24)

In the case of Ceausescu's Rumania, these inherent mechanisms and responses have been supplemented by an elaborate, codified complex of mechanisms focused on centralizing media control and making professionals control themselves and their colleagues. From far less concrete data, it appears that this basic organization exists in all "uncensored" Communist media systems. On the one hand, a cultural council for "directing, guiding, and providing unified control over all cultural and educational activity in the Rumanian Socialist Republic" was formed in 1977. It was responsible for (1) guiding publishing houses and exerting control over their output by issuing journalists' cards and publishing authorization; (2) distributing "paper quotas to publishing houses . . . and periodicals" and exerting "control over the way this paper is utilized;" serving

> as a central records office providing the editors of newspapers and periodicals, radio and TV and publishing houses with the lists prepared by ministries and other national agencies of the type of data and information which, according to the law, may not be published;

and (3) monitoring "the way in which periodicals and other printed matter have conformed to and respected the provisions of the Constitution, the law on state secrets, as well as other valid laws and legislative acts."(25)

On the other hand, by setting up pseudo-self-management boards at every level, a system of "mutual censorship" also was established. Individuals' careers depended on the ideological merits of the organization with which they were affiliated. So approval for articles and coverage comes from fellow writers and workers (cum Party representatives) assigned to individual boards.(26) Experiences of the late 1970s show that this, in a situation where the stakes are high and the rules vague, has been a far more repressive form of censorship than formal, institutionalized prereading by professional censors.(27)

Control without prior censorship in all but the most democratic Communist societies predetermines authors' decisions from the very beginning of the journalistic process. Risk taking is decreased as the possibility of censors serving as a safety net is removed. For this more restraining system to function, however, there can be no dramatic shift in or out of the profession. Instead, journalists must be socialized gradually into correct political judgments. In addition, the political leadership must be stable, for, as happened in Hungary in 1956, a battle in the leadership brings with it the transformation of the media into a political battleground that encourages the population to vocalize its discontent.(28) This system offers no controls whatsoever against the fragmentation of media messages when the leadership itself divides.

Political Monitoring Mode

The model of Polish media control that has existed since 1957 has been the most developed and active system of formal prepublication control in the Communist bloc. At the same time, it is the product of the weakest Communist Party penetration. Thus its existence and strength is mandated by this failure of the Party to penetrate the population and gain basic legitimacy. What it does is substitute artificial controls for journalists who have taken the controls to heart: Polish journalists have experienced periods in which they were comparatively independent. They also work in a society where the pays legal and the pays real are not even comparable. As a result, they continually see themselves not as mouthpieces of the Party but as professional reporters and critics. Because of this, censors not only have to remove information forbidden in detailed daily instructions but also make individual political judgments on the overall tone and character of the media. Normally, these political interventions represent half of all censors' decisions.(29)

In this system, the normal controls of the media production process and the directions of the Party and state organs are supplemented by a separate Office of Control of Press, Books, and Public Performances, nominally a state organization but actually under the Party. As in the Soviet and in the initiation models, all publications from visiting cards to books, all performances and exhibits, and all broadcasts must be approved by a censor and stamped with his number. In Poland, though, the censor becomes involved only at the final stages of production. Journals and books and broadcasts, for instance, are given to the censors when they are set in type or ready to go on the air. This allows the censor not only to read for specific violations of the regulations he receives from his superiors but also to check for general content and overall tone. It allows journalists and editors to have their articles read less closely and in the context of other articles included to "balance" the coverage. Normally, too, the censors know that questioning any journal holds up the publication process so they are restrained in their actions.(30)

In this uniquely Polish model, the fact that censors often use their own judgment in deciding what should and should not be censored gives editors and writers the leeway to appeal their decisions. Particularly for editors who have enough political power to protect themselves from any dissatisfaction with their decisions, appeals to high-ranking officials in the Main Office of Control or to their contacts in the party hierarchy are a regular part of the editorial process. Beyond this, the Main Office of Control enters into the political process by serving as a channel for the top leadership to get information about issues raised by journalists that are considered important but not publishable. This has, according to both journalists and officials who have been interviewed, been an important factor in some policy decisions.(31)

The impact of this institutionalized censorship process is, at best, to give some sort of stable veneer to the media in Poland even during periods of factional infighting. But because so much depends on individual censors' judgments, and most of the censors' guidelines are deliberately kept from journalists and editors in order not to discourage them from researching issues, the process can be highly unpredictable. Under the Gomulka leadership, when there was little interest in the media as a tool in politics, the censors were left on their own and frequently had to make decisions about which requests from Party leaders or organizations to follow. Censorship in this system was often unexpected but almost always appealable.

With a change of leaders and leadership policy, censorship took on an entirely different character. Gierek treated the media as his own tool to promote his interests and not to question his decisions. As a result, the Main Office became a direct agent of the Party Press Department, which initiated its regulations, sent out special directions when there was a critical issue with which to deal, and reviewed its work. In addition, all of the institutions of control were expanded.(32) The result was that censorship became less unstructured and less appealable. It also ceased to function as the channel for public opinion and information under Gomulka. Ultimately, this restrained the Polish media. But the reliance on control rather than direction and self-control also left it devoid of advocacy and filled with simply passable articles.

With a censor to filter out what is unacceptable, journalists and editors could afford to generate their own ideas and worry only about how to mold them so that they would slip through. Without a censor, journalists have to depend on the leaders' guidance from the very inception of a story because they know beforehand what is to be printed and are responsible for their work. In Poland, the profession never relinquished its desire for independence enough to be freed from prior censorship: When journals edited by leading Party figures were exempted from censorship, their articles quickly became so controversial that censorship was reinstituted after six weeks.(33)

Revolutionary Mode

In every "revolutionary" situation in Eastern Europe, media management has been a cause, a target, and, initially, an easy compromise. With the exception of the workers' movement in Poland in 1980, every major period of liberalization (Hungary, 1956; Poland, 1956; and Czechoslovakia, 1968) has been preceded by a period of gradually increasing media criticism and discussion. Controversial articles appeared first in limited circulation journals and then, as a result of the precedents that were set, in mass journals. Their appearance encouraged further public questioning of the Party and its policies. They suggested to the population that the Party leadership was factionalized and paralyzed. Through the media and the discussions it facilitated, a momentum of increasingly daring demands was generated. After each previously unprintable demand was published, another more daring one was submitted. Ultimately, these demands and the revelations that accompanied them challenged the very tenets of the system and the process was brought to an end with the return of strict media control and direction.(34)

The major liberalization spokesmen in each of these periods were the journalists who had appeared to "toe the line" and to have been properly trained in earlier years. In all of these cases, journalists took their cues initially from the Party leadership, which was either so factionalized that individuals sought to court journalists to improve their own positions or sought increased professional discussion to resolve difficult issues. Once journalists had responded to these pressures, though, their writings opened a "Pandora's box" of public demands for more and sharper criticism. As their positions and their work were challenged, journalists responded with even more daring articles. And in situations where the leadership was divided and public discussion indicated that it had no authority, journalists felt themselves compelled to take positions of political leadership.

The opening through which all of this could occur was a weakening of control by the leadership. In no case was this intentional. In the Hungarian case, the leadership was divided so that it continually sent out conflicting signals to journalists and editors. Gradually, the battling leaders protected journalists who wrote articles attacking their opponents. In this battle, too, old journalists who had been jailed and formerly taboo topics suddenly reappeared: All of this called into question the ideology journalists had been taught and told to propagate. As this occurred, journalists increasingly took it upon themselves to initiate criticism. Their internal censors disappeared as did the significance of the sanctions that the leadership had always threatened to impose.(35)

In the case of the popular upheaval in Poland in 1956, a similar leadership division led to conflicting orders. There, though, the leaders gave both journalists and censors conflicting orders. The result was that censors no longer felt sure that they would be supported in their decisions or that they knew what was to be said. Increasingly, the censors simply did not censor. Finally, in the fall of 1956, the censors gathered together for a stormy all-night session, ending in a vote to disband themselves. Journalists were then free of any restraints except economic ones. But because of the threat of a Soviet invasion, they organized an ad hoc committee of journalists and government officials to review the media and suggest to those who had become too daring that they tone down their work.(36)

In the Czech case, censorship had been revised and toned down in 1966 in an attempt by the authorities to court favor with the intellectual community by appearing to limit censorship. In point of fact, the new Press Law was vague enough to have allowed for any level of control had the leadership of the Party not been seriously divided. Much like their colleagues in Poland and Hungary, journalists were initially "liberated" by their involvement in internal Party battles and then became critical actors on their own. Censorship simply ceased to function in late 1967. But, unlike their Polish predecessors, journalists did not seek the protection of a review board. They continued on in their criticism and voicing of proposals.(37)

The case of Poland in 1980 and 1981 is significantly different from the movements that preceded it. Until the granting of the Gdansk workers' demands (of which one of the top three was free access to the media and information),(38) the Gierek leadership was not visibly divided and kept a tight hold on the mass media. As a result, there were programmatic discussions to preface the changes. Platforms grew up in reaction to workers' demands and their gains. The censorship that Gierek had built up continued to function, following orders to be more or less liberal from its Press Department instructors.(39) Because there was a general agreement that the total abolition of censorship was not feasible, the battles over the media centered around access by the Solidarity union to its own media and to television time as well as the codification of strict and detailed limits on censorship. On the issue of legalizing censorship, the leadership came to a compromise after nearly a year of negotiation. On the issue of access, there was never an agreement for Solidarity's use of the broadcast media.(40)

In all four of these cases, the loss of control over the mass media was a major concern for the Soviet Union. According to the USSR's own statements on Poland, Hungary, and Czechoslovakia, the freedom of the media was a major cause for its actions. When it invaded Hungary and Czechoslovakia, the mass media were prime targets of attack. In Poland in 1956, Gomulka was told by Khrushchev, as he reported to representatives of the journalism called to speak to him, that continued escalation of media freedom would necessitate a Soviet intervention.(41) In Poland in 1981, one of the primary actions of the martial law regime was to close down all but two journals, impose total censorship, and force journalists to undergo "political verification" and sign loyalty oaths.(42) In all of these cases, the new media freedoms were quickly reduced to levels comparable to that of early periods of Stalinist repression. And in all but the Polish case of 1956, there was a major turnover in the journalism cadres to bring in new, untainted blood. This, of course, necessitated a return to initiation censorship.

THE TARGETS OF CONTROL

What is censored is evidence of both the posture and fears of the regimes in Eastern Europe. Most often, there is either no clear articulation of what is publishable or the regulations are kept strictly secret. As a result, what journals and subjects are controlled is visible only in the voids that appear.

Under normal circumstances, little needs to be said explicitly. Journalists and editors are conscious of the strictures of the societies in which they live. They also have the personal and professional connections that allow them to anticipate political shifts in their writings. The desire to maintain their positions ensures their self-restraint unless they know the Party leadership is fragmented and no authority exists to control them. At these times they test the limits ("the Soviet factor, the party dictatorship and personalities"), first in limited circulation intellectual journals that are always the most independent. Then similar criticism spills into more mass and more closely controlled media.

In stable times, detailed regulations do exist on what information can and cannot be published. There is only one set of these regulations available in the West. These 700 pages of the Polish censors' internal instructions and reports from 1974 to 1976 provided individual censors with explicit prohibitions and instructions for information ranging from negative mention of the Shah of Iran and his entourage to information on factory and children's camp accidents.(43)   This evidence from Poland indicates that the targets at least of explicit censorship are not national security issues but images of domestic realities. For example, in the first two weeks of May 1974, 45.9 percent of the interventions involved social issues, 14.6 percent economic issues, 11.9 percent culture and history, 6.2 percent religion, and only 12.4 percent "protection of the state."(44)

These same regulations are more detailed than those apparently required in other systems.(45) However, in substance they represent the kinds of controls found elsewhere in Eastern Europe. Censorship prohibitions are not consistent. Some organs are deliberately allowed to be more critical than others on subjects of special interests to their readers. As a result, there is an inverse relationship between the extent of criticism allowed in an organ and its audience. In addition, it is clear that no prohibitions must be issued to keep questions of the legitimacy of Communist rule from being raised. Journalists and editors simply do not try to publish such things. In less significant areas, though, prohibitions are not permanent.   Rather, regulations are often valid for only a limited period of time and are then removed.(46) After this, the criticism of information is allowed, although it is usually no longer timely.

MEDIA MANAGEMENT AND POLITICAL CONTROL

The orchestration of the media is far more than simply an element of government organization. It is a critical factor in political life in these societies. The character of media direction and control is a reflection of individual leaderships' perceptions of their positions and the critical issues for their societies. It is also a product of their cohesion and ability to lead. At the same time the orchestration affects the relationships of the leaders to each other and to their populations. Finally, for the population and journalism professionals, media control and direction are critical political issues themselves.

Media control in Eastern Europe was originally necessitated by the low level of support for the Communist takeovers.(47) Once the Communist regimes moved to rule and not just control the basic levers of power, they actively tried to transform their societies. For this, the media were the primary channels for instructing and threatening the population, as well as the major instruments for promising improvements. To do these things, the Communist leaders felt there could only be a single line presented to the population so that no questions would be raised. This required direction as well as control because of the disparity the images allowed, the promises made, and the reality lived.(48)

This imperative continues today. It is not, therefore, surprising that the two countries in which the media are the most critical and informative (Hungary and Yugoslavia) are also the countries with the most reformed and viable economies narrowing the gap between expectations and reality. The countries where special institutional structures are required to control the mass media (Czechoslovakia, Poland, and Rumania) are, conversely, the countries with the largest gaps between what the population expects and what exists. On a narrower scale, this same relationship holds. The least information and criticism appear on subjects and in areas where the regimes are the most committed and sensitive about their failures. So, for instance, as the economies declined in Poland and Rumania during the 1970s, economic information and discussion virtually disappeared.(49) Only the massive Polish workers' revolts in August 1980, with their focus on the demand for free information on Poland's situation forced the Polish Communist leadership to reveal the failings of the past and allow unorchestrated discussion of the future.

The inability of the media to mirror reality acurately, and the directives that they must create a positive image of society, ultimately only serve the interests of the Soviet Union. When the media reflect the real problems in the society, veiled or direct critiques of communism and Soviet dominance are inevitably made. This threatens the image and invincibility the Soviet elite has tried to maintain for itself. It also involved the exposure of information about Eastern European societies, economies, and their relations to the Soviet Union, as well as internal information about the Soviet Union that Soviet leaders do not want presented to the West or to their own populations. Thus, any deviation from restrained media brings with it veiled or direct criticism from the Soviet Union and ultimately a forced end to the critical Eastern European discussions.

For the Eastern European leaderships, the comfort of being presented positively in the media carries with it the underlying risk of losing touch with society. And, at the same time, when these positive images do not reflect reality, they erode the political elite's authority. So, although the leaders themselves seldom rely on the media for information on domestic or foreign affairs,(50) they depend on journalists for accurate information on administration and on public attitudes. Over the years, however, the limits on what can be public have discouraged journalists from exploring or reporting problems when they know it will not be published. As a result, that link between the population and the rulers disintegrates, and top leaders become increasingly dependent on the bureaucrats around them to report their own failings. In the end, the only images these leaders receive are those they have ordered. This leaves them to make decisions on the basis of skewed information.(51)

This enforced unreality does not, as they intended, increase the authority of the leaders and their policies. Instead, when the leadership insists on a positive image being presented even in bad times, its authority is diminished. Readers come to depend not on their domestic media but on gossip and Western broadcasts.(52) They use domestic media for information but, according to surveys done during periods of liberalization, they assume that the media are not completely truthful.(53) By extension, because most of their contacts with political leaders come through the mass media, they also assume that their leaders do not tell the truth. All of this leaves those leaders who demand positive media images in the face of serious problems in their societies with none of the authority that they sought to ensure by media control.

Equally as important, the controls and direction on the media block professionals and specialists from engaging in discussions as to the direction of policy. Not only do they not have access to basic information required to make decisions but they also do not know what other groups of professionals or specialists are saying on any given issue. Ultimately, discussions can only occur among limited groups who are usually in the same field or of the same political persuasion.(54) This limits the quality of the discussions. The forced reliance on private channels for intellectual discussion also leaves workers with no sense of the intellectuals as a group that could generate new ideas, as a group that could provide some viable alternative leadership. So only when media controls break down before workers act can intellectual discussions be published and provide a framework for broader social discussions. In the Polish case, where the media remained tightly controlled until after the workers' strikes, intellectuals were, therefore, never fully trusted as leaders. This left the movement without a clearly agreed upon platform.

Finally, in addition to all of its negative effects on the process of effective governance, the control and direction of the mass media, when it leads to a misrepresentation of reality, is an irritant for the population itself. One of the first demands made by all social groups in any period of liberalization is for the mass media to be free to provide more accurate information and critical discussion. And, as was particularly clear in the Polish case, this involves not only reduced blocks on media coverage but also increased access for a variety of groups in the society.

The ultimate irony of the various forms of media direction and control in Eastern Europe is they simply have not worked. Public opinion has been created not be carefully orchestrated media images but by the realities of everyday life. As readers and viewers have been educated in these Communist systems, they have grown more aware of the gaps between the media messages and reality. This has made them more dissatisfied with their leaders and reduced the authority of those leaders. In societies where reality and media messages are consistent because leadership policies have been successful, control and directions are tolerable. And the leadership is willing to allow relatively open discussion. But in other societies where reality is less presentable, direction and control of the media merely serve to increase the division between the leaders and the led. And when that leadership is internally weak, it serves to spark discontent.

NOTES

1. Carl J. Friedrich and Zbigniew Brzezinski, Totalitarian Dictatorship and Autocracy (Cambridge, Mass.: Harvard University Press, 1956), pp. 9-10.
2. On this and other details of media control and censorship, comparable and reliable information is not available for all of the Eastern European states. This is, in part, a product of the prohibitions in these systems against any open discussion of censorship. It is also a direct result of Western research on the mass media and its controls. This article uses detailed research on Poland done by the author and Dr. A. Ross Johnson of the Rand Corporation; interviews with current and emigre journalists from Poland, Czechoslovakia, Hungary, and East Germany; the censors' documents brought out of Poland in 1977; available Western research on the other states; and Eastern European statements and legal documents as well as scholarly and

autobiographical articles published in the West.

3. J. L. Curry, "The Professionalization of Polish Journalists and Their Role in the Policy Process," Ch. III, unpublished manuscript.

4. Interview data, 1980.

5. Interview data, 1975-76. In most cases, half of the journalists' salaries come from "piecework rates" for work beyond the minimum required from journalists.

6. Poland Today (Armonk, N.Y.: M. E. Sharpe, 1981), pp. 53-54.

7. See, for example, discussions of media making in the West, John W. C. Johnstone, Edward J. Slawiski, and William W. Bowman, The News People (Urbana: University of Illinois Press, 1976); David R. Bowers, "A Report on Activity by Publishers in Directing Newsroom Decisions," Journalism Quarterly 44 (Spring 1967); David L. Grey, "Decision-Making by a Reporter Under Deadline Pressure,"Journalism Quarterly 43 (Autumn 1966); and Ben Baggdikan, "Shaping Media Content: Professional Personnel and Organizational Structure," Public Opinion Quarterly 35, no. 4 (Winter 1973-74): 569-79.

8. Interview data, 1979-80. J. L. Curry, "The Media and Intra-Elite Communication in Poland: The System of Censorship," Rand Corporation Note, December 1980, p. 22-23.

9. Interview data, 1975-76.

10. Interview data, 1979.

11. "The Fourth Day: Afternoon," in The Czechoslovak Reform Movement (Santa Barbara, Calif.: ABC-CLIO, 1973), pp. 237-38.

12. Ibid., p. 291.

13. Ibid., p. 237.

14. V. Kusin, From Dubcek to Charter 77 (New York: St. Martin, 1977), p. 100. Other aspects of the "normalization" of the Czech media included "new staffing of party-supervised media . . . closure of newspapers by governmental decree, dispersal of defiant party branches in editorial offices, disbandment of sections of the Journalists' Union and takeover of the Union's Central Committee by a handful of trusted lieutenants, and even some arrests."

15. "Improvement of Journalistic Standards Urged," Radio Free Europe Research Report, Czechoslovakia/29, July 23, 1975, p. 2.

16. Kusin, Czechoslovak Reform Movement, p. 257.

17. Paul Lendvai, The Bureaucracy of Truth (Boulder, Colo.: Westview Press, 1981), p. 51.

18. Interview data, 1981.

19. Gertrude Joch Robinson, Tito's Maverick Media (Urbana: University of Illinois Press, 1977), p. 27.

20. Ibid., p. 148.

21. Ibid., p. 149.

22. Dimitor Bochev, "Orfografiia i Orfoepos, ili vseobshchaia vina i anonimuyi vinovnik," unpublished manuscript; "DieFrage der Zensur in der DDR. Eine Erklarung des Schriftstellers Heym," Frankfurter Allgemeine Zeitung, April 26, 1979; Paul Goma, "The Rumanian Labyrinth," Index on Censorship 7 (November–December 1978): 41–43; and "Additional Information on the Rumanian Censorship System," Radio Free Europe Situation Report, Rumania/1, January 19, 1978, p. 22.

23. Interview data, 1981.

24. "Hungarian Cartoonists Satirize Censorship," Radio Free Europe Situation Report, Hungary/22, June 23, 1976, p. 7.

25. Rumanian Situation Report/1, p. 23; and "Amended Law on Press Activity Published," Foreign Broadcast Information Service, February 15, 1978, pp. 62–80.

26. Goma, op. cit., p. 43.

27. Ibid.

28. Paul Zinner, Revolution in Hungary (New York: Columbia University Press, 1962), pp. 189–94, 273–74.

29. For a more complete discussion of the censorship process in Poland, see Curry, "The Media and Intra-Elite Communication in Poland," and Curry, The Black Book of Polish Censorship (New York: Random House, 1983).

30. Ibid.

31. Interview data, 1975–76 and 1979.

32. Interview data, 1979.

33. Michal Radgowski, "Cytelnicy o 'Polityce': Miedzy Biegunami," Polityka, August 25, 1979, p. 3.

34. See, for example, the collections of documents from Hungary and Czechoslovakia: Paul Zinner, National Communism and Popular Revolt in Eastern Europe (New York: Columbia University Press, 1956); and Robin Remington, Winter in Prague (Cambridge, Mass.: MIT Press, 1969).

35. Interview data, 1975–76.

36. Ibid.

37. Frank I. Kaplan, Winter Into Spring: The Czechoslovak Press and the Reform Movement (Boulder, Colo.: East European Quarterly, 1977).

38. Radio Free Europe, "August 1980: The Strikes in Poland," October 1980, p. 223.

39. Dariusz Fikus, "Niech Kazdy Mowi, O Co Ma Na Sercu," Prasa Polska (February–March 1981), p. 7.

40. A censorship law was agreed upon August 21, 1981, after nearly a year of negotiations [Ustawy o Kontroli Publikacji i Widowisk," Zycie i Nowosci, August 21, 1981, p. 4]. The issue of access continued to bedevil the negotiations between Solidarity and the government right up to the declaration of martial law. Solidarity regularly demanded access to television time in which

it could produce its own programs. Because the union could not get this access, and because it did not agree with the coverage it was receiving, it blocked Polish television from covering its convention in August and September 1981.

41. Transcript, National Congress of the Polish Journalists Association, 1956.

42. "Martial Law: A Chronology of Events," Radio Free Europe Situation Reports, Poland/1, January 22, 1982, p. 2.

43. Lendvai, Bureaucracy of Truth, p. 118, as well as the English translation of the entire set of documents, Curry, Black Book of Polish Censorship.

44. Ibid., p. 115.

45. In other systems, much of this is unstated. But, for instance, in Rumania there is a detailed test of prohibitions — all vague enough to allow almost anything to be sanctionable — in Section II of Rumanian Press Law (F.B.I.S., February 15, 1978). In East Germany and Bulgaria, when critical and difficult situations arise, domestically or internationally, instructions are cabled out to editors. In Yugoslav law, there also had been a general listing of forbidden topics (Robinson, 1977).

46. Curry, Black Book of Polish Censorship.

47. Zbigniew Brzezinski, The Soviet Bloc (Cambridge, Mass.: Harvard University Press, 1960), pp. 3-22.

48. Ibid.

49. Interview data, 1979. See also the economic prohibitions listed in Curry, The Black Book of Polish Censorship, and Poland Today, p. 53, 159-66.

50. Curry, "The Media and Intra-Elite Communication in Poland."

51. Interviewers said, for instance, that, in the Polish case, Gomulka by 1968 was dependent on an essentially one-page press summary prepared for him by an aide who supported an opposing faction.

52. Lendvai, op. cit., pp. 158-60.

53. Jaroslaw Piekalkiewicz, Public Opinion Polling in Czechoslovakia (New York: Praeger, 1972); and unpublished research by the Center for Public Opinion Research of Polish Radio and Television showing that only 23 percent thought Polish television presented factual information about the actual situation in Poland.

54. One example of this is the initiative forming a discussion group (Experience and the Future of Poland) to share information and opinion among groups of intellectuals. Limited almost completely to Warsaw-based intellectuals known to each other, after one meeting even this was prohibited. For samples of the opinions exchanged subsequently in informal surveys, see Poland Today, which is an English translation of the first two memoranda of the groups and a discussion of their inception.

CHAPTER 6

The Chinese Communist
Press as I See It

BY LU KENG

Being a journalist is the only job I have taken in my life.
Though I also taught reporting at a university, that was really a
sideline, or "guest starring." You may say that journalism has
become my life. Unfortunately, because of my almost
superstitious pursuit of an ideal of press freedom, I buried most
of my "prime time" in jails. In April 1949, I was in a Nationalist
jail in Canton. In December 1949 and August 1958, twice I was
in Communist jails, altogether totaling 22 years. Nevertheless, I
have taken all these as the God's arrangements. My interest in
journalism has never subsided. One thing I have felt proud of is
that, even when I was without any freedom, I edited a newspaper
for other inmates. This was really incredible. Of course, that
newspaper was a great mockery of press freedom. This
experience, however, enabled me to gauge the very nature of the

This article is a translation of a speech given by the author
to the Journalism and Communication Society of the Chinese
University of Hong Kong on October 4, 1979. Except for the
omission of several jokes toward the end of the text, which,
though translated, would be difficult for English-speaking
readers without any knowledge of Chinese, no attempt has been
made by the translator to change the informal tone of the oral
presentation. The author, an outstanding journalist who came to
Hong Kong from China last year, is chief commentator of The
Centre Daily, a Hong Kong-based independent newspaper. Opinions expressed are those of the author and do not reflect those
of The Asian Messenger.
Reprinted from Asian Messenger, vol. 4, no. 2, 3 (Autumn
1979-Spring 1980), pp. 44-53, with permission of the Center for
Communication Studies, Chinese University of Hong Kong.

press under "proletarian dictatorship." Besides, during the six
years when I was not a prisoner, the Communists treated me as a
"democratic personage." Being their "guest," I had the opportunity to have some direct contact with them, to discuss problems
with them, and to observe and study the press under the Chinese
Communists.

Certainly, this opportunity was not available to the common
people, not to mention the prisoners. Since I never worked at
any Communist press agencies, what is presented here may be
limited and one-sided. However, whatever I say is based on a
journalist's conscience. I shall speak from facts and not political biases.

DIFFERENT IDEOLOGIES, DIFFERENT PRESS SYSTEMS

First, I want to emphasize that we must never look at the
Chinese Communist press from Hong Kong's angle. According to
the Chinese Communists, the press in Hong Kong, for the most
part, belongs to bourgeois journalism. What they want is a
proletarian journalism. Regrettably, up to now, this proletarian
journalism has not been established. Until this very day —
October 4, 1979 — not a single book on proletarian journalism
has ever been written by the Communists.

The People's Republic of China is a country under the
leadership of the Chinese Communist Party. Since the polity of
this country is proletarian dictatorship, its press is also inscribed
with dictatorship.

Mao Tse-tung said: "The force at the core leading our cause
forward is the Chinese Communist Party. The theoretical basis
guiding our thinking is Marxism-Leninism." Thus, the ideology
guiding the press under the Chinese Communist Party was copied
from the Soviet Union. Or, more appropriately, given by the
Soviet Union. In his "On the People's Democratic Dictatorship,"
Mao said: "The salvos of the October Revolution brought us
Marxism-Leninism." The very basis of this ideology is the grasp
of class struggle as the key link. Everything is for class
struggle. Everything must obey the principle of class struggle.
In the West, journalism more or less reflects the social
responsibility theory, in which the function of the press is to
satisfy the people's cultural needs, to promote understanding and
social progress, and to improve the well-being of the people.
From the Communist point of view, however, the major function of
the press is to carry out class struggle between the proletariat
and the bourgeois. In his "On the Nature of Our Newspapers,"
Lenin iterated that class struggle will be carried out in the
newspapers against the protectors of the bourgeois. He said
that the proletarian press should look like a "revolutionary press"

and "the mouthpiece of class dictatorship." "This class is now using actions to demonstrate that the resistance of the bourgeois and the protectors of the bourgeois will be smashed by its iron fists," Lenin said.

Mao Tse-tung fully subscribed to Lenin's concept of proletarian dictatorship. Not only did he inherit Lenin's conceptualization of the press as a tool for class struggle, he developed it further. In his "Talks at the Yenan Forum on Literature and Art," Mao said that "in the world today all culture, all literature and art belong to definite classes and geared to definite political lines." "To defeat the enemy, we must rely on the army with guns. But this army alone is not enough; we must also have a cultural army, which is indispensable for unity in our own ranks and defeating the enemy." During the Cultural Revolution, Mao's handpicked heir-apparent, Marshal Lin Piao, further elaborated this concept. He said, "Carrying out a revolution is inseparable from two barrels, one is the barrel of a gun and the other, the barrel of a pen. To establish a political power, we must depend on these two barrels." Thus, from this viewpoint, the press is a component of the proletarian dictatorship machine. Like the army, police, jails, and courts, the press is a tool and weapon for proletarian dictatorship. It would be a great honor if a journalist should become a small "screw" in this machine of dictatorship. In the eyes of the proletariat, the so-called "crownless king" and "voice of the people" are nothing but lies used by the bourgeois to cheat the people. In Mao Tse-tung's words, "this windy nonsense" must be stopped.

FUNCTIONS OF THE CHINESE COMMUNIST PRESS

In scholarship, we usually begin by learning from others. This is also true with running a newspaper. From the very beginning, the Chinese Communist press has been learning from the Russians. It is neither the traditional intellectual endeavor nor the Western free enterprise, but an organ of proletarian dictatorship. Its propaganda functions, as prescribed by the Party, are to carry out the Party's intentions and to look upon the materialization of communism as its highest goal. During the present stage, it must struggle for the materialization of socialism and the consolidation of proletarian dictatorship.

1. To propagate policies: In his "Talk to the Editorial Staff of Shansi Suiyuan Daily" Mao Tse-tung said, "Questions concerning policy should as a rule be given publicity in the party papers or periodicals." "The role and power of the newspapers consists in their ability to bring the Party program, the Party line, the Party's general and specific policies, its tasks and

methods of work before the masses in the quickest and most extensive ways."

2. To educate the mass: In the same talk, Mao unequivocally pointed out: "You comrades are newspapermen. Your job is to educate the masses." In the inaugural statement of China's Worker (Chung Kuo Kung Jen Pao), a daily launched in Yenan in 1940, Mao made it clear that "China's Worker should become a school for the education and training of workers."

3. To organize the mass: Mao Tse-tung always emphasized that "the people need us [Communists] to organize." In addition, Mao also regarded the press as a tool for organizing the mass. He said, "To strengthen the Party's ties with the masses through the newspapers — this is an important question of principle in our Party's work which is not to be taken lightly."

4. To mobilize the mass: In the talk to the editorial staff of the Shansi Suiyuan Daily, Mao also said that "we must arouse the people to fight for their own emancipation." Later in Yenan and Peking, Mao said several times that the goals for struggle and the slogans for fighting should be advocated through the newspaper to unite the people and mobilize the people.

What, then, is the purpose of propaganda, education, organization, and mobilization? The purpose is to "attack the enemy and eliminate the enemy," or, in a word, to carry class struggle to the end. There was one vivid example. In 1957 around the time of the antirightist struggle when Mao Tse-tung was masterminding his "open plot," under Mao's direct instruction the Chinese Communist newspapers were engaged in a series of "insidious plots." On June 8, 1957, Mao drafted for the Communist Party Central Committee an "inner-Party directive" entitled "Muster Our Forces to Repulse the Rightists' Wild Attacks." In this directive Mao said:

> Get each of these parties to organize forums with the Left, middle and Right elements all taking part, let both positive and negative opinions be voiced, and send reporters to cover these discussions. We should tactfully encourage the Left and middle elements to speak out at the meetings and refute the Rightists. This is very effective. The Party paper in each locality should have dozens of articles ready and publish them from day to day when the high tide of the attacks begin to ebb there. . . . But before the tide is on ebb, Party papers should restrict the number of articles expressing positive views. . . . Better let the reactionary professors, lecturers, assistants and students spew out their venom and speak without any inhibitions. [emphasis added]

This resulted in the trapping of an uncountable number of intellectuals known all over the world.

Wasn't this unbashful use of the newspaper as a tool for class struggle too exciting? Well, according to Mao Tse-tung's thought, it was not a question of excitement. He would do it whether it was exciting or not because they were all reactionaries. "Only by boosting our own morale and dampening the enemy's can we isolate the reactionaries so as to defeat them or replace them."

THE CHINESE COMMUNIST PRESS SYSTEM

Basically, the Chinese Communist press includes two levels: the central press and the local press. The local press an be further divided into the provincial, district, and county press. In fact, there are very few district newspapers. And the county newspapers are even more few and far between.

Major central level newspapers are the People's Daily, Kuang Ming Daily, Worker's Daily, Liberation Army Daily, and the China Youth Daily, plus the small China Pioneers Daily. Each of these newspapers is under a different command system. The People's Daily, the mouthpiece of the Party Central Committee, is under the jurisdiction of the central Politboro. Its editorials, which toward the later half of the Cultural Revolution were jointly published in the People's Daily, the Liberation Army Daily, and the Red Flag journal, speak for the Party Central and must be studied by all of the people. It had then become an unwritten law for all the other newspapers to reprint its editorials. At that time the Party Central iterated that even such specialized journals as Health News (Chien Kang Pao) or Oral Cavity Journal (Kuo Chiang Ko Cha Chi) also had to carry out propaganda in line with major political events.

The Kwang Ming Daily, formerly the mouthpiece of the Democratic League, was taken over by the Chinese Communists in the 1957 antirightist struggle. Run by the Party Central's Department of Propaganda, this daily focuses on the propaganda of cultural, educational, and scientific content. The Liberation Army Daily is run by the General Political Department of the Ministry of Defense. The paper is distributed to military units and state institutions. No individual subscription is permitted. The Worker's Daily is the mouthpiece of the National Workers Union. The China Youth Daily is the mouthpiece of the Central Committee of the Chinese Communist Youth League. The China Pioneers Daily, also run by the Chinese Communist Youth League, is published for the young pioneers (generally known as the "red scarfs"). All these newspapers are under the unified leadership of the Party Central Committee.

As for the local level press, each of the 29 provinces and municipalities has a daily of its own under the direct leadership of the respective Chinese Communist Party Committees. Before the Cultural Revolution, some of the Party's regional bureaus also published their own newspapers. For instance, the South China Bureau published the Southern Daily (Nan Fong Jih Pao) in Canton and the Central-south Bureau published the Yangtze Daily (Chang Chiang Jih Pao) in Wuhan. The Southern Daily and Canton Daily (Kwang Chou Jih Pao) were later merged to become the mouthpiece of the Kwangtung Provincial Party Committee.

Each provincial newspaper is named after the province and is published in the provincial capital. For instance, Hopei Daily is published in Shihchiachuang, Shensi Daily in Sian, Liaoning Daily in Shengyang, Honan Daily in Chengchow, and so on. However, there are exceptions. The mouthpiece of the Kiangsu Provincial Party Committee published in Nanking, for instance, is not called "Kiangsu Daily" but Hsinhua (New China) Daily. The mouthpiece of the Shangtung Provincial Party Committee published in Chinan is not called "Shangtung Daily" but Ta Chung (Popular) Daily. These newspapers have kept their historical names. To the Chinese Communists, the Hsinhua Daily has a glorious history in the struggle against the Nationalist Party. At the time of the Huannan (Southern Anhui) Incident, Chou En-lai himself peddled the Hsinhua Daily on Chungking streets. Ta Chung Daily, established in 1947 in Shangtung's liberated areas, was the brainchild of General Chen Yi.

Before the Cultural Revolution, there were six evening newspapers in the country. Among the better known were Peking Evening News (Pei Jing Wan Pao), Shanghai's Hsinmin (New People) Evenings News, and Canton's Yangcheng (Canton) Evening News. Chengtu, Lanchow, and Harbin each had an evening daily.

Besides the Worker's Daily, other specialized newspapers include the quarto-sized China Farmer's Daily (Chuang Kuo Nung Min Pao), the Physical Education Daily (Ti Yu Pao, issued daily except Sunday), and Health News (issued every three days).

Local Newspapers

Generally, each province or municipality has a newspaper. In places where economy and culture are more developed, there are more than one. In Shanghai, for instance, in addition to the Liberation Daily (Chieh Fang Jih Pao) and the Wen Hui Pao, there are other smaller quarto-sized papers like the Youth News (Ching Nien Pao). A few provinces also publish a local farmer's paper. In Yunnan, for instance, there is a quarto-sized Yunnan Farmer's Daily (Yunnan Nung Min Pao), published in Kunming. In areas populated by the minority nationalities, newspapers are also published. In Hungtai and Chinpo Autonomous Chow, there is the Unity News (Tuan Chieh Pao), which propagates unity among nationalities and socialist constructions in areas populated by minority nationalities.

From the central to the local level, there are a little more than 40 newspapers in the country, averaging about one for every 20 to 25 million people. Compared to Hong Kong, where there are more than 120 newspapers, the number is far too small. Except for the People's Daily, which publishes one and a half sheets, the rest only contain one sheet a day. In addition to the limitations imposed by policies, there is a severe shortage of newsprint. The Cultural Revolution, in particular, saw the almost crazy printing and issuing of Selected Works of Mao Tse-tung and the so-called "Red Treasure Book" (Quotations from Chairman Mao Tse-tung)(1) as well as the almost crazy posting of tatsepao (big character posters). These activities had drained the country's domestically produced paper. Even with paper imported from abroad in great quantities, the demand still far exceeded the supply. As a result, even school textbooks could not be printed.

During the first few years after the liberation, the Chinese Communist newspapers allowed circulation abroad included the People's Daily and the Kwang Ming Daily in Peking, plus the Libertion Daily and Wen Hui Pao in Shanghai. In addition to these four newspapers, now the China Youth Daily, Peking Daily, and Nan Fang Daily are also permitted for export.

Before and during the Cultural Revolution, no local newspapers were allowed for sale overseas. They were classified as "third degree secret" (san chi chi mi). Some of the less capable Nationalist agents, being unable to obtain any Communist intelligence, paid a high price for these local newspapers in Hong Kong, Macao, or the Yunnan-Burma border area. During the Cultural Revolution, in the Yunnan-Burma border area, a copy of Yunnan Daily could sell for 100 Jen Min Pi, or 300 Hong Kong dollars. Copies with special features were even selling for as high as 1,500 Hong Kong dollars. Through this channel the agents could easily report to the Nationalist's Mainland China Work Committee that the mission had been accomplished. For the speculative but needy residents however, as long as they were not caught, one bundle of used newspapers might bring them as bag full of Seiko watches. Thus, the attraction was still very great.

The People's Daily is the newspaper with the largest circulation. In addition to free and exchange copies, it has a circulation of 6,200,000 copies. However, there is a quarto-sized paper whose circulation exceeds the People's Daily by some 3 million copies. This paper is called Reference News (Tsan Kao Hsiao Hsi). It was a semipublic paper suggested by Chou En-lai and authorized by Mao Tse-tung. Chou had wanted to "open the eyes of the people" a little bit more. He said, "We have neglected our left and right neighbors too much." A closed-door policy was too dangerous. Though Mao Tse-tung had given his approval, at one meeting he sarcastically referred to the endeavor as "a case of a Communist Party publishing a newspaper for imperialism." At first, the circulation of this paper was strictly restricted but was later gradually expanded to more than 10 million copies by 1977 and 1978, becoming the paper with the largest circulation in China.

In addition to Reference News, there is the Reference Materials (Tsan Kao Tse Liao), generally known as ta tsan kao, or "big reference." A bound sextodecimo, with a morning edition and an afternoon edition, it is especially edited for the eyes of high-ranking Communist cadres (the thirteenth rank and above). What, then, is the difference between the "big reference" and the "small reference"? The "small reference" reprints stories by the various international wire services and important articles in foreign newspapers. The "big reference," with a much higher confidentiality, carries a lot more stories or articles about Taiwan and Hong Kong. Reports sharply critical of the Communists are also often printed.

"Internal Reference"

Since the Chinese Communist press puts the Party in the first place and demands a strict secrecy, there are some conditions which they would like to have the high-ranking personages informed, but not the common people. Thus, both Hsinhua (New China) News Agency and the People's Daily issued their own "internal reference" (nei bu tsan kao, abbreviated as nei tsan). For instance, Hsinhua's internal publication is called Trends of Journalistic Work (Hsin Wen Kung Tso Tung Hsiang), which stipulated Hsinhua duties as follows: (1) to report to the Party Central, and (2) to guide the work of lower levels. This publication also frequently carried the opinions of the various provincial and municipal Party committees, usually about some touchy problems. The internal publication of the People's Daily is called Brief Reports on the People's Daily's Work Conditions (Jen Min Jih Pao Kung Tso Chin Kuang Chien Pao). Problems not suitable for publication or those whose publication is yet to be decided for some time are included in it. As for minor problems, they are published in the Life in the Editorial Department (pien chi bu sheng ho). These problems include letters from readers as well as the exchange of experience.

If someone should ask: Is there any privately owned newspaper in the mainland? The answer is no.

In the first few years after the liberation, Ta Kung Pao and Hsi Min Pao (New People's Daily) were still permitted to publish. The Democratic League also used Wen Hui Pao and Kwang Ming Daily as its mouthpieces. Before long, however, the Chinese Communists launched a total "adjustment." Hsin Min Pao was assigned to publish as an evening paper in Shanghai. Ta Kung Pao, on the other hand, was assigned to cover news about light and handicraft industries. Later, it was renamed Ching Pu Pao (Progress News). But there was not much "progress." The papers soon ceased publication. Luckily, Fei Yi-ming had some foresight, for he had also started a Hong Kong edition. Otherwise, this once Missouri Journalism Award-winner paper would have become a historical name. Both Wen Hui Pao and Hsin Min Pao were taken over by the Chinese Communists after the antirightist struggle.

One episode deserves mentioning. When Mao Tse-tung went to Shanghai for the first time after the liberation, out of whim, he asked about Sheng Pao. Mao was told that it had been closed. Mao shouted, "What a pity!" To flatter him, someone said: shall we resume the paper? Mao replied, "Forget it! Resumption of the paper will be restoration of the old!" Thus, one of China's oldest papers can only be viewed in the library by officials who have obtained permission.

Therefore, when we talk about the press system in mainland China, there is only one system. That is, the Chinese Communist press system. This was at least the case in the seventies. We can only hope that it will become different in the eighties. Recently, it was said that Ta Kung Pao and Hsin Min Pao had requested permission to resume their papers. Their reports had been forwarded to the Party Central Committee's Politboro, though no further word has been heard yet.

ORGANIZATION AND PERSONNEL OF THE CHINESE COMMUNIST PRESS

The People's Daily is not run by the director, but rather by an editorial committee headed by the editor in chief. Membership of this committee has varied from time to time, ranging from five to more than ten. Receiving instructions from the Politboro, this editorial committee decides the paper's policies and personnel and supervises the daily operation.

Inner organization of the paper is confidential. There are two channels through which we come to know about it, though still very little. First, we know through cumulated material scattered here and there. Second, we know through the exposés during the Cultural Revolution when many Chinese Communist inside stories were being dragged out.

The office of the editor in chief in the People's Daily gives out orders and serves as the command headquarters. The editorial division is the executive unit. It includes the following departments:

- Theory Propaganda Department: This department is responsible for the materialization of "politics taking command." For instance, the study of "using practice to test truth as the sole criterion" is now its major thrust.
- Reporters Department: It commands the paper's reporters stations, the People's Daily dispatches correspondents, and establishes stations in all provinces and municipalities as well as major agricultural and industrial bases like Tachia and Taching.
- Other departments are politics and law, rural villages, industry and transportation, finance and economy, cultural and educational, literature and art, international, and mass work. The Literature and Art Department edits the "literary supplement page" (fu kan) while the International Department handles international news and the Mass Work Department, letters from the readers. In addition, there are a Domestic Morgue and an International Morgue.

The paper has a gigantic administrative structure. Under the editor in chief and the deputy editor in chief, the secretary general supervises all the routine work. In the office of the editor in chief, the director handles all the administrative routines within the editorial division. As for the editors, some are responible for rewriting and polishing, others for editorial layouts or postpublication checks.

In a recent talk with Mr. Watanabe, director of Japan's Asahi Shimbun, Hu Chi-wei, editor in chief of the People's Daily, said in the Mass Work Department alone some 80 persons were responsible for the handling of letters from the readers. Still the staff was too small for the job. It is not unusual at all for the whole newspaper to have more than 2,000 or 3,000 people.

Unlike their counterparts in Taiwan or Hong Kong, all editors and reporters in the People's Daily, the Hsinhua News Agency, and other newspapers, agencies, and radio or television stations are state employees, enjoying privileges as Party or state cadres, and they are paid according to their rank in the Party or the government.

Originally, there were 30 ranks in the Chinese Communist cadres; now there are 25. The first rank cadres are paid 600 Jen Min Pi while the thirtieth rank, 22 Jen Min Pi. The first rank is further divided into two levels. Only Mao Tse-tung was classified as a first-rank first-level cadre. The five vice chairman — Liu Shao-chi, Chou En-lai, Chu Teh, Chen Yun, and

Lin Piao — and Party Secretary General Ten Hsiao-ping were classified as first-rank second-level cadres so as to distinguish slightly the latter from the chairman, since Mao never wanted anyone equal to him. Below the second rank, there are no divisions into levels. Teng To, one-time editor in chief of the People's Daily, was said to be an eighth-rank cadre, paid 300 Jen Min Pi a month. In the mainland, quite a few of the provincial governors are only ninth-rank cadres. This illustrates the importance of the unique role the People's Daily occupies.

The recruitment of personnel is based on political background, usually requiring a three-generation political clearance.

Where do these journalist cadres come from? There are three sources: The first group of journalistic cadres were trained during the Yenan years by the various newspapers in liberated areas or by the Hsinhua News Agency. These newspapers included Liberation Daily (Chieh Fang Pao), Shansi Suiyuan Daily (Chin Sui Jih Pao), Chin-Cha-Chi Daily (Chin Cha Chi Jih Pao), and the Ta Chung Daily in Changtung. Quite a few of these journalists were the students of Hu Chiao-mu, while many others were trained by persons like Teng To, who was well versed in Chinese classics. The second group consists of underground Chinese Communist journalistic workers in Nationalist-controlled areas. Quite a few of them were able to penetrate into Nationalist newspapers or newspapers run by Nationalist reporters. These Communist journalists later were charged with very important duties. For instance, a young journalist who worked for me was a Chinese Communist underground agent assigned to the Nanking Central Daily News. A graduate of the Department of Journalism of the National Cheng-chi University, Lee Lien-chun changed his name to Li Lien when the Chinese Communist troops entered Nanking on April 23, 1949. On behalf of the Communists, Li took over the Nanking Central Daily News. The third group are those recruited after the liberation among college graduates with relatively good family backgrounds (workers, peasants, and soldiers). After the liberation, college departments responsible for the training of journalistic workers were the Department of Journalism of Futan University in Shanghai and the Department of Journalism of Peking University, which had incorporated the department at Yenchin University. Later, journalism departments were established at the Chinese People's University and the Peking Broadcasting Institute. Students at these institutions all have to go through a very selective screening procedure. The Chinese Communist policies stipulate that "Backgrounds are important, but not by themselves only. The important thing is political performance." But, in fact, all the people entering the journalistic teams are picked first of all for their backgrounds. Political performance comes second, and talents, last. This was at least the case before the Cultural Revolution.

CONTROL OVER THE PRESS BY THE CHINESE COMMUNISTS

In short, the control is absolutely strict. The tight control over the Chinese Communist press is inseparable from Mao Tse-tung's conceptualization of the functions of the press. Mao said:

> To overthrow a political power, it is always necessary first of all to create public opinion, to do work in the ideological sphere. This is true for the revolutionary class as well as for the counterrevolutionary class.

Thus, to the Chinese Communists, or at least to Mao Tse-tung, the press has become a very sensitive issue.

Facts also have proved the importance of "grabbing the barrel of a pen." When the Gang of Four were rampaging in the mainland, under their control was really nothing but the media. With the propaganda tools in their hands, however, they were able to turn the whole mainland upside down.

Having fully understood the importance of the media, Mao Tse-tung maintained that all propaganda tools be under the absolute leadership of the Party. The first principle the media must observe is tang hsin, or Party allegiance. From a given viewpoint, Mao's call for "the whole Party to run the press" has been accomplished. In this respect, it must be admitted that the Communists have done better than the Nationalists. At least, the Communists were far more serious and paid far more attention to the media than the Nationalists.

For two years I was the deputy editor in chief and city editor of the Central Daily News in Nanking, the mouthpiece of the Nationalist party Central Committee. The Nationalist party was picky only after the newspaper had been published. They would then tell you what should not have been printed. This practice was really tying up the party's own hands and legs. In news reporting, the Communists, however, impose far more restrictions on the press than the Nationalists do. All important news is under Hsinhua's unified release, and so is all international news. This control is carried out all the way from the top to the very bottom. In terms of editorials, authority can thus be established for the Chinese Communist press. Important editorials or features in the People's Daily like "On the Historical Experience of Proletarian Dictatorship Revisited," "Long Live Leninism," and so on all had to go through a strict procedure. The Politboro drafted the outlines and submitted them to Mao Tse-tung for approval. When finished, the editorial would be studied word for word as well as again and again. Then it would be resubmitted to the Politboro for review and authorization for publication. During the eight years when the People's Daily was under Teng To, 46 editorials and commentaries were written or revised by Teng To himself and reviewed by Mao. Another 153 editorials and commentaries were reviewed by Chou En-lai. As far as I can recall, the Nationalists never did this. From the viewpoint of press freedom, this practice was not admirable at all, but from that of establishing authority for the Chinese Communist press it was not unacceptable. I have often thought that this was perhaps one of the reasons why the Communists could drive the Nationalists out of the mainland.

The five comments on the U.S. White Paper issued by Hsinhua in the autumn of 1949 were written by Mao Tse-tung. Even after the Communists had taken over the mainland, some of the editorials and editor's notes in the People's Daily were still being written by Mao. For instance, the preface and editor's notes to "Material on the Counter-revolutionary Hu Feng Clique" as well as "Wen Hui Pao's Bourgeois Orientation Should Be Criticized," which was the editorial in the People's Daily that raised the climax of the antirightist struggle, all precipitated the coming of a storm. Whether or not you approve it, you cannot but pay attention to it.

During the civil war, Mao Tse-tung himself also wrote news stories. For instance, the news about the crossing of the Yangtse River by the Communist troops was written by him. Of interest was that he unbashfully included his own name in this news. Toward the end of his news story, Mao wrote: "The People's Liberation Army is now fighting in its own heroic style and resolutely executing the order of Chairman Mao and Commander-in-Chief Chu [Teh]." Mao was really good at propagating himself. Mao emphasized so much the class character of the press that when Teng To advocated just a little bit of human interest so as to liven up the newspaper a little bit Teng was criticized by Mao as "a scholar running a newspaper, and a dead man running a newspaper" and was removed from his post.

Among the members of the Politboro and secretaries of the Party General Secretariat, one was responsible for propaganda. Before the Cultural Revolution, Lu Teng-i was in charge. After the Cultural Revolution, it was Kang Sheng when Lu had been removed. When Kang Sheng was sick, Yao Wen-yuan was "grasping" the work. When the Gang of Four failed to form a cabinet during the convention of the Fourth National People's Congress, to hasten Chou En-lai's death, the Gang purposely submitted the People's Daily's editorials and other important articles to Chou for review while Chou was lying in bed being treated for cancer. Because of this, Chou issued a call urging that his energies be relieved of correcting schoolchildren's miswritten words. Teng Ying-chao, Chou's wife, finally had to plead that no more articles be sent to Chou for review. To the delight of the Gang of Four, Yao Wen-yuan soon took over as the propaganda czar.

Chou En-lai was much more restrained in handling the press propaganda. On February 16, 1959, the New York Daily News reported that the U.S. Secretary of State, John Dulles, was sick, and possibly from incurable cancer. Many newspapers in the mainland reprinted this story. The headline in Szechuan Daily read: "A stubborn man has a stubborn disease, Dulles's cancer worsens." In Hunan Daily, the headline was: "Such a man with such a disease; Dulles contracts deadly cancer." In Fukien Daily, the headline said: "West wind is to take its last breath; the advisor has an incurable cancer; Dulles's cancer recurred." Later, learning about all these, Chou criticized that it was wrong. He said, "We must not sneer, and nor must we curse. Dulles had refused to shake hands with Chou at the Geneva Convention. If people should recall this, they would surely admire Chou's statesmanship even more.

On November 12, 1956, the ninetieth anniversary of Dr. Sun Yat-sen's birthday, the People's Daily published a commemorative article by Shao Li-tse, a former Nationalist member who later turned Communist. Not only the headline was set in very small type, but also the article was purposely placed in an inconspicuous corner. When the Chinese People's Political Consultative Conference held its commemorative meeting that day, Chou publicly criticized Teng To: "Why was Mr. Shao's article treated so inconspicuously. You people have no respect for the articles by democratic personages." This seemed to suggest that Chou En-lai did assume a relatively more open attitude toward these problems.

Not only does the Party Central leadership attach much importance to the media, but the provincial and municipal Party committee secretaries do also. In the autumn of 1956, at a dancing party in Tsui-hu (Grassy Lake) Guest House in Junming of Yunnan, I met a Party secretary in charge of propaganda by the name of Ma Chi-kung. During intermissions, I saw Ma reviewing an editorial to be published the following day in the Yunnan Daily. The Chinese Communist press emphasizes leadership by the Party Secretary. Besides taking directive from him, all newspaper workers, in their relationship with leadership units, are required to assume a responsible attitude in seeking instructions, in discussion with him, in reporting the situations to him, and in voicing opinions. In the Communist eyes, the press not only can be helped by the leadership institutions but also can help the leadership institutions. In fact, the press itself is a gigantic investigation, research, and control institution. The press not only seeks instructions from the Party Secretary but also uses research results it has obtained to investigate, report, and make suggestions to him.

Before the Cultural Revolution, not a single news story or article in the Chinese Communist press ever violated the intentions of the Party Secretary. Hu Feng's criticism that there was a "uniformity of public opinion" was not without any basis. During the Cultural Revolution, because of the intensification of faction struggles, especially after the Gang of Four's slogan of "grasping revolution by kicking away the Party Secretary," were there cases of violations. But still, the press was under the absolute control of the factions.

OPERATION OF THE CHINESE COMMUNIST PRESS

Operation of the press follows the practice of "walking on two legs." In the People's Daily, for example, on the one hand it depends on Hsinhua for news, while on the other hand it also reprints all the good materials in local newspapers. Besides, the paper also utilizes its correspondence network, for example, the various reporters' stations. As for international news, all comes from Hsinhua.

As for local newspapers, they are cast in the same mold as the People's Daily's. There is very little local uniqueness. When the Gang of Four was at its height, there was a widely circulated saying in the mainland: "The big papers [referring to the People's Daily and other local papers] copy the small papers [referring to Journal of Peking University and Journal of Tsing Hua University]; small papers copy Liang Hsiao [referring to the writers' group organized by Chiang Ching at Peking University and Tsin Hua University. Members included such well-known professors as Chou I-liang and Fung Yu-lang.]"

During this period, Liang Hsiao's articles were guiding the whole political life in the mainland. As for news, the soul of a newspaper, it was compressed to a very miserable position.

In 1958, Mao Tse-tung proposed a socialist general line: "Muster all energies, swim up the stream and construct socialism in a massive, quick, good and economic way (to, kwai, hua, sheng)." The opposites of "massive, quick, good and economic" are "scarce, slow, bad and wasteful" (shao, man, cha, fei). These four words can best describe the news in Chinese Communist newspapers and radio broadcasting. This was especially the case during the Cultural Revolution.

Scarce — According to statistics obtained by the Department of Journalism of the People's University, before the Cultural Revolution, news only accounted for about 60 percent of all the newspaper space. During the Cultural Revolution, it dropped to about 40 percent and sometimes to as low as 30 percent. Nevertheless, what could be regarded as news was in fact very meager. Most of the space was "hegemonized" by lengthy and dull articles.

Slow — That the Chinese Communist news is slow has been a widely known fact. The Lin Pao incident was not announced until a full month later. The arrest of the Gang of Four on October 6, 1976 was first broadcast on October 9, 1976 in London. However, the people in the mainland were still kept in the dark. It was not until October 15 did we people in Kunming see Tatze-Pao, a newspaper in mainland China, saying "hail the crash of the 'Gang of Four.'" Still, people were half suspicious and half believing. It was not until October 18 that Hua Kuo-feng's talk on this incident was circulated. By then the people had already lost their interest in knowing the exact date the newspaper first carried the story.

Bad — Quality of the news is so bad that it can hardly be regarded as news. When Chou En-lai died, the mainland was in a mourning atmosphere. To divert the people's attention, the Gang of Four ordered their "running dog" at Tsing Hua University, Chih Chun, to orchestrate a news story headlined "Great Debates Bring Great Changes." At the very beginning, the story said that people were very concerned with the debates at Tsing Hua University, suggesting that they did not care about Chou's death. Then several thousand words were used to describe the debates at Tsing Hua. This was no news at all. It was nothing but playing political games and sheer nonsense. From a journalistic point of view, it was not news at all. Headlines like "Grasp Spring Ploughing," "Resist Drought and Protect Saplings," "Great Harvest Expected," "Annual Quota Surpassed," and so on would appear annually in the newspapers in turns and in the same format. Even by proletarian journalistic standards, such news could not be regarded as "good." It can only be regarded as "bad."

Wasteful — It is not uncommon for the Communist press agencies to spend mountains of efforts on a single meaningless item. For instance, in covering a certain provincial conference, the reporter must submit his completed report to the conference secretariat. It will first be reviewed by a secretary in charge of news release and then passed on to the conference secretary general, who will then submit the article to the Provincial Party Secretariat's office. If the secretary general of the Party Secretariat's office is also very careful, he will ask a provincial Party Secretary to review it. When the article returns to the newspaper, it goes to a department head first, who then assigns an editor to handle the "news." If it should be published at all, the item would have gone through several checkpoints and been chopped up several times. In this tedious reviewing process, the persons in charge, to show that they are responsible, will have changed a few words or deleted a couple of sentences.

This is the handling of ordinary news. When it comes to important news, before publication both Hsinhua and the People's Daily will have to submit it to the Party Central for review and approval. As for local newspaper, articles will have to be submitted to the standing committee of the provincial Party Committees for discussion. Thus, news has already become "old" or even history.

THE CHINESE COMMUNIST REPORTERS

Since all Chinese Communist reporters are classified as Party or state cadres, they lack the independence of professionals. During the Nationalist years in Chungking and Nanking, reporters were often seen walking proudly in and out of the residences of powerful personages. This scene can no longer be found in the present-day mainland. Nevertheless, the Communists have adopted a different system, in which news not suitable for publication is released as "internal reference news." Much of this internal reference news covers the dark side of Party and state cadres and can often reach the "heaven," that is, the highest leadership. It was said to be Mao Tse-tung's must for daily reading. Even when he was too ill to do any reading, he had it read by his niece, Wang Hai-yung. In addition to Mao, members of the Politburo also read it. Since the articles by Hsinhua or People's Daily reporters may be read by the "heaven," they occupy a very special status in the people's eyes. In fact, when people want to "kao yu chuang" (that is, "make a plea with the emperor," meaning pleading with the highest authorities), they will try all means to get their complaint to a Hsinhua or People's Daily reporter. This is exactly what the editor in chief of the People's Daily, Hu Chi-wei, said in his talks with the director of Asahi Shimbun: "The People's Daily has its own authority. It will demand concerned departments to investigate into many things and get them resolved."

In spite of their special status, well-cultivated reporters who cherish ethics usually will not behave in a conceited way. On the contrary, realizing their responsibility, they will behave rather moderately and cautiously. However, there are reporters who behave like "imperial ministers" and shout "You watch out! I will get you reported in the 'Internal Reference'!"

When the Gang of Four were rampaging in China, journalistic personnel recruitment followed a kind of "henchman policy." Mean persons and henchmen took charge. As a result, the Chinese Communist press was further molested into pieces. The press, radio, and television were all filled with lies, empty talks, big talks, useless talks, and conventional talks (huang hua, kun hua, ta hua, fei hua, and tao hua).

The funniest figure was Lu Ying, then editor in chief of the People's Daily. Lu Ying was given this important job because of his loyalty to the Gang of Four and Chiang Ching's promotion. Lu left many jokes behind him and is still being talked about.

Lu Ying used to work for Ta Chung Daily in Shangtung. Later he became the director of the office of the editor in chief in the People's Daily in charge of some administrative duties. Because he was also born in Shangtung, Chang Chun-chiao recommended him to Chiang Ching (also from Shangtung). As a result, Lu was given the authority to run the People's Daily. Unfortunately, he had received too little education. It was said that he could not distinguish many Chinese words. When I was in Peking in the spring of 1978, I heard a lot of jokes about him. Once I asked a leftist friend: "Was he really so dumb?" My friend said rather sentimentally that there might have been some exaggeration. But he added that the people recruited by the Gang of Four were really abominably bad; otherwise, they would not have collapsed so fast.

When Hua Kuo-feng and Teng Hsiao-ping took power, Lu Ying and other followers of the Gang of Four in the press circle were said to have been sent to a labor reform farm of Hsinhua and the People's Daily. Though Hua and Teng have been working very hard, the serious effects left behind by the Gang of Four have given the impression of irreversibility. In the press particularly, though the "Gang cliches" (pang pa ku) were crashed, the phantoms of "party cliches" (tang pa ku) are still haunting around. Whether they can be removed will depend on whether Hua and Teng have the determination and how Tseng Tao, Chu Mu-chi, and Hu Chi-wei will be doing in the future.

NOTE

1. About 1 million copies of the Quotations from Mao Tse-tung of various sizes were printed, approximately one copy for every member of the population. This was really a great disaster for the people.

PART III
PRESS CONTROLS IN THE DEVELOPING WORLD

CHAPTER 7

Press Censorship and the
Military State in Brazil

BY JOAN R. DASSIN

INTRODUCTION

As the English sociologist Philip Schlesinger has observed, the debate about the media reporting of unofficial terrorism in Western capitalist democracies has primarily developed in the context of the psychological warfare aims of the state.(1)   In Latin America's Southern Cone, information policy as a whole is governed according to such psychological warfare aims.   After military takeovers in Brazil (1964), Chile (1973), Uruguay (1973), and Argentina (1976), these aims were established as national objectives.   They were officially enforced by extraconstitutional legislation creating perpetual "states of emergency" and systematically implemented by covert practices like prior political censorship and torture of political prisoners.   Throughout the region, a unique "National Security Doctrine" has shaped all aspects of government policy, including information management. To date, this process is largely unstudied.(2)

The purpose of this chapter is to examine information repression in the Latin American national security state.   Press censorship in Brazil from 1964 to 1978 will serve as the model. It is representative because the Brazilian coup d'etat was not only the first of the military takeovers in the Southern Cone but many of its "national security" features were reproduced. Moreover, because political censorship of the press officially ended in Brazil in June 1978, it is easier to document than any other case of information repression in the region.

Censorship persisted longer in the electronic media.   Although all Brazilian media are largely in private hands, the broadcast media are directly dependent on the state for franchising, licensing, and to a much lesser extent, programming.   In regulating broadcasting, the state has been able to exert continuing political control. Hence, despite the undeniable importance of radio and television in Brazilian society, a complete study of information repression in these media is as yet unfeasible.(3) Finally, political censorship of all media prevails in the rest of the region. Information about this repression is itself censored.

Specifically, this chapter opens with a discussion of the origins and key tenets of the National Security Doctrine that provided the rationale for information repression in the Southern Cone. In the main body of the study, the semiclandestine political system of press censorship in effect in Brazil from 1968 to 1978 will be reconstructed. A consideration of the nature of the evidence for this system is a necessary prelude to an analysis of its principal features: its historical development and relation to events in the larger political order; its organization, including the training, methods, and identity of the censors; and finally, its differential impact on various print media. The issues raised by this analysis suggest further questions about the ways in which press censorship was systematic, effective, and consequential in Brazil. These are considered in the final section.

It should be made clear that this system was independent from, but complementary to, the legal structure of political censorship based on extraconstitutional national security legislation. Restraints on expression were codified in the 1967, 1969, and 1979 versions of the National Security Law, the cornerstone of all emergency legislation in the Brazilian national security state. They were legalized somewhat differently in the explicit fusion of politics and morals established by Decree Law 1077 of 1970, which permitted prior censorship of all publications and entertainment. In addition, other restrictive legislation promulgated by the military in the post-1964 period regulated both individual expression and the means of communication. All of these systems of political censorship, whether applied to the press or broadcasting, were nonetheless perfectly consistent with the objectives of the Brazilian military government in its creation of a national security state.

It should be noted also that information control in the Southern Cone has not been limited to semiclandestine or even legal censorship. Although this cannot be done here, the study of national information policy in these countries should ideally include an analysis of the state role in information production. In Brazil, the state has created various propaganda agencies to oversee patriotic public relations campaigns conducted through government advertising in mass media publications, radio and television spots, and short films. Argentina carried propaganda dissemination to the international sphere by hiring Burson-

Marsteller, a New York-based public relations firm, to counter its negative image as a human rights violator with positive publicity about its development potential.(4) Also in Brazil, the state has planted false news in the media — reporting deaths under officially sanctioned torture as suicides or disappearances, for example. Indeed, the systematic torture of political prisoners by security forces is a major way the Brazilian state obtained information relevant to its policy goals. This practice has been extensively documented throughout the region, although it declined noticeably in Brazil after 1976 and especially after the opposition campaign for political amnesty in 1977 and 1978.

In addition, the military states in the Southern Cone have sought political control of consumer product advertising and mass media entertainment by economic means. In Brazil, for example, although advertising agencies, movie companies, and radio and television networks — like the press — are primarily in private hands, the government ensures their political compliance through direct investment, generous credit incentives, liberal tax breaks, and other financial "favors." Thus the government has extended its political information control beyond the information structures of its own agencies, departments, and propaganda organizations into the private sector.

The content of mass media advertising and entertainment has also directly bolstered the Brazilian regime's economic and social policies. For millions, the trade-off between economic development and political rights has been made more palatable by seductive mass media images of celebrities and popular fictional characters enjoying luxurious consumer goods. On television, in particular, the typical Brazilian family is portrayed as upper middle class. But this promise of economic development is itself false. In reality, the military's economic policies are based on the extreme concentration of national wealth, a heavy dependence on foreign investment, and the wage-squeeze of workers. Insofar as illusive mass media products have disguised this contradiction, they have been important to the Brazilian regime's strategy of power. Indeed, throughout the region, official policies of information control have included the manipulation of mass media content.

The theoretical implications of this case study are also not explored here. Nonetheless, this material could easily serve as an empirical test of the major theories about legitimacy in the contemporary Latin American military state.(5) It could also test the control capacity of these so-called bureaucratic-authoritarian regimes.(6) In a broader application, this material might also contribute to the debates in political communications regarding the diffusion of political information in society and the development of a comparative framework for the analysis of media-state relations.(7)

THE DOCTRINE OF NATIONAL SECURITY

In Brazil, the Doctrine of National Security has been elaborated in courses offered by the Higher War College (Escola Superior de Guerra, ESG), as well as in speeches of the military presidents and chiefs of staff, published statements of military policy, and to a much lesser degree, in articles and books. The ESG course documents are unpublished; the speeches generally appear in Brazilian newspaper articles.(8)

Best known among the published sources is General Golbery do Couto e Silva's Geopolítica do Brasil, published in 1967. The founder of the Brazilian National Intelligence Service (Servico Nacional de Informação, SNI) during the first revolutionary government, Golbery was the Minister of the Civil Household under Presidents Ernesto Geisel and João Figueiredo. But it was his early elaboration of the concepts of "total," "global," "permanent," and indeed "apocalyptic" war — directed above all at the state's internal enemies — that secured his reputation as the ideologue of the Brazilian revolution.

By extension, Golbery's concept provided a rationale for the suppression of dissent by any means. It became the indirect basis for the systematic torture and elimination of the regime's critics in Brazil, as well as the justification for similar "dirty wars" waged in the 1970s by security forces in Chile, Argentina, and Uruguay.

Golbery's "total war" concept, as Armand Mattelart points out,(9) obliterated the distinctions between peace and wartime, civilians and the military, civil society and the battleground. Americans are familiar with a modified version of this view, which has justified their own cold war politics. In the Southern Cone, however, the cold war became the state's raison d'être. The Christian Western world and the Communist Eastern world are seen in permanent conflict. At stake are the values of occidental civilization, summed up in the name of an influential right-wing Brazilian group: "Tradition, Property, and Family."

The total war to preserve or attack these values is waged on all levels of individual and community life. Every individual is a combatant, either for or against. All aspects of national life can be arms in the struggle, from the official state business of diplomacy, pacts and counterpacts, treaties, commercial agreements, sanctions, boycotts, loans, embargoes and foreign aid to the more obviously political weapons of propaganda and counterpropaganda, slogans, and other techniques of international persuasion such as blackmail, threats, and even terrorism. The battle lines are drawn not only along military but also political, economic, and psychosocial lines. Information and the means of communication, according to military proponents of the scheme, are deployed on this last front.

In his <u>Geopolítica do Brasil,</u> Golbery spells out what he means by "total war":

From a strictly military conception, war has now been converted into total war, a war that is economic, financial, political, psychological, and scientific, as well as being a war of armies, naval forces, and aviation; from total war to global war, and from global war to indivisible war, and why not admit it, permanent war.(10)

What Golbery calls "national power" — the total physical and human resources of a nation — must be mobilized by the state in this war. Each citizen must therefore subjugate his own aims to the struggle against the state's enemies. This defense of national security is the paramount national objective in the rigid order imposed by the military state. It is limitless and absolute.

"National security" itself was clearly defined by Brazil's first military president, Marechal Castelo Branco. The strategic importance of political information for both the regime and its opponents is clear in his definition:

The concept of national security . . . includes the global defense of institutions, and takes into consideration <u>psychosocial aspects,</u> preservation of development and internal political stability. In addition, the concept of security . . . takes into account internal aggression, manifested through <u>infiltration, ideological subversion,</u> and <u>guerrilla movements.</u> All of these forms of conflict are much more likely to occur than foreign aggression.(11) [emphasis added]

The institution behind both Golbery and Castelo Branco was the Higher War College. Above all, this so-called Brazilian Sorbonne shaped the National Security Doctrine and proposed it as the basis for a new militarized state. Founded after World War II by Brazilian officers who fought side by side with U.S. troops in Italy, the ESG was itself highly influenced by U.S. military thinking. Numerous public safety and technical assistance programs, in reality counterinsurgency training, further strengthened U.S.-Brazilian military ties.(12)

Nonetheless, as Mattelart further notes, "The theory of the military state is the result of practices and doctrines that do not refer exclusively to the Pentagon's military praxis and philosophy."(13) Indeed, Mattelart convincingly demonstrates that elements of Prussian and Nazi geopolitics, American McCarthyism (represented by the 1947 National Security Act and anti-Communist legislation passed in the 1950s), and the French experience in Algeria and Indochina are also key reference points in the Southern Cone.

Despite its many shared tenets, the National Security Doctrine has not been uniformly applied by the region's military leaders. In Chile, for example, the rhetorical accent has fallen heavily on extreme right "Christian" values. The discourse of the Chilean generals reflects the importance of the Catholic integralist movement in Chilean society. Although this movement has also been powerful in Brazil, the Chilean leaders have made much more explicit reference to the "Christian tradition of the Fatherland" than their Brazilian counterparts. The latter in their "revolutionary" discourse characteristically stress Brazil's future course and their determination to institute "indispensible means for the economic, financial, political and moral reconstruction of Brazil."(14) The former, in contrast, stress the need to follow "the direction of historical traditions and . . . respect for symbols representing the Fatherland."(15)

Nonetheless, the basic characteristics of the National Security Doctrine can be identified for the entire Southern Cone. The Doctrine welds cold war politics and right-wing Christianity into the basis for an absolute state. Conceived of and implemented by the military, the Doctrine permits supersession of national constitutions and renders the legislative and judicial branches of government subservient to executive power. Executive power is itself a manifestation of the hegemony of the military-police machinery within the state apparatus, although factionalism often develops among the various armed services or among military men with conflicting ideological positions. In Brazil, for example, nationalistic economic policies versus those favoring multinational interests have often been at issue among the military, as have "hard-line" versus "soft-line" political and social policies.

This type of military rule has been dubbed "bureaucratic authoritarianism" by social scientists. It is seen as a new phenomenon in Latin America, different from the traditional forms of military domination in the region. In contrast to rule by a single strongman, the bureaucratic-authoritarian state is run by the institutionalized military. In both Brazil and Argentina, there has been an orderly transfer of power from general to general. Throughout the Southern Cone, military bureaucracies have assumed control of state administration.

Bureaucratic-authoritarian regimes also differ from European fascist states of the 1930s and 1940s. These regimes depended on mass support, whereas today's Latin American military states fear both mass mobilization and popular political activity. Instead, the creation of mass apathy and the political demobilization of all classes aside from the ruling elites are instrumental in the formation of state policy.

To ensure their domination of the political process and achieve their authoritarian goals, these states have dismantled political parties, professional associations, trade unions, and other representative civil organizations. They have generated a number of military and civilian "information and security" services that in reality became organs of political repression. Also on the information front, they have sought to control news flow through the means of communication. In Brazil, this control was exercised through two political censorship systems, one legalized by revolutionary decrees and other national security legislation and the other semiclandestine. The story of the first rightly belongs to a separate study of national security legislation. Recounted here is the less known development of semiclandestine political censorship.

THE POLITICAL CENSORSHIP SYSTEM

The Nature of the Evidence

In Brazil, the web of national security legislation as well as civil and criminal laws regulating individual expression and the means of communication constitute a formidable legal arsenal upon which the state could draw to punish and even prevent political "abuses" of information. Nonetheless, unlike some other repressive governments, which rely on publicly acknowledged formal censorship bureaucracies, the Brazilian military preferred to censor "secretly, by means of verbal orders . . . psychological coercion . . . and veiled threats,"(16) as one journalist put it.

Of course this "secret" system, in effect from 1968 to 1978, was well known to news professionals, at least insofar as it interfered with their work. To a much lesser degree, the public was also aware of political censorship, having been alerted by disguised references in the press. In fact, the system's real secrecy lay in its dubious legality and its arbitrary enforcement in concert with other forms of officially sanctioned intimidation and repression. The government's silence and half-truths compounded the mystery. Nonetheless, bits and pieces of legal and historical evidence now in the public domain can be brought together to explain much of this once-secret system.

It is on record, for example, that the government, when challenged by newspapers in Brazilian courts, curiously did not defend political censorship on the specific grounds provided by the substantial body of relevant emergency legislation written by the military between 1964 and 1967. Instead, the government chose to base its defense on Institutional Act No. 5 (A.I. 5) of December 13, 1968. This decree had formalized the "coup within the coup" perpetrated by the hard-line military. For the next ten years, it "legally" permitted them to suspend normal constitutional guarantees. Obviously, A.I. 5 was imposed on the country illegally, at least when judged by democratic standards that equate legality with constitutionality.

The divergence of the two is clearly demonstrated in the provisions allowing censorship. A.I. 5, in Article 9, specifically empowered the president to adopt the "coercive measures" foreseen in lines "d" and "e" of Paragraph 2, Article 152, of the 1967 constitution.(17) Line "d" permitted "suspension of freedom of assembly and of association." Line "e," directly relevant here, permitted "censure of correspondence, printing, tele-communications, and public amusements."(18)

According to the constitution, however, these "coercive measures" could only be authorized by the president of the republic during a declared "state of siege." A "state of siege," for its part, could be decreed only in two cases: "(I) Serious disturbance of order or threat of the outbreak of such disturbance; or (II) War."(19) According to A.I. 5, however, the president could impose these coercive measures if they were "necessary to the defense of the Revolution"(20) [emphasis added]. In other words, A.I. 5, like the authoritarian constitution of 1937 that marked Getulio Vargas's Estado Novo, expressly permitted prior censorship without the specific conditions warranting the formal declaration of a state of siege. Thus the 1967 constitution, although it had been promulgated by the military itself just one year prior to A.I. 5, was considered too restrictive of executive power.

In fact, the military did not bother to decree a state of siege in Brazil in 1968. On the strength of the discrepancy between A.I. 5 and the constitution, then, several important suits were filed by newspapers against the government. Lawyers arguing on behalf of the Rio opposition weekly Opinião in 1973 and the Catholic weekly O São Paulo in 1977 sought to prove that censorship was unconstitutional, even in light of the military's own constitution.(21) Although Opinião did win an initial victory, the decision was later overturned by a higher court. Both suits were ultimately denied.

The results convincingly demonstrated the strength of the draconian A.I. 5. It in effect established an extraconstitutional governmental structure, granting the president absolute powers and enabling him to act without the possibility of restraint by Congress or the courts. Indeed, on the strength of A.I. 5, the president ordered the Congress closed several times during this period. Nor did political censorship require specific grounds. After A.I. 5, even prior restraint could be implemented by an unconditional executive decision. Proof in writing was supplied during the Opinião case in 1973, when the government produced a dispatch, curiously dated 1971, which justified political censorship of the paper on the basis of executive powers granted under A.I. 5.

Political censorship, therefore, was officially recognized by the state as a key tactic in defense of the revolution. It follows, then, that a centralized chain of information control was organized by the highest levels of the military. Two principal forms of political censorship emerged: a system of telephoned and written orders that prohibited press treatment of certain issues and a system whereby military officers and then, later on, police censors reviewed page proofs prior to publication.

Prepublication review was predominantly employed at the beginning of the 1968–78 period, while the system of specific prohibitions reached its height from the second half of 1969 to early 1975, roughly during the years of the Médici administration (1969–74). Direct censorship by means of prepublication review was maintained throughout the period as a punitive measure, however, and applied for varying lengths of time to a variety of publications, including the prestigious daily O Estado de São Paulo, the alternative opposition weeklies Opinião of Rio de Janeiro and its offshoot, Movimento, from São Paulo, as well as the diocesan newspaper O São Paulo and the sensationalistic Rio daily, A Tribuna da Imprensa.

Two kinds of evidence support the view that political censorship was created by the highest echelons of the military. First, the orders dealing directly with national security matters contain much inside information, particularly in the prohibitions on clandestine security force activities and bans of news about the 1973 internal power struggle over the presidential succession. Secrecy on both issues was considered so vital to national security by the military that even orders prohibiting related news had to have originated in the very centers of power.

The second kind of evidence is administrative. While the Federal Censorship Bureau publicly admitted only to conducting "morals" censorship of public entertainment, leaving political censorship of news and information to the Federal Police Department, both bureaucracies have direct ties to the military. Thus the Federal Censorship Bureau is actually a division of the Federal Police Department, and the Federal Police Department, nominally subject to the Ministry of Justice, was in fact headed by an army general or colonel during this entire period.(22)

Both written and telephoned orders as well as the criteria for prepublication review, then, most likely originated in the Army Information Center or the Federal Police Department headquarters in Brasília. It is true that some later orders reflected parochial concerns and were probably emitted not by the president of the republic, but by the minister of justice, the minister of the army, the general director of the Federal Police Department, or commanders of the military regions,(23) or even by officials in various government departments and agencies, local officials, political figures, or influential citizens. Similarly, the military officers who first carried out prior censorship by means of prepublication review were by all accounts politically consistent with the policy goals of the state. The police censors who replaced them, in contrast, were notoriously unqualified, often censoring on the dubious criterion of "when in doubt, cut."(24) Thus power fragmented and led to its own abuse.

Nonetheless, as first conceived by the military, the political censorship apparatus was designed at the highest levels of the state to implement the national security objectives of the revolution. In practice, this meant banning news of dissent and protest over the military's handling of the country's political, economic, and social affairs. Censorship was enforced, moreover, by the threat of government sanctions against individual journalists and news organizations. Legal indictments and convictions of both under an arsenal of national security legislation, as well as seizures of editions and invasions and closures of newspapers and radio stations, were frequent enough to substantiate these threats. Even more intimidating were well-known blacklists maintained at news organizations, public testimonies of torture upon arrest, and the suspension of habeas corpus for those charged with political crimes. As Paulo Marconi has observed, censorship was institutionalized during a period in Brazil when "anyone could be imprisoned, kidnapped, tortured, and sometimes made to disappear forever."(25)

This overall picture of the political censorship system is finally emerging, despite silence or evasions on the subject by government spokesmen and the censors themselves. Official explanations, when made, have hardly been revealing. Indeed, only reports made public by newspapers and individual journalists have documented the process. Similarly, no torturer freely admitted to his job. In fact, although torture of political prisoners in Brazil was an official state policy from 1964 to at least 1976, only the public disclosure of victims' testimonies brought it to light.

Even recent official statements claim ignorance about political censorship. Testifying before a congressional sub-committee in 1979, Jose Vieir Madeira, director of the Public Entertainment Department of the Censorship Bureau of the Federal Police, refused to speak about political censorship, as he could not answer for "things past." He preferred to speak about the future agenda: classifications in entertainment censorship, which are justified on the clear grounds of "morality and public decency" provided by the Brazilian constitution. While Vieira implies that political censorship of both news and entertainment existed, he certainly was not going to elaborate.(26)

Testifying before the same committee, the former head of the same department took the same position. Rogério Nunes, censorship director for seven years during the "state of exception," stated that his official work had nothing to do with press censorship. His censorship, he insisted, was of public entertainment, "foreseen in Brazilian law and inscribed in the constitution." Press censorship, he added, was based solely on A.I. 5, now a dead letter. Therefore, he concluded, he had nothing to add to the previous discussion by journalists testifying before the committee.(27)

This position completes a circle of evasion, as officials did not commonly acknowledge press censorship during the time of A.I. 5, either. In 1974, for example, a censorship instructor at the National Police Academy wrote the following definition: "To censor," said Coriolano de Loyola Cabral Fagundes, "is to examine and classify public entertainment within a determined age group."(28) Any mention of news or information is conspicuously absent.

Official statements obviously reveal little. Personal and published testimonies of newspeople and other cultural figures still provide the most comprehensive description of political censorship.(29) Some written materials are also useful. In October 1978, for example, a National Congress for Freedom of the Press was held in São Paulo. In May 1979, a national meeting of the self-designated Permanent Commission of the Struggle for Freedom of Expression of the Brazilian Press Association was held in Rio de Janeiro. On both occasions, participants produced detailed accounts of the legal, historical, and professional aspects of the political censorship system.(30)

The Brazilian Press Association newspaper, Boletim ABI, and Unidade, the São Paulo Journalists' Union newspaper, provide additional data.(31) Both reflect the profession's concern with press freedom issues, and neither was directly censored. The legal documentation from Opinião and O São Paulo cases is also available,(32) as are transcripts of congressional hearings on censorship, held in May and June of 1979.(33) The investigating committee sought to analyze the practices and institution of censorship and explore the possibilities for a legally regulated system.

The most documentary evidence of political censorship is found in records of telephoned and written censorship orders kept by journalists. More than 500 were recorded for the national press between 1968 and 1978.(34) They indicate both the range of censored topics and how so-called sensitive issues either changed or remained constant over time. In addition, copies of general press guidelines issued by the authorities before specific written orders came generally into use(35) in 1972 have been published. They indicate the initial relationship of censorship to the early objectives of the revolution. Finally, actual censored materials preserved by journalists and editors in various newspaper archives demonstrate the subject matter, style, and tone of "unacceptable" information.(36) These materials clearly reveal that the criteria for political censorship were discriminatory, depending on the readership and ideological orientation of the censored publication.

This wealth of data however, has some important limitations. In addition, further research and analysis may be jeopardized by professional difficulties facing journalists in Brazil today. Indeed, this essentially historical study may itself be affected by changing historical conditions. The first limitation is the lack of historical perspective. This makes the assessment of military censorship in Brazil more difficult. The second is that our informants are often professional rivals, at times producing conflicting versions of events. The third is more serious. Unlike dissidents who have been granted political asylum elsewhere, our informants cannot speak with impunity. The information about censorship in Brazil is largely provided by journalists, jurists, and other opponents of the military regime who still live and work in Brazil. Although in recent years there have been changes in leadership, the restoration of some civil and political guarantees, the reformulation of a multiparty system, the growth of a significant trade union movement, and above all, a formidable challenge to the state by progressives in the Catholic church, the regime responsible for repression in past years still holds sway. It is true that the Brazilian government has publicly repudiated its excesses of the 1968-78 period. Nonetheless, not a single torturer has been held to account. For those who have exposed and condemned political censorship, there may be an increasing professional and political risk.

Journalists, in particular, face a difficult professional situation. The job market is increasingly saturated. Some outspoken opponents of the regime, including top-flight experienced professionals, have been squeezed out of the establishment press and even from the alternative media. These independent organs, extremely effective as the vanguard of the opposition campaign for amnesty and liberalization, have themselves suffered from concerted government pressures.

In 1979, a bitter and divisive strike at the prestigious daily O Estado de São Paulo ended with the firing of more than one hundred journalists. No longer were newspaper owners, editors, and less well-paid reporters united against the censor, their common enemy. Indeed, the government strategy to reestablish the traditional press-state alliance — disrupted during the period of censorship — was successful. By lifting censorship, the government actually created a more compliant press. In this professional environment, plain speech about past or present government pressures can hardly be encouraged. Nonetheless, to the credit of many courageous journalists, debate has continued.

The political climate is equally inhospitable. The press as a whole has been harassed by the government and attacked by right-wing terrorist groups. Repeated bombings in the past several years have damaged and destroyed kiosks selling opposition publications. In 1979, the military's secret plan to pressure these publications was leaked by the Estado de São Paulo.(37) In 1980, a bomb demolished the editorial offices and printing plant of A Tribuna da Imprensa. In 1981, in the aftermath of the bombing incident resulting in the death of one military officer and the wounding of another outside a crowded Rio meeting hall, the press concluded that only a premature explosion had saved the crowd. An official inquiry, however, concluded that the thwarted bombers were "leftist terrorists." The press, too, was denounced as "leftist infiltrated." After this affair, government harassment of the press intensified: Journalists were condemned by military courts, newspapers were seized and suspended, and the military charged the press with sensationalism and irresponsibility.(38)

This precarious situation is reflected in the larger political order. Events of late 1981 — the conviction of trade union leaders on national security charges, the interference in universities by state officials, the tampering with election rules by means of government "packages" designed to weaken and divide the opposition parties — indicate that the liberalization is by no means irreversible. In the present light, moreover, it is easier to see that the 1978-79 period was one of euphoria produced by significant opposition victories in national elections and human rights. The safe return of many political exiles further buoyed opposition spirits. Significantly, this was also the historical moment when most of the testimony about censorship went on record. If that moment elicited this testimony, the current one may well discourage more. Full knowledge of the political censorship system in Brazil may only slowly come to light.

The Nature of the System

Despite these obstacles, three major features of the political censorship system in Brazil can be reconstructed in some detail. First, a chronology of events can be compiled, and a basic periodization established. This scheme reveals that the censorship system developed in response to decisive events in the larger political order. Second, the censorship bureaucracy can be described. The training, methods, and identity of the censors are all part of the picture. Finally, the impact of the system on various print media can be assessed, allowing for a general evaluation of censorship in terms of the military's national security goals, on one hand, and press performance, on the other.

Obviously, this analysis presupposes that there indeed was a censorship system. This assumption runs counter to a popular impression in Brazil among both newspeople and the public that censorship was arbitrary and erratic. These are logical perceptions for those who experienced it piecemeal: an anonymous phone call to a newsroom; a political story interrupted by non sequiturs; participation in an unreported demonstration. Do these events form a coherent pattern? Answering that question is the task at hand.

Chronology of Political Censorship

The chronology of political censorship reflects the key events of the post-1964 period in Brazil. Historical consensus has it that the first two military governments under Castelo Branco and his successor Costa e Silva were committed, at least in theory, to freedom of the press. There was in fact no direct censorship until 1968. Nonetheless, many journalists and editors were imprisoned during the first four years of military rule. The case of Hélio Fernandes, for example, is well known. For his outspokenness, the controversial editor had been deprived of his political rights for ten years. The penalty included denial of the right to make political statements. This prohibition notwithstanding, Fernandes wrote and signed articles that were violently critical of ex-president Castelo Branco, who had died in an airplane crash shortly after his successor Costa e Silva took office. In retribution, the government imprisoned Fernandes, for some days in 1967, on the remote island of Fernando de Noronha.(39)

Also in the 1964-68 period, many leftist and pro-Goulart newspapers were invaded and destroyed, for example, the small tabloids Politica and Folha da Semana. Nor were the established newspapers exempt. Across the country, editorial offices of the newspaper chain that employed the most journalists in the country, Ultima Hora, were literally devastated. A police invasion also damaged Correio da Manhã, Rio's venerable hundred-year-old daily.

The story of the Correio is an important one. The paper had been among Goulart's most powerful opponents in the days preceding the military coup. Indeed, its famous editorials, "Basta" ["Enough"] and "Fora" ["Out"], demanded his ouster. But the new regime's undemocratic tactics, especially the abrogation of constitutional guarantees in a series of institutional acts and the torture of political prisoners, soon caused a turnabout. The Correio quickly became the single most important opposition voice in Brazil.

From 1964 to 1968, the paper systematically denounced the regime. Editions were coveted and sold throughout Brazil. Confronted with this resistance, the government struck back. Rather than forcibly closing the prestigious Correio, however, it pressured advertisers to withhold their business. The resulting revenue loss, combined with management problems and the exodus of its top journalists, crippled the paper and eventually caused it to fold. Furthermore, this method of pressuring the Correio was indicative of an important government position. Rather than declare an open dictatorship, the regime chose to maintain nominal freedom of the press as a symbol of its "democratic" intentions — thus providing an excellent international image with little cost to the regime. Márcio Moreira Alves, a key opposition political figure and also a journalist for the Correio, explains why. Commenting on the government's rather puzzling tolerance of the Correio's antitorture campaign in his own banned book Torturas e Torturadores,(40) Alves wryly notes that an opposition newspaper or two with a daily circulation of less than 350,000 was ultimately of little consequence in a country of some 40 million illiterates.

Nonetheless, the government saw the Correio as a formidable foe. Even after 1968, the paper was warily handled, although the economic boycott had been successful and the Correio was hardly the opposition voice it had been. True, in late 1968 and early 1969 it suffered a veritable reign of terror: a bomb attack, the confiscation of an entire edition, the imprisonment of staff members and directors, and the interdiction of editorial offices and the physical plant by police. Owner-publisher Dona Niomar Bittencourt herself spent 70 days in prison, 23 of them incommunicado. Nonetheless, she was subsequently acquitted on charges of violating the National Security Law by insulting President Costa e Silva.(41) Albeit heavy-handedly, the government was apparently trying to demonstrate that a "responsible" press could still function in Brazil.

On the whole, however, the regime completely abandoned its concern with democratic credibility in the late 1968–72 period, during which additional repressive legislation regulating the press was written. A.I. 5 of December 13, 1968, as noted, provided the official justification for political censorship, particularly prior restraint. It was cited specifically to justify Decree Law 1077 of 1970, which authorized the federal police to exercise prior censorship of material "contrary to morality and public decency,"(42) as well as to justify the government's 1973 rejection of Opinião's suit protesting censorship on constitutional grounds.

But the decree also had an immediate impact on the country's newspapers. Alberto Dines, then political editor of the Rio daily O Jornal do Brasil, recounts the events that followed the emission of A.I. 5.(43)   On December 13, two army majors occupied the paper's editorial offices.   On December 14, journalists and editors put out what became a historic protest edition by making substitutions for approved material in the composing room.   As a reprisal, the number of military censors was increased to five.   They remained for some 20 days, until January 5, 1969.   One officer, Dines recalls, was a Marcuse specialist;   all, once they understood the mechanics of newspaper production, could not be deceived and efficiently carried out their duties.   During those days, also, both Dines and the general director of the newspaper, Sette Câmara, were arrested. They were released soon afterward.

After this initial period, self-censorship was instituted at the Jornal do Brasil.   A "gentlemen's agreement" was made stipulating that the censors would leave the newsroom if editors and journalists would comply with general press guidelines.   Dines notes sadly that the paper accepted the condition with little hesitation. Federal police agents who dealt directly with editors soon replaced the military censors who had transmitted the official orientation to the newspaper's directors.   But they were not stationed in the newsroom.   This state of affairs continued until 1972, when the guidelines were superseded by sequential written orders specifically related to ongoing events.(44)

A look at the 1969 guidelines themselves is instructive.   In language similar to that found in the 1969 National Security Law, they prohibited newspapers from publishing "false news," "demoralizing the government," or "contesting the regime." These prohibitions also included "sensationalist news," "publicity about communist nations," "criticisms of state governors, seeking to demonstrate unsound appointments by the Federal Government," and the "exaltation of immorality, with news about homosexuality, prostitution and drugs."   In addition, no reporting of tensions between the Catholic Church and the state or of "agitation in the labor and student movements" was allowed.(45)

Clearly, the authorities sought to keep the small-scale urban guerrilla war then being waged out of the press.   Public knowledge of guerrilla actions like the kidnapping of ambassadors, politically motivated bank robberies, and armed assaults was particularly feared.   Government suspicion of the press increased when the kidnappers of the American ambassador left instructions for gaining his release at the Journal do Brasil offices. Suspicion turned to rage when it was discovered that one of the kidnappers was a journalist, once employed at that very paper.(46) Yet it is also clear from the content of the guidelines that the authorities' prohibitory zeal extended to almost every aspect of political, economic, and social life.

This wide range of prohibited topics can only be an indication of how many actual events or tendencies were considered subversive or objectionable by the military. It is true that the regime was in fact challenged in some quarters. Still, its response on the information front was to declare no less than the "total war" envisioned by national security ideologues. Was this overkill? Would banning news or dissent really make dissent itself disappear? Would a press image of a perfectly static society with no social conflict convince citizens that national goals had been achieved? The answers are unclear. The fact remains, however, that at least in the short run, the regime scored a tactical victory. Newspapers submitted to censorship.

In the aftermath of A.I. 5, those in Rio were hit hard. Within months of the crackdown, all the city's major newspapers were effectively silenced. The Correio da Manhã, already emasculated, was invaded. The Jornal do Brasil was intimidated. Hélio Fernandes, imprisoned in 1967, was arrested again. His combative newspaper, A Tribuna da Imprensa, had in fact been invaded by military censors two months before A.I. 5. It would remain subject to uninterrupted censorship for nearly ten years. O Globo, another leading Rio daily, was considered virtually a government organ, although it is privately owned. Clearly, A.I. 5 allowed the government to strike at the Rio press as it had struck at the Congress, in an all-out effort to liquidate political opposition to the regime.

Throughout Brazil, the crackdown struck hard at the press. Carlos Chagas, press secretary to President Costa e Silva and one-time political editor at the Estado do São Paulo, fills in the events in Brazil's other major city. In spite of Dines's assertion that "the papers of São Paulo, including O Estado, had every liberty of publication" and were subjected to censorship only two years later,(47) Chagas recalls that an edition of O Estado was confiscated immediately after A.I. 5, because of an editorial entitled "Institutions in Tatters" that protested the decree.(48) In fact, Chagas describes many of the same censoring measures that Dines does: military censors installed for short periods in newsrooms and radio and television stations as reprisals for noncompliance, backed up further by the threat of invasion by radio patrols, and a continuing barrage of telephoned and orally transmitted censorship orders.

At the end of 1968 and in early 1969, references to the state of exception, public protests, and street battles, as well as to political disappearances, were prohibited in the São Paulo press. By the second half of 1969, however, censorship had broadened, increased, and become less politically consistent. In the first months of the Médici regime, the immediate responsibility for censorship was transferred from the military to the federal police. With less effective police control and execution, various authorities began to censor in accord with their own interests. In comparison, military censorship appeared competent, intelligent, and even objective. For Chagas, this period of police phone calls, censorship orders, and newsroom appearances was a "negative mark" in the history of censorship. Across the country, it had become a "snowball that carried us to the bottom of an abyss."(49)

A turning point in São Paulo came on August 24, 1972, when 12 police radio patrols invaded the Estado newsroom. According to Chagas, they were armed with machine guns and grenades, as well as with orders to stop an edition of the paper that allegedly contained an editorial or manifesto launching the candidacy of General Geisel for the presidency. Chagas claims the article never existed. Nonetheless, it served as a pretext for the invasion and an occupation by censors. Clearly, any leaks of news about President Médici's possible successors were an anathema to unity-minded officers who preferred that their internal power struggles be kept private.

After this incident, the paper refused to submit to self-censorship. For more than two years, until the paper's centennial on January 5, 1975, a team of censors read O Estado line by line. Their prepublication review included the sports page, the economics section, and even the obituary page, as well as political news. Consequently, each edition of the paper was delayed. In addition to the censors, journalists and editors had to obey a barrage of censorship orders. These arrived in great profusion from 1972 to 1975, constituting a distinct period in the chronology of censorship.

Copies of many of these orders were made by journalists and have been analyzed in some detail. In 1978, Elio Gaspari, former political editor of the Jornal do Brasil, published the texts and an analysis of a series of 270 sequential written orders, dating from September 14, 1972, to October 8, 1975. Silio Boccanera, now the Washington correspondent for the same newspaper, studied orders from this same "Black Book." His conclusions appeared in an unpublished master's thesis written at the University of Southern California in 1978. Several years before, Alberto Dines made a preliminary study of 288 orders received at the Jornal do Brasil from September 1972, to December 4, 1974. His interpretation appeared in an unpublished manuscript prepared for Columbia University in 1975. All three analyses attempt to isolate the principal targets of political censorship during this period, by classifying and recording the varying frequencies of censored topics.(50)

Boccanera, for example, arranged the censored topics (including those prohibited by the general guidelines cited above) into 14 categories, listed here in descending order of frequency: police activity, domestic politics, international news, subversion, the Catholic Church, criticism of authorities, the media, economics, education, censorship, prisons, health, urban problems, and intelligence and security. Gaspari, for his part, pinpointed the activities of the security apparatus and the succession of President Médici as the two principal targets. Dines, in his account, observes that of 288 orders, 24 dealt with the political opposition, 26 with terrorism, 24 with economic matters, 18 with political prisoners and torture, and 12 with student activities. Twenty, or just under 10%, were designed to keep censorship itself secret.

Despite the different classification systems employed, it is nonetheless possible to generalize from these analyses. All three suggest that police matters, the activities of the security apparatus, and news of domestic politics, particularly armed resistance to the regime, as well as peaceful protest, were of greatest concern to the censors. In addition, as Dines notes, orders regarding economic policy banned news of wage fixing, problems of supply (a serious meat shortage had occurred during this period), and most importantly, the sensitive "politics of petroleum." News of the so-called "risk contracts," which opened Brazil to foreign oil exploration, was particularly sensitive.

Another sensitive area involved the Catholic Church, which had emerged after 1968 as the chief critic and indeed the conscience of the regime. Although the hierarchy was by no means united, outspoken clerics were singled out by the censors. Recife Archbishop Don Helder Câmara, disparaged as the "Red Bishop of Brazil," was specifically named in at least 28 orders.(51)

It is also clear from these analyses that news of censorship itself was repeatedly banned. In theory, at least, as the saying goes, "the devil's best device is to make us believe that he doesn't exist." Similarly, the reduced news diet had to appear natural. This preoccupation with denying censorship led to some ironic prohibitions. When the Estado de São Paulo, for example, protested the written censorship orders, the protests were repeated by opposition congressmen. Government leaders denied the charges, claiming that there was no censorship in Brazil. But an order made liars of them all: "Federal Censorship," read that evening's note, "prohibits the publication of the speech of Majority Leader Filinto Muller, denying there is censorship in Brazil."(52)

It is tempting to confuse the absurdities and contradictions of the system with its principal intent. Yet that intent is clear. Censorship was designed to aid in the creation of a sanitized Brazil, cleansed of "terrorist" acts, "subversive" movements, divisions in the armed forces, and splits in the government. It was supposed to create press images of a functioning "national security state" enjoying an "Economic Miracle." Of course these were official fictions, not accurate descriptions of reality. Ultimately, censorship could no more make the fictions real than the regime's repressive political and economic policies could in fact create political stability or prolonged economic growth.

But what of the absurdities and contradictions? How did they affect the overall course of censorship? During this period, the system clearly went out of control. As noted, censorial power fragmented. Correspondingly, the range of prohibited topics broadened. Not only politically logical prohibitions but also cases of civil corruption, military misdemeanors, local intrigues, and even diseases were banned from the news. Not only controversial churchmen but the Pope himself, the daughter of the American president, Brazilian congressmen, generals, and local leaders were "x-ed" out.

The official truth, moreover, was to be written in accord with verbose orders that permitted some commentaries, banned others, allowed some photographs to be published, cut others, let some controversial items pass, but banned explanations, and so forth. In addition, the orders became increasingly imperious. By 1974, for example, Paulo Marconi found that 100 percent of 308 orders made no mention of any censoring body. They simply declared "It is prohibited . . ." or began with the words, "By superior order. . ."(53) Thus, in its zeal, censorship became unworkable and unenforceable, despite the fact that most newspapers had simply accepted the system, and despite a pervasive climate of fear in the country, which had made resistance, even minimal or symbolic protests, nothing short of heroic.

Recognizing this situation, the authorities lifted prior censorship from the major dailies and newsweeklies in 1975 and 1976. The number of written and telephoned orders also sharply decreased after late 1975. But it was not until June 8, 1978, that prior censorship was lifted from the alternative and diocesan press and from the daily Tribuna da Imprensa. (Prior censorship was lifted from radio and television in late 1978. As noted, however, the broadcast media are still subject to a variety of direct state controls.)

In regard to the press, this lag is very significant. It indicates that between 1975 and 1978, the prime objective of censorship was to stifle the opposition press and, through those organs, the opposition itself. During this period, the government became concerned with the growing number of small, independent publications like the São Paulo weekly Movimento, which was "born censored" in 1975. By 1978, according to one source, 4.5 million words had been cut by censors from page proofs of Movimento.(54)

The paper was certainly an outspoken critic of the regime. It even denounced the "slow and gradual liberalization" that many opposition groups eventually welcomed and that the establishment press, certainly by 1978 and 1979, lauded. Even during the period of prior censorship, Movimento insisted on running whatever stories it could about the internationalization of the economy, agrarian questions, and the exploitation of industrial workers. In addition, it led the way with stories about torturers and police violence. These were picked up and legitimized by the establishment press during the 1977-78 amnesty campaign, but Movimento had the scoop.

Like its predecessor Opinião, which had "died censored" in 1977, Movimento was especially irksome to the new regime. Both papers were subjected to punitive prepublication review. They were also often barred from running stories that had appeared elsewhere in the Brazilian press. Movimento finally died in 1981, amid much controversy. Not the least of its problems was a series of devastating bombings of newsstands where the paper was sold.(55)

Some explanation is also in order for why O São Paulo, the official organ of the São Paulo archdiocese, was subject to prior censorship from 1972 to 1978. Throughout this period, the church was engaged in the organization of so-called base communities throughout the country, but particularly in the slum areas and huge industrial parks outside São Paulo. O São Paulo, written in simple language and designed for group reading in churches and community centers, reported on this organization, as well as on the activities of São Paulo's tireless archbishop, Dom Paulo Evaristo Arns. Dom Paulo has been an especially active defender of human rights, explicitly denouncing the regime's abuses and coming to the aid of its victims. He is also an ardent defender of workers' rights, opening churches to workers and supporting illegal strikes on many occasions. Generally, the church antagonized the state with its defense of peasant land rights and criticism of threats to Brazil's ill-treated Indians. Especially before the reformulation of political parties was permitted in late 1979, the church, along with São Paulo's burgeoning independent trade union movement, was the most powerful institution contesting the state. It thus took on an explicitly political role, to the consternation of both government officials and conservative churchmen. It is no surprise, then, that the government attempted to hamper church communications. Radio Nove de Julho, the official church station in São Paulo, had in fact been closed for "technical reasons" as early as 1973.

This periodization indicates that the censorship system evolved with, and reflected changes in, the regime during the ten-year period of arbitrary rule, from 1968 to 1978. In the 1968-78 period, the threat of invasion and occupation by military censors kept newspapers largely respectful of general press guidelines. This use of intimidation corresponded to the wholesale repression launched by the regime.

The 1972-75 period began with unchecked government repression, but ended with some political gains for the opposition. The Brazilian Democratic Movement (Movimento Democrático Brasileiro, MDB) made a significant showing in the 1974 national elections. Renewed military factionalism during this period also contributed to the realignment of ruling elites that would later result in even more sweeping changes. In March 1974, General Ernesto Geisel assumed the presidency. But a "slow and gradual opening" was in fact begun during his administration. The relaxation of censorship in 1975 led the way.

Changes in the censorship system during this period reflect this transition. On one hand, censorship orders were more frequent, more specific, and more formally transmitted. On the other, the system became increasingly unwieldy as various authorities interfered with the centralized chain of information control, and the orders themselves proliferated wildly. Also, if increased censorship was a last-ditch attempt to conceal the military's internal divisions, once Geisel's selection as Médici's successor was known, in June 1973, a top secret was out. Furthermore, the system was debilitated by the increased resistance of journalists who were finally provoked into action. At the Estado de São Paulo, for example, both explicit denunciations and sabotage of censorship were routine. Thus the very growth of the system hastened its demise. In the same way, the excesses of the regime caused its retrenchment as the military sought new strategies for staying in power.

The final period of censorship began in 1976, when Geisel edged out the hard-line military. The decisive confrontation came in March of that year, when Geisel fired Second Army Commander General Ednardo de Mello. Ironically, because this was a victory for the moderates, the firing was reported but commentary of Geisel's motives was forbidden. Nonetheless, after Geisel's victory, both torture and censorship declined. Like the nominal freedom of the press in the 1964-68 period, the renewal of relative press freedom served to promote the regime's newly "democratic" image. The banner of a free press, in fact, was so important that it was the first of the major civil and political rights to be restored.

With General Figueirdo's presidency in March 1979, another phase of press-state relations began. Without semiclandestine political censorship, the regime nonetheless continues to control information. National security legislation, though amended, is still in effect. Under some legal articles, the government retains broad censorship powers. In addition, the government invests heavily in its own information agencies and has attempted, so far unsuccessfully, to maintain a cabinet-level information ministry, a state radio network, and a national wire service. It pours funds into privately owned information businesses and has become a major media advertiser and creditor.(56) This shift from information repression through political censorship to information control through government involvement in the information industry corresponds to a major feature of the liberalization. Although the government has relinquished its exclusive control of the political process, nonetheless it continues to control the state apparatus. This gives many Brazilians reasons to fear a retrocesso, or "stepping back," after each political crisis. Indeed, for some, the abertura, or "opening," is already over.(57)

The Censorship Bureaucracy

What do we know of the censorship bureaucracy? Who were the censors? What training did they receive, and what methods did they use? The first point has already been made. Although various military officers and police investigators signed their names to the written censorship orders, and agents identified themselves on a first-name basis over the telephone, it is likely that the most important of the orders originated at the Army Intelligence Center or the Federal Police Headquarters in Brasília. Others were nonsensical or parochial and no doubt emanated from local officials. On national security matters, however, the orders revealed an intimate knowledge of state policy that would have been accessible only to the highest-ranking officers.

To support this view, Elio Gaspari notes that 74 orders relative to security matters had been emitted by the time of Geisel's inauguration on March 15, 1974, with no "errors."(58) Nonetheless, it must be admitted that the government has never publicly disclosed the details of the political censorship operation. Still, the evidence would seem irrefutable that at least the crucial orders were determined and authorized at the highest levels of the military government. This is tantamount to proof of a centralized censorship system with an institutionalized chain of command.

What about the agents who exercised prior censorship? One suspects they were chosen from among the censors working in the Public Entertainment Censorship Division of the Federal Police Department, officially the central censorship bureaucracy in Brazil. Its function as defined by law is to "plan, coordinate, execute and control . . . the censorship of public entertainment, in all of national territory."(59) Its specific tasks are to regulate the transport of films across state borders and review television programs and plays. It is in practice subject to the Ministry of Justice and in theory to a Higher Censorship Board (Conselho Superior de Censura), established in 1968. This body was supposed to make all final decisions regarding the censorship of shows and public entertainment. It was also supposed to set the norms and criteria for censorship. As of 1979, however, the board was not yet functioning, although it was an expressed priority of then Justice Minister Petrônio Portella, the civilian architect of the liberalization.

According to one source, as of 1975 over 400 censors, including "political censors," worked in the Public Entertainment Censorship Division.(60) Before 1974, high school diplomas were sufficient preparation. After that time, as a result of waves of criticism about the low level of the censors, a college degree was required. All "public entertainment" censors study at the National Police Academy in Brasilia. They take courses in social psychology, sociology, communications, techniques of censorship, film technique, art and theater history, national security, and censorship legislation. Entrance to the censor's course, moreover, is highly selective. Candidates are required to pass a public competition. In 1974 in São Paulo, only 40 of 3,500 candidates were admitted. Professor Fagundes of the National Police Academy speaks of his censors with pride. In Brasilia, he claims, censors hold university degrees in literature, pedagogy, philosophy, communications, history, the social sciences, and psychology. Others have even done graduate work, and many are journalists forced to seek a "related" career because of the limited journalism job market.

Of those who became political censors, records are scarce. We do know that political censors comprised a specialized department within the bureaucracy. They were even isolated physically. In São Paulo, according to one recent magazine article, (61) the political censors occupied a special room on the fifth floor of a common office building in the old commercial center of the city. Over the door, there was a no entrance sign. Inside, in a room with a half-dozen tables and telephones, six almost unknown civil servants emitted the irrevocable orders of prior censorship to editorial offices of newspapers, magazines, and radio and television stations. The "regular" censorship office, with 24 censors overseeing the "morals" censorship of public entertainment, was upstairs.

The reporter also recounts how Dr. Richard de Bloch, director of the São Paulo political censors, responded to some questions. "My work is secret," said Bloch, "it is subject to regulations." Still, the reporter ascertained that "Dr. Richard" worked independently of the normal hierarchy of the Censorship Division, receiving his ,instructions directly from the justice minister's office in Brasília or from local military authorities.

Known only by their first names, these political censors were omnipresent figures in the early 1970s. Journalists challenged and harassed them as much as possible, and they report a high level of shame and defensiveness among censors. Rather whimsically, journalists categorized censors into three types: mediocre ones, who feared transfer to remote places if they made an error in judgment; sadistic ones, born to x-out whatever they disagreed with; and progressives, who discussed cuts with journalists.(62) Whatever the attitude of the censor, journalists agree, criteria for suppression were erratic and arbitrary. Stories of inept censors abound. Nonetheless, information about how the censors worked is admittedly sketchy. To date, it is based on the recollections of journalists. From officials, only accounts of "morals" censorship are heard. One waits, perhaps in vain, for a former political censor to fill the picture.

The Impact of Censorship

As mentioned, censorship was less detrimental to the established press than to so-called alternative or opposition newspapers. Criteria for censorship were thus not uniform. Although items relating to national security in the broadest sense were universally banned, much information regarding social, economic, or local political issues was allowed to pass in some publications, yet was banned in others. This leads to the conclusion that certain publications, like the opposition Rio weekly Opinião, its São Paulo offshoot, Movimento, the Catholic weekly O São Paulo, and Hélio Fernandes's Rio daily A Tribuna da Imprensa were special targets of the regime.

Indeed, the establishment press enjoyed more license than a literal reading of the official censorship guidelines or the written orders would indicate. In the major dailies and newsweeklies, for example, there was considerable sabotage of the ban against signaling censorship to newspaper readers. Symbolic protests captured both the professional and public imagination, and examples have become part of the folklore of resistance. One well-known anecdote concerns the Rio daily, Jornal do Brasil. In a protest edition of December 14, 1968, printed the day after the passage of A.I. 5, journalists fooled the military censors who had occupied the newsroom by filling the paper with ominous metaphors about the repression, although direct references were forbidden. Most inventive was the weather forecast: "Dark clouds stalk the country." The censors, at that time army majors from General Staff Headquarters, quickly got both wise and even. They insisted that only routine news replace the cut items, foiling the journalists' efforts to signal readers with ambiguous or metaphorical messages hidden in regular columns or even classified ads.

This cat-and-mouse game delighted not only journalists, editors, and newspaper owners but also the more discriminating public. It continued at the newsroom of O Estado de São Paulo, when the military censors were installed in 1972. In retaliation, editors began to substitute cut items with photographs of flowers. These were accompanied by texts instructing readers how to cultivate roses. This ploy had its risks: Some literal-minded ladies were so moved by the paper's campaign to beautify the city that they asked the mayor to join in. Poetry was next: the Lusiads, Camões's great epic poem, ran 26 times from 1972 until 1975, when press censorship was lifted from the Estado. In the Jornal da Tarde, the Estado's afternoon sister paper, recipes for inedible dishes were substituted for censored news. An entire page was run entitled "Alfredo's Specialties" — the pun referring at once to a well-known São Paulo restaurant and the minister of justice.(63)

There were also direct denunciations. In 1972, Rui Mesquita, an influential member of the Estado de São Paulo's owning family, sent a blistering telegram to then Justice Minister Buzaid, railing that censorship of his paper had reduced Brazil to "any old Uganda" or banana republic. Mesquita warned that one day the unfortunate minister would not only lose his position, as did Hitler, Mussolini, and Stalin, but also that the truth would not be contained forever. Ironically, the telegram was censored from the entire Brazilian press. The Porto Alegre daily Correio do Povo tried to publish it, but the edition was confiscated.(64) Still, an influential newspaper publisher and traditional government ally had gone on record against the regime. The government's intractability had forced Brazil's leading daily into an adversary position.

This example illustrates how political censorship of the establishment press backfired. Rather than thoroughly intimidating the press and forcing it to espouse the government line, censorship instead mobilized the journalists' resistance, thus spurring the normally conciliatory establishment press to protest.

Did the press also attempt to run more coverage of controversial issues than the censors would have liked? Obviously, or censorship would not have persisted as long as it did. In this sense, the development of the system demonstrated the government's weakness, not its strength. But how much was attempted relative to what got through? Two lines of research could produce a precise answer: (1) the reconstruction of a representative sample of newspapers by the addition of preserved censored materials to published editions;(65) and (2) a close reading of that same sample as it in fact appeared, with particular attention to sensitive areas like church-state relations and human rights.(66) The sheer mass of material involved, however, makes these impractical tasks for the moment. At present, the impact of censorship must be assessed on the basis of historical interpretation.

Some Larger Questions

This general assessment can be divided into three questions. Was political censorship in Brazil systematic? Was it effective, and in what areas of national life? Will it be of continuing consequence?

On the first count, one could say that political censorship in Brazil was systematic in regard to national security issues. Eccentricities of the system — orders banning news of "streaking," for example — are evidence of a by-product of censorship: the power to censor. At times, that power was exercised ineptly, sadistically, or for its own sake. Just as torture was used for ends far beyond extracting information, censorship was used to intimidate individuals and threaten the journalistic community and the public. In addition, the personal vindictiveness, vendettas, and biases of particular censors provoked abuses of power. Nonetheless, censorship was a key weapon in the military's "dirty war," fought against internal "subversion."

As to the system's effectiveness, there was obviously a gap between design and execution. Enough protests and leaks appeared in the press to render it highly inefficient, at best. But the system must be seen over the short and long term. Even in the short term, the system was not totally effective. On one hand, news of dissent was in fact suppressed, especially during the Medici administration (1969-74). Yet, on the other, even during this period and certainly after 1975, there was some reporting of sensitive topics, as well as resistance against censorship in the form of symbolic protests, suits brought by newspapers challenging the government's right to censor, and the determined growth of the alternative press. These independent news organs, much more than their establishment counterparts, consistently challenged the government's Pollyanna version of events.

Over the long term, censorship was on balance ineffective. Since 1975, nearly all the prohibited stories — including those about guerrilla warfare, torture, and censorship itself — have broken anyway. It is true that controversial stories broke in print, often in small magazines and specialized journals with very limited circulations. The mass public, which depends on radio and television for political information, still receives little, because political controls have been built into state regulation of broadcasting. The public affairs programming that does appear is notoriously superficial. But at least for the literate middle classes and ruling elites, censorship did not obliterate reality. Over a ten-year period, in fact, the military's effort to rewrite history, rationalized elaborately by the National Security Doctrine, failed.

The impact of censorship in Brazil is thus ambiguous. Despite its temporary effectiveness, even in the short run censorship also worked against government aims. It unified the journalistic profession against the military government, making newspaper owners as well as journalists into temporary champions of press freedom. Among readers, too, the impression they were reading censored texts created a culture of skepticism and encouraged them to imagine the worst about the regime.

In the longer run, the government understood that censorship was alienating even its natural supporters. From 1975 to 1978, it changed tack and took the calculated risk of gradually ending prior political censorship of the press. This halted the contrary effects and proved a major tactical victory. The action permitted the regime during this period to claim legitimacy as a democratizing system with a free press. This preemption of a major opposition demand in turn increased support for the government's own liberalization timetable.

In addition, the end of restrictions for the establishment press allowed the government to continue its discriminatory censorship of the alternative press with relative impunity. In effect, it "bought off" the major newspapers and magazines with their own freedom. There were other consequences, too. Although the government granted itself broader censorship powers in the amended version of the 1979 National Security Law,(67) it still did not lose its credibility with much of the establishment press. Nor was the government above exploiting the divisions among newspaper owners, editors, and reporters that had been temporarily forgotten when military or police censors were in the newsroom.

From the viewpoint of the opposition, it must also be said that the relative freedom of the press, however grudgingly or underhandedly granted, turned out to be the watchdog of other basic freedoms in Brazil. The ability of the press to denounce human rights abuses was particularly important in the restoration of habeas corpus for political crimes. In this way, the end of censorship allowed the press, for a time, to take a vanguard role in the opposition campaign for liberalization. Key articles on torture, police violence, corruption, collaboration of Southern Cone security forces, and the internal security apparatus unquestioningly broke ground for the rebirth of national political institutions.

It is clear, therefore, that the effectiveness of censorship in Brazil can only be judged on largely political grounds. The judgment must take into account the play of forces in political repression and the resistance it engendered. Curiously, there is no direct correlation between the power to censor and the power of the state. On the contrary, the government's calculated relaxation of press censorship was a strategy for maintaining power, not relinquishing it. At present, the government still controls the state apparatus and could reimpose political censorship at will. Political factors, however, would make this a costly move. Only the outcome of the political process will finally determine the effectiveness of censorship. For now, it is an ongoing question.

In the 1968–78 period, however, censorship clearly had its most impact on political life in Brazil. Its intent was to perpetuate the regime by suppressing news of national political events, particularly divisions within the military, the activities of the security apparatus, and resistance to the regime. Censorship also impaired the citizens' knowledge of social reality. For example, detailed news about the lack of municipal services and deteriorating urban conditions, which have produced a critique of public policy, was also often banned.

Censorship was also important as a tool for suppressing debate about government economic policies. It can also be argued, however, that the major dailies and newsmagazines and especially the broadcast media needed little coercion in this area. Both Opinião and Movimento, consistent critics of the regime's "denationalization" of resources, as well as the "anti-multinational" Tribuna da Imprensa, were subjected to punitive prior censorship for expressing this view. The establishment press, however, received fewer economic than political orders.

It may also be significant that both the Jornal do Brasil and the Estado de São Paulo built luxurious new physical plants during the so-called "Economic Miracle." These became showcases for the government's economic policies, which could then hardly be criticized in the papers the plants housed. Perhaps the enormous debts incurred during the construction — some from government loans — also contributed to the newspapers' reluctance in this regard.

On the psychological level of Brazilian society, censorship did contribute in a major way to the "culture of fear"(68) prevalent in all the Southern Cone countries. As part of the repressive apparatus that operated without seeming restraint, it helped create a pervasive climate of uncertainty and intimidation. Self-censorship on the part of both journalists and other individuals was a common result. On the other hand, resistance to arbitrary authority, self-examination, self-criticism, and a reassertion of high critical standards for journalistic and artistic excellence were also by-products of censorship.

Will this period of censorship have lasting consequences in Brazil? Judging by the immediate aftermath, the most important effect so far seems to be a broader understanding of the ideal role of a free press in a democratic society. Above all, state censorship made many journalists aware of other, more subtle forms of press control. In journalists' union meetings and gatherings of their professional associations, these controls have been denounced. The censorship imposed by news organizations on their staffs, self-censorship by individual journalists, and the unequal access to media resulting from illiteracy and poverty in Brazil head the list.

In addition, the internal organization of the journalism profession, including training, ideology, sexual discrimination, the restricted job market, inadequate salaries and research facilities, and the unequal pay scale, have all come under scrutiny. A broad range of other political questions have also been debated: the political consequences of the monopolistic structure of media ownership, the role of the alternative press, and Brazil's dependent position in the world news order, characterized by a near-total reliance on foreign wire service for international news and a very high penetration of foreign advertising monies in the national press. The growing role of the state in almost every aspect of news production is also warily observed.

Common to all these debates is a dual perception of the press as both an industry with interests of its own in a given economic system and a key political institution capable of playing an important contestatory role in a dictatorial state. The inevitable conflict between these two identities helps to explain the complex behavior of the media in Brazil. Journalists, for their part, have put the issue more directly. Will the press align itself with established power or with the forces for social change?

NOTES

1. Philip Schlesinger, "'Terrorism,' the Media, and the Liberal-Democratic State: A Critique of the Orthodoxy," Social Research, special issue on violence, October 30, 1980, p. 8.

2. To my knowledge, there is no systematic case study of the impact of national security ideology on state information policy in Brazil. Nor has any such study been done for the other Southern Cone countries. Several other kinds of secondary studies on information policy in Latin America in general have been done, however, and deserve mention here:

1. There are some case studies of communications policies in individual Latin American countries. Many have been commissioned by UNESCO. An example is Nelly de Camargo and Virgilio B. Noya, Communications Policies in Brazil (Paris: UNESCO, 1975).

2. Two recent surveys of media-state relations have appeared in English: Marvin Alisky, Latin American Media: Guidance and Censorship (Ames, Iowa: Iowa State University Press, 1981); and Robert Pierce, Keeping the Flame: Media and Government in Latin America (New York: Hastings House, 1979).

3. There are also a number of studies specifically about political censorship in the post-1964 period in Brazil. The only published book-length study is Paulo Marconi, A Censura Política na Imprensa Brasileira (São Paulo: Global Editora, 1980). There are several unpublished manuscripts and theses. These include Albert Dines, "Censorship of the Press in Brazil," Columbia University, Spring 1975; Jim Brooks, "Information Control in Brazil," M.A. thesis, Yale University, 1977; Silio Boccanera, "An Experiment in Prior Restraint: Press Censorship in Brazil, 1972-1975," M.A. thesis, University of Southern California, 1978; Luiz R. Gonzaga Motta, "Censorship in Brazil and Changes in Press Content," M.A. thesis, Indiana University, 1974; and Aureliano Biancarelli and Alberto Villas, "La Censure de Presse au Bresil — 1968/78," Institut Français de Press, Université Paris II, Juin 1979. Another thesis of interest is Maria Cristina Pinto Torres, "La Stampa Alternativa in Brasile (1964-1978)," Università Cattolica del Sacro Cuore, Scuola Superiore delle Comunicazioni Sociali, 1977/78.

4. Among a number of published articles on Brazilian censorship, several interpretive pieces stand out. They include Perseu Abramo, "O Sistema de Censura do Sistema," Revista de Cultura Contemporânea, 1, no. 1 (July 1978); Joan Dassin, "Press Censorship — How and Why," Index on

Censorship: Brazil 8, no. 4 (July/August 1979); Antonio de Souza, "Forced Into Silence: How Pre-Censorship Works in Brazil," Index on Censorship 6, no. 3 (May/June 1977); Christopher George, "Press Freedom in Brazil," Index on Censorship 1, no. 1 (Spring 1972); and Elio Gaspari, "Os Documentos da Censura," Jornal do Brasil, June 18, 1978.

5. There is also some mention of the Brazilian information policy after 1964 in a number of Brazilian sources. Most detailed are Antonio Costella, O Controle da Informação no Brasil (Petrópolis: Editora Vozes, 1970); and Cariolano de Loyola Cabral Fagundes, Censura e Liberdade de Expressão (São Paulo: Editora e Distribuidora do Autor, 1975).

6. Many details about political censorship in Brazil are also found in documents written and distributed in very limited numbers by Brazilian journalists. Additional data appear in the official newspapers of the Brazilian Press Association and the São Paulo Journalists Union (Boletim ABI and Unidade, respectively). All of these materials are considered primary sources and are discussed in this text.

3. Even a few statistics indicating media diffusion patterns in Brazil underscore the ramifications of government broadcasting control. Journalists have estimated, for example, that no more than 10 percent of roughly 124 million Brazilians have direct access to newspaper, while 85 percent have access to radio and television. Cf. Fernando Morais, "As Pressões do Governo Brasileiro Contra a Imprensa Independente," Document for the Conselho Parlementar de Defesa dos Direitos Humanos, 1979 p. 4. Another source counts 20 million newspaper readers, still a small figure when compared to the 85 million reached by radio and the 45 million by television. Cf. Dacio Nitrini et al., "Censura a Rádio e Telvisão," Document for the Congresso Nacional de Liberadade de Imprensa, 1978, p. 3.

These statistics in turn explain why the state has maintained persistent control of broadcasting through station concession, licensing, and the required transmission of certain government programming. These matters are administered by the National Telecommunications Council (CONTEL), the official regulatory body for broadcasting in Brazil. It is made up of political appointees from various government ministries as well as the Brazilian postmaster general. Its president is directly named by the president of the republic. CONTEL would not be all that different from the Federal Communications Commission in the U.S., except that it is buttressed by the 1962 Telecommunications Code, which was amended and amplified in 1967 to contain many of the national security crimes spelled out in other national security legislation. Under all of this legislation, individual broadcast journalists can be accused of state-defined "political" crimes.

One more comment is in order. Widespread illiteracy, the high cost of publications relative to average income, and the concentration of media in urban centers are among the principal factors contributing to the media diffusion patterns outlined here. Linkages between state information policy and its political outcomes should be developed and analyzed along these lines. Such a project could incorporate basic statistical research already conducted and readily available in publications of the Getúlio Vargas Foundation, UNESCO, and the World Bank.

4. See Todd Shapera, "The Burson-Marsteller Public Relations Campaign for Argentina," Paper for Columbia University seminar, "The Press in Latin America," November 1981.

5. Provocative speculations about the changing strategies for legitimacy are found in two unpublished papers by Fernando Henrique Cardoso: "Political Regime and Social Change (Some Reflections Concerning the Brazilian Case)," October 1980, and "Political Transition in Latin America?" n.d. Douglas Chalmers and Craig Robinson have attempted to construct a political model for liberalization in an unpublished paper, "Why Power Contenders Choose Liberalization Perspectives from Latin America." This model attempts to account for changing criteria of legitimacy. In Brazil, the work of Bolívar Lamounier has addressed this issue, and in the U.S., it was discussed in a major conference on liberalization in Latin America held in Washington, D.C., at the Wilson Center in 1981. Among the published sources, one of the most developed arguments is found in Guillermo O'Donnell's essay, "Tensions in the Bureaucratic-Authoritarian State and the Question of Democracy," in The New Authoritarianism in Latin America, David Collier, ed. (Princeton, N.J.: Princeton University Press, 1979).

6. The most complete bibliography on bureaucratic-authoritarianism is found in David Collier, ed., The New Authoritarianism in Latin America (Princeton, N.J.: Princeton University Press, 1979).

7. See Steven H. Chaffee, "The Diffusion of Political Information," and Jay G. Blumler and Michael Gurevitch, "Towards a Comparative Framework for Political Communication Research," in Political Communication: Issues and Strategies for Research, Steven H. Chaffee, ed. (Beverly Hills, Calif.: Sage Publications, 1975), pp. 85-128 and 165-93, respectively.

8. The most complete bibliography and study of these sources for all of Latin America is found in Fr. Joseph Comblin, A Ideologia de Segurança Nacional: O Poder Militar na América Latina, trans. A Veiga Filho, 2nd ed. (Rio de Janeiro: Civilização Brasileira, 1978).

9. Armand Mattelart, "Notes on the Ideology of the Military State," trans. Colleen Roach, in Communication and Class Struggle, 1., Capitalism, Imperialism, Seth Siegelaub and Armand Mattelart (New York: International General, 1979) pp. 402-27.

10. Ibid., p. 406.

11. Ibid.

12. See A. J. Langguth, Hidden Terrors (New York: Pantheon Books, 1978).

13. Mattelart, op. cit., p. 409.

14. "Ato Institucional No. 1, de 9 de abril de 1964," in Constituição de República Federativa do Brasil, ed. José Bushatsky (São Paulo: Livraria e Editora Juridica José Bushatsky Ltda., 1975), p. 87.

15. Cited by Mattelart, op. cit., p. 408.

16. Flávio Galvão, "O Estado de São Paulo," de 22 de fevereiro de 1970, cited in Antonio Costella, O Controle de Informação no Brasil (Petrópolis: Editora Vozes, 1970), p. 148.

17. "Ato Institucional No. 5, de 13 de dezembro de 1968," in Bushatsky, op. cit., p. 107.

18. Constitution of Brazil, 1967 (Washington D.C.: Pan American Union, General Secretariat, Organization of American States, 1967), p. 60.

19. Ibid.

20. "Ato Institucional No. 5," in Bushatsky, op. cit.

21. For documentation and analyses, see José Antonio Pinheiro Machado, Opinião x Censura (Porto Alegre: L & PM Editores, 1978); and José Carlos Dias and Arnaldo Malheiros Filho, Contra a Censura Prévia: Mandado de Seguraça no Supremo Tribunal Federal (São Paulo, 1977).

22. Marconi, manuscript for A Censura Política na Imprensa Brasileira, p. 48.

23. Ibid., p. 52.

24. Ibid., p. 89.

25. Ibid., p. 49.

26. José Vieira Madeira, Director of the Bureau of Public Entertainment Censorship of the Federal Police Department, Transcript of Testimony at the "Simpósio Sobre Censura," conducted by the subcommittee of Deputado Israel Dias Novaes of the Brazilian Congress, April 29, 1979, p. 40.

27. Rogério Nunes, Chief of the Civil Cabinet of the Federal District Transcript of Testimony at the "Simpósio Sobre Censura," April 22, 1979, unpaginated.

28. Censura e Liberdade de Expressão (São Paulo: Brusco & Cia., 1974), p. 129.

29. Most of the published sources have been cited in note 2. In 1978 and 1979, I conducted personal interviews with a number of journalists and critics. Although not formally structured, the following points were covered in all interviews: career histories; personal experiences with censorship; overviews of the censorship process; and the mechanics, key moments, and political objectives of censorship. In addition, the interviewees were asked general questions about the Brazilian press, the political conjucture, and the future of the liberalization.

30. (1) Documents from the Congresso Nacional Sobre Liberdade de Imprensa, sponsored by the Brazilian Press Association and local journalists' unions, include "A Censura e o Mercado de Trabalho," "Censura a Rádio e Televisão," "Formas de Censura: Censura do Estado, Censura da Empresa, Autocensura," "Legislacão e Liberdade de Imprensa," "Liberdade de Informação e Direitos Humanos," "O Monopólio de Informação e as Alternativas para Combate–lo." (2) Relatorio Final do I Encontro Nacional Pela Liberdade de Espressão, Rio de Janeiro, 21 de maio, 1979, prepared by the Comissão Permanente de Luta pela Liberdade de Expressão, Brazilian Press Association.

31. The following runs have the most information about censorship: (1) Boletim ABI, Órgão Oficial da Associação Brasileira de Imprensa, 1975-78. (A relevant selection of articles from the Boletim ABI was prepared and distributed by José Gomes Talarico under the title Documentos da ABI em Torno da Defesa da Liberdade de Imprensa e dos Direitos Humanos, in 1978 and 1979.) (2) Unidade, Órgão Oficial do Sindicato dos Jornalistas Profissionais no Estado de São Paulo, Nova Fase, Ano 1, No. 1, agosto 1975 — No. 24, agosto 1977 (bound: plus unbound numbers for 1978-81).

32. See Note 21. See Note 41 for additional relevant legal documentation.

33. The complete collection of transcripts may be available in Brasília. My personal collection includes transcripts of testimonies by Celso Luiz Amorim, Diretor da Embrafilme, 5/30/75; Ayrton Luiz Baptista, Jornalista, 6/20/79; Oliveira Bastos, Jornalista, 6/07/79; Flávio Cavalcanti, Jornalista, 6/05/79; Carlos Imperial, Compositor, 6/19/79; Eduardo Seabra Fagundes, Presidente da Ordem dos Advogados do Brasil, 6/12/79; Fernando Gasparian, Jornalista, 6/06/79; José Vieir Madeira, Diretor do Departmento de Policia Federal, 5/28/79; Plínio Marcos, Dramaturgo, 5/31/79; Carlos Guilherme Motta, Professor, 5/17/79; Rogério Nunes, Chefe do Gabinete Civil do Governo do Distrito Federal, 5/22/79; J. Pereira, Jornalista, 6/13/79; Eduardo Portella, Ministro da Educação, 5/25/79; Carlos Chagas, Jornalista, 5/16/79.

34. In his research for A Censura Política na Imprensa Brasileira, Paulo Marconi found copies of more than 500 messages in various newspaper, radio, and television archives, as well as in documents prepared by journalists. Elio Gaspari, in "Os Documentos da Censura," reports 270 orders at the Jornal do Brasil for the four-year period 1972-75. Alberto Dines, in his 1975 Columbia University manuscript, refers to 288 orders recorded at the Jornal do Brasil from September 1972 to December 4, 1974. As more research is conducted for all major press organs, additional orders will undoubtedly come to light. (See Note 2 for full references.)

35. There is a debate as to when sequential written orders came into use. Dines does not systematically distinguish between telephoned and written orders. He simply states that in September 1972, the censorship orders became so numerous and contradictory that he as editor in chief of the Jornal do Brasil had to collect them in a "Black Book." Elio Gaspari, later political editor of the same newspaper, holds that specific written orders came into use in September 1972. Previously, from December 18, 1968, when A.I. 5 was emitted, to the first written order of September 14, 1972, general restrictions were enforced. These were backed up by the threat of censors who could be sent to newsrooms for prior inspection of page proofs.

Carlos Chagas, press secretary to President Costa e Silva and later political editor of the Estado de São Paulo, states in testimony before the congressional investigating committee on censorship that the first written order was brought to the newsroom of the Estado de São Paulo on September 13, 1972. Before that time, orders were telephoned to the paper or orally transmitted by federal police agents. Immediately after A.I. 5, O Estado was occupied by military censors, but only for a short time. Finally, Marconi, like Dines, does not systematically distinguish between written and telephoned orders. Rather, he contrasts both methods to the prior censorship system, which involved prepublication review of materials by military officers and then police agents. In contrast to the other accounts, however, Marconi claims that on occasion, telephoned orders replaced written orders. This less troublesome method was equally effective, because the press was so cowed it could be forced into submission over the phone.

36. I have personally analyzed censored materials from the archives of A Tribuna da Imprensa, Jornal do Brasil, Movimento, O Estado de São Paulo, Opinião, O São Paulo, Pasquim.

37. For a full account of the plan, see "As Pressões do Governo Brasileiro Contra a Imprensa Independente," Conselho Parlamentar de Defesa dos Direitos da Pessoa Humana da Assembléia Legislativa de São Paulo, prepared by Deputado Fernando Morais et al., 1979.

38. Unidade, June/July 1981, p. 5.

39. Antonio Costella, in O Controle da Informação no Brasil, makes the point that while Justice Minister Gama e Silva justified Fernandes's imprisonment on the basis of the Institutional Act, which prohibited cassados (those deprived of their political rights) from making political statements, the imprisonment was nonetheless indefensible, since the promulgation of a subsequent constitution had superseded the Institutional Act in question. Fernandes himself, in a memoir entitled Recordações de um Desterrado em Fernando de Noronha (Rio de Janeiro: Editora Tribuna da Imprensa, 1967), argues that the Institutional Acts were applied because the other exceptional legislation in effect

could not punish him for the content of his articles. Alberto Dines argues that the real reason for Fernandes's confinement in such a remote spot was to prevent attacks on the journalist's person. Carlos Chagas comments that guaranteeing Fernandes's physical safety was in fact a pretext of the justice minister to disguise the real nature of the attack against the press. Dines concurs that there was no legal basis for the imprisonment.

40. Rio de Janeiro, 1967. On the eve of the book's publication, most of the first edition was confiscated by the federal police, by order of the minister of justice. It was released soon afterward, under a provision of the 1967 Press Law, which forced the government to submit its action for review to a federal tribunal. The confiscation was ruled illegal, despite the justice minister's concerted campaign to prove that the work, which documents more than 80 cases of torture suffered by political prisoners after April 1, 1964, "offended the dignity of the Armed Forces," among other violations. Alves also points out that most of the material had already appeared in the press, especially in the Correio de Manhã, where Alves himself was a prominent journalist in an antitorture campaign.

The case of Torturas e Torturados turned out to be important in several respects. First, the issue of whether the regime systematically tortured its opponents has never been satisfactorily or completely documented and resolved. Second, Alves himself became a principal actor in the events surrounding A.I. 5. Later, in exile, he would remain an important opposition leader.

41. Marconi, op. cit., p. 44. For the controversy and legal issues of the case, see Heleno Cláudio Fragoso and Tude Neiva de Lima Rochas (Dona Niomar's defense attorneys), "Em Defesa de Niomar Moniz Sodré Bittencourt," published document dated September 18, 1969.

42. Marconi, op. cit.,p. 38.

43. "Censorship of the Press in Brazil," Columbia University, Spring 1975, pp. 29ff.

44. The reader is reminded of the debate on this point. See Note 35.

45. "Regras Gerais da Cenaura," "Os Documentos da Censura," Jornal do Brasil, June 18, 1978.

46. Dines, op. cit., p. 33.

47. Ibid., p. 30.

48. Carlos Chagas, Testimony for the "Simpósio Sobre Censura," May 16, 1979, pp. 29ff.

49. Ibid., pp. 33, 35.

50. See Note 2 for complete references.

51. Chagas, op. cit., p. 40.

52. Ibid., p. 39.

53. Marconi, op. cit., p. 53.

54. Chagas, op. cit., p. 48.

55. For a rundown of the controversy, see Raimundo Periera, "Cinco teses sobre o fim do 'Movimento,'" Unidade, no. 64 (December/January 1981-82): 13-14.

56. See Nassif, "O Poder e o Controle de Imprensa," Jornal da Tarde, December 12, 1979.

57. Pereira, op. cit., p. 13.

58. Gaspari, op. cit.

59. Fagundes, op. cit., p. 77.

60. Peter T. Johnson, "Academic Press Censorship Under Military and Civilian Regimes: The Argentine and Brazilian Cases, 1964-1975," Luso-Brazilian Review 12 (Summer 1978): 9.

61. "A Beira do Corte," Veja, April 11, 1979.

62. Ibid.

63. Chagas, op. cit., p. 53.

64. Ibid., p. 56.

65. See Note 36.

66. One of the most complete collections of the Brazilian press from 1968 to 1978 on these issues is Father Charles Antoine's Diffusion de L'Information Sur Amèrique Latine (D.I.A.L.) Archive in Paris. It has been indexed by Professor Ralph Della Cava in Religião e Sociedade (Rio de Janeiro) 5 (Junho 1980) and 6 (Dezembro 1980), respectively, entitled "Fontes para o Estudo de Catolicismo e Sociedade no Brasil," pp. 211-40, and "Arquivo Charles Antoine: Igreja e Estado no Brasil — 1971/1974," pp. 189-220. The index to the complete Antoine collection is forthcoming in the Cadernos do ISER (Rio de Janeiro, Instituto Superior de Estudos da Religião).

67. See "Nova Lei de Segurança torna penas mais brandas," Jornal do Brasil, October 18, 1978.

68. This "culture of fear" has been conceptualized and discussed in provocative detail in a seminar of the same name, organized by Professor Juan Corradi under the auspices of the Social Science Research Council in 1981-82.

CHAPTER 8

The Middle East Press:
Tool of Politics

BY MUNIR K. NASSER

INTRODUCTION

Although the Middle East encompasses a large number of
societies subscribing to diversified cultural, sociological, and
political norms, still their press systems share a fundamental
characteristic. Middle East journalism tends to be closely
merged with politics, and reporters are expected to reflect a
partisan view and judge, evaluate, and discuss events from a
position of commitment. The role of journalists as objective
reporters of facts continues to be a fragile one. As private
citizens, intellectuals may favor a detached position when they
are not working for the government. But when they become
reporters or editors of a publication for a government, a party,
or a revolutionary movement, they have to develop a new
commitment. In the minds of many people in the Middle East,
the press must convey an idea, usually with political and
ideological tone.(1)

The assumption that the press is a tool of nationalism and
politics is accepted by both the mass public and governments of
the Middle East. Today, government control of the press goes
far beyond occasional censorship. The Western concept of a
newspaper's purpose being to inform and entertain is replaced by
the aim of using the press to put over a political message and
"educate" the masses. To many Arab leaders, this is a necessity

---

This chapter was written before Egyptian President Anwar
el-Sadat's assassination on October 6, 1981. An update appears
as the postscript to the chapter.

as their countries pass through the stages of "revolutionary transformation." Most countries of the Middle East view the mass media as instruments of national policy, devices by which the goals of the national state or the government in power can be furthered.

Middle Eastern governments often claim that freedom of the press endangers national security and the welfare of the state. They justify their control of the press on the grounds that the majority of the people are ignorant and irresponsible, and a free press would expose the state to the danger that some could play upon the ignorance of the people and incite them to irresponsible actions. Government officials usually argue that in a situation where the majority of the people are illiterate and owe their allegiance to their families, clans, and tribes more than to the nation, the conditions that justify a free press do not exist.

This explains in part the absence of political, social, and intellectual freedoms in most countries of the Middle East. The Arab world is living through a period in which journalists and writers find it more difficult to say the truth or speak against repressive regimes. Most Arab leaders are intolerant of any criticism and have been cracking down on anyone who would dare write or publish against the central state authority. The best writers and journalists of the Arab world have been either detained, jailed, murdered, co-opted, or forced into silence.

This situation is particularly true in the seven Arab states that call themselves socialist: Egypt, Syria, Iraq, Libya, Algeria, the Sudan, and South Yemen. Each of these regimes has assigned a "mobilization" role to the mass media and gives them guidance on government goals and on news presentation and interpretation. The press in these countries has been structured and centralized in support of socialist programs, and newspapers faithfully reflect the party line of the regime or the ideas of the ruling elites.

In the nonsocialist countries of the Arab world, such as Jordan and Saudi Arabia, the press largely remains in private hands, but government influence and controls over the press are direct. Government control of the press in Jordan, for example, is manifested in many ways. The Press Law of 1973 legislates standards of taste, ethical conduct, and legal controls of the press. These include licensing of newspapers and regulating their staff, size, sale price, advertising rates, and editorial content. The law also prohibits the press from publishing certain topics, such as news about the king and the royal family, unless cleared by government officials, or articles attacking friendly heads of states. Violations of these provisions are penalized by imprisonment or fines.

In the less authoritarian Arab countries, such as Kuwait and Lebanon, the press exhibits a relative degree of freedom and diversity. In recent years, however, the press in both Kuwait and Lebanon has come under great pressure. In 1976, the Kuwaiti government dissolved the National Assembly and suspended articles of the constitution providing for a free press. As a result, the government was given power to suspend nationalist newspapers. The Lebanese press, in contrast to the controlled press of the Arab world, was until 1976 one of the most vigorous and competitive in the Middle East. Before the outbreak of the civil war in 1975, Lebanon was the commercial, cultural, and information center of the Arab world. The war destroyed Lebanon's liberties along with much of its population. The war-torn country came under the care of an Arab peacekeeping force dominated by Syrian troops that forcibly closed several newspapers and imposed strict censorship. Some of the Lebanese publishers could not tolerate the strict censorship code and left Beirut to resume publication in Paris and London. Kidnapping and murdering of journalists by opposing factions have become commonplace in Beirut. In 1980, Riad Taha, president of the Lebanese Press Association, and Salim el-Lozi, a prominent editor and publisher, were gunned down by groups opposed to their brand of journalism.(2)

EGYPT: "ALL THE NEWS THAT FITS THE PRESIDENT"

The marriage between press and politics is no more vividly illustrated than in Egypt under President Anwar el-Sadat. Although Egypt has most of the characteristics of the socialist Arab states, the Egyptian press deviates from the typical mobilization model discussed above and presents a unique illustrative example of the press-government relationship.

Under both Presidents Nasser and Sadat, the press in Egypt has been more supportive than critical of the political establishment. Since the press was nationalized in Egypt in 1960, the ownership of newspapers has been transferred to the state. Unlike the press in other authoritarian countries, the Egyptian press has a unique situation in that it is controlled and partly owned by the Arab Socialist Union, Egypt's only political party until the emergence of the multiparty system in 1976. The senior editorial posts are in effect under the control of the president, who uses his power to dismiss editors who do not support his policies. Sadat called on the press to become part of the establishment as a true fourth estate. In reality this has meant that all people holding the "strings" in the press have to be appointed by the government. Once in charge, these appointees own their allegiance to the authority that appointed them and cannot criticize that authority without fear of dismissal.

Although under tight control, the press-government relationship in Egypt is much more relaxed than in other Arab countries. Egyptian newspapers exhibit more style and vitality and criticize government officials who fail to execute policy. This criticism, however, usually comes in the wake of critical remarks already made by the president himself. Editorials critical of the basic state policies, such as the peace treaty with Israel, are not allowed. The press has become docile and subservient in the face of political realities in Egypt.

After assuming power in 1970, Sadat was eager to liberalize the political structure of Egypt, including that of the press. Yet criticisms of the press and the drastic actions taken against dissident journalists have had a great impact. To Sadat, the press has "grown into a fearful and huge industry that should not be left to private citizens to run." Sadat believes the press has developed into a state institution with authority equivalent to that of a fourth estate. The function of this institution, he believes, is to represent the people in watching over their government through free writing and constructive criticism. Yet, according to Sadat, the press must not be given complete freedom before reforming itself and adopting a code of ethics, "because every thing in this world, even freedom, must be controlled."(3)

Sadat's experiment with democracy since 1976 has brought mixed results. In a national referendum in May 1980, the people of Egypt endorsed a number of constitutional changes that would guarantee democracy. One of the amendments dealt with the adoption of the multiparty system that Sadat introduced in 1977. Sadat has always underscored this development as symbolizing the degree of "liberalization" he introduced to Egypt after Nasser.

Many of Sadat's critics, however, point to the measures he has taken against political parties and their newspapers as being undemocratic. They say that the 1977 law of political parties restricts party activities in a way that will make the rise of a true opposition movement a remote possibility. They see certain legal restrictions as limiting the freedom of expression. The strict code of ethics adopted by the Egyptian Press Syndicate is seen as imposing severe restraints on journalists and discouraging any paper from criticizing Sadat or his policies. Also, Sadat can always silence his critics by invoking the controversial Law of Shame, which makes antisocial behavior an indictable offense, or the Law of National Unity, which prohibits publication of articles "attacking the national interest of the state or propagating the spirit of defeat."(4)

The press situation in Egypt seems to have created a dilemma for Sadat in his experiment with democracy. For one thing, he has permitted opposition political parties to function but has been unwilling to allow them complete freedom of expression. It was inevitable that these parties use their newspapers to criticize Sadat's policies, but it is clear he is finding their criticism intolerable. He has solicited public support and introduced laws to silence the press, but in doing so, he is facing the dilemma of admitting that his experiment in democracy has failed.

PRESS CONTROLS IN EGYPT: A CASE STUDY

The press-government relationship in Egypt provides a unique case in information control and management. Aside from direct censorship of the mass media by the government, information control takes a variety of forms. Direct censorship procedures include press laws, codes of ethics, dismissal of journalists, seizure of papers and books, and withholding newsprint from opposition papers. Subtle forms of censorship range from self-censorship to scare tactics against dissidents to public criticism of government opponents by the president. The following case study examines these procedures in detail.

When Gamal Abdul Nasser and other army officers overthrew the monarchy in Egypt in 1952, they abrogated the constitution and promptiy dissolved political parties and imposed press censorship. They chose to impose political, social, and economic controls to protect the regime against external threats and to carry out their planned transformation of the Egyptian society. As soon as the new regime was declared, the press dramatically shifted its support from the deposed king to Nasser and his revolution. They repeated the slogans of the regime: "Unity, Freedom, and Socialism." Claiming a desire to mobilize the press in the service of the public, the government started a newspaper of its own. The license of the new paper, Al-Gumhouria (The Republic) was issued to Nasser himself, and Anwar el-Sadat, one of the Free Officers who helped Nasser, was named its first editor.

The first confrontation between government and the press came in 1954, when Nasser briefly lifted press censorship that had been in effect since the British imposed martial law on Egypt in September 1939. Nasser's critics took advantage of this opportunity and attacked him fiercely for failing to allow democratic institutions in the country. This prompted the government to reimpose censorship one month later and to warn journalists against spreading suspicion and doubts against the revolution. In 1956 a new constitution was enacted and Nasser was proclaimed president. Article 45 of the new constitution stated that "freedom of the press, publication and copyright is safeguarded in the interest of public welfare within the limits prescribed by the law."

Nasser Nationalizes the Press

Despite press censorship and publication of government newspapers, Nasser remained unhappy with press performance in general. In the late 1950s, he was embarking on his plan of nationalizing private and foreign banks and corporations. At this time he said that the press must be organized to take part in the process of social and economic transformation and to "liquidate the interests of privileged groups who were exploiting the Egyptian people at a time when annual per capita income did not exceed $25."(5) On several occasions, Nasser himself publicly expressed discontent with the press for devoting more space to sensational accounts of crime, divorce, and sex than to government development programs. At one meeting with newsmen, he urged that they offer constructive criticism and devote more space to serious articles.

Using state-controlled media, particularly radio, Nasser was able to communicate directly with the masses, arousing their passions and motivating them to strive for the national goals. The press, however, was still in private hands and could not be as effectively mobilized. To solve this problem, Nasser issued on May 24, 1960, a presidential decree of 13 articles nationalizing the press. Under this decree, the Press Organization Law, five major publishing houses had to surrender their private ownership to the National Union, now known as the Arab Socialist Union. The decree stated that owners were to be compensated for their properties in government bonds yielding 3 percent interest over 20 years. Working journalists would have to obtain a license from the National Union, which would also establish press institutes and designate boards of directors to manage the publishing houses.(6)

The decree was accompanied by an explanatory note written by Mohamed Hassanein Heikal, then editor of Al-Ahram and a close friend of Nasser. Heikal played a significant role in influencing Nasser's views toward the press. The note said organization of the press was necessary to stop capitalists from controlling the press and to restore ownership of the media of social and political guidance to the people. The note also said that the press was part of the whole national structure and was not controlled by the executive branch of the government. The press, according to the note, "is an authority whose function is to guide the people to actively participate in building their society, exactly as does the People's Assembly [The Parliament]."(7)

Initially, the impact of nationalization was not felt in the press because little change in editorial and management positions was made. A committee representing the National Union was formed of editors and owners to run the nationalized press. Editors and columnists had to abide by the new directives and guidelines of the National Union and to promote themes such as Arab unity, Arab socialism, and revolutionary spirit, while attacking themes such as imperialism, Zionism, and "reactionary elements." In 1964 a number of Marxist and socialist writers were given important editorial positions in the press to help the government sell the Arab socialism concept to the masses. Criticism of Nasser and the regime, however, remained taboo, and the press acquired a reputation for uniformity in handling domestic issues. Most journalists seemed to have accepted the official justification that the press was "socialized," not nationalized. They practiced self-censorship because they feared government reprisal or because the new system was more financially rewarding. Profit bonuses made it possible for many journalists to receive salaries high enough to support a life of luxury.(8)

The Press Syndicate

Nasser also used the professional syndicates in Egypt to mobilize the support of the professionals for the new socialist society. He recognized the need to use the Press Syndicate to ensure the acquiescence of journalists to his rule. The Press Law of 1955, for instance, reorganized the legal status of the Press Syndicate previously governed by bylaws approved by its members. The new law gave the Press Syndicate the role of censor and made it a tool to purge journalists. During the 1950s and 1960s, however, the Press Syndicate resisted these measures and tried to rally its members against government pressure and press censorship. Following nationalization of the press in 1960, the Syndicate came under increasing government control. It was denied permission to hold its general assembly in 1962 and 1963, and elections were postponed. Four members of the Syndicate's board of directors resigned in protest over the illegal delay of the elections. Finally the government gave in and the Syndicate was allowed to elect a new board.(9)

Another threatening situation to the press came in 1964, when the Arab Socialist Union announced its intention of bringing the press under its control by establishing a Supreme Press Council within the Union itself. The new press council was intended to set new rules for press development and assign a political role for the press. The Press Syndicate rejected these proposals at its annual meeting in 1965, but the National Assembly, under pressure from the government, canceled the

Syndicate's decision and declared it ineffective. The Syndicate, however, continued to fight against the Arab Socialist Union's attempts to control the press by electing in 1966 and 1967 board members known for their antigovernment positions. On both occasions, the government and the Arab Socialist Union intervened and dissolved the elected boards and appointed new members.

The June war of 1967 shook the foundations of Nasser's regime and exposed the flaws in the political system. Many critics of the regime called for reform and political freedoms. The government admitted implicitly the need for more freedoms in its March 30, 1968, program. One year later, the government introduced in the National Assembly a bill favorable to the press. Eventually, this bill was passed as Law No. 76 in 1970. The law, signed by Nasser before his sudden death in September 1970, abolished the Press Syndicate Law of 1955 and established a new Press Syndicate. The new law was meant to regulate the press as a profession and to make sure that journalists would conform to the government line. Article 3 of the law promised to "guarantee freedom for journalists in carrying out their journalistic mission, and to ensure that professional ethics, traditions, and principles are closely observed."(10) Article 65 of the law provided that journalists would not be permitted to practice journalism unless they became registered members of the Press Syndicate. Among the basic functions of the Syndicate was to adopt a code of ethics following its approval by the government and the Arab Socialist Union.

Article 72 of the law dealt with the duties and obligations of the Syndicate members who had to promise to keep their professional conduct in line with the "principles of honesty and professional ethics." Journalists accepted as members had to recite the following oath in front of the Syndicate's board: "I swear in the name of God the Almighty to protect my country's interests, to carry out my journalistic mission with honesty, to honor the secret of the profession, and to respect its ethical standards and traditions." Those who broke this oath were subject to disciplinary action by the Syndicate. Penalties included warnings, fines, or dismissal from practicing journalism for a period not exceeding one year. A disciplinary committee of two Syndicate members and one member from the Ministry of National Guidance investigated accusations against journalists and issued its decisions in secret session. The accused, however, had the right to appeal their cases to court.

Sadat's "Free Era"

The stable press-government relationship from 1960 until Nasser's death in 1970 was interrupted only by occasional shuffling in editorial or management positions. There were no drastic changes in the press until 1973, when the Egyptian society underwent a series of shocking events as a result of the fourth Arab-Israeli war.

When Sadat succeeded Nasser in 1970, he made it clear that he wanted to run the country by institutions. He stressed the significance of the press and the positive role it had to play in the new era. In 1971 he was planning a major shake-up in the press in order to dismiss extreme leftists. The opportunity came in May, when he was the target of a plot by his cabinet members led by Vice-President Ali Sabri. Soon after the crisis was over, a purge of Communists and leftist elements took place in the government, the Arab Socialist Union, the broadcasting service, and the press.

By mid-1972 Sadat began to relax press controls by opening up news sources to reporters. Press censorship continued, however, and all newspapers had resident censors to whom all copy was submitted. These censors were civilian government officials responsible to the Ministry of Information. In 1972 the Press Syndicate appealed to the government for the immediate lifting of censorship of newspapers except in military matters involving national security. The Syndicate recalled in a statement that Sadat had promised to lift censorship as soon as the journalists adopted a code of ethics. The code was adopted unanimously by the Syndicate's general assembly in February 1973.

Instead of fulfilling his promise, Sadat took drastic actions against the press. He charged in February 1973 that several Egyptian journalists were making contacts with foreign correspondents "with the aim of spreading unrest and tarnishing Egypt's reputation by supplying foreign mass media with false information."(11) As a result, 64 intellectuals were dismissed from the Arab Socialist Union and automatically lost their jobs in newspapers, radio, television, and the theater. Clearly, the purge was primarily directed at people working in the mass media or otherwise capable of influencing public opinion at home and abroad. Twenty-seven of them were journalists working for daily newspapers, and among these were four top editors of Al-Ahram.

Sadat's thinking with regard to the press started to change as a result of the October war of 1973. In the first days of the war the Egyptian forces astonished the world by crossing the Suez Canal, storming the formidable Barlev Line, and pushing the Israeli troops back into Sinai. For the first time in its recent history, Israel was on the defensive. Sadat emerged as a hero who was able to destroy the "myth of Israeli invincibility" created by Israel's victory in 1967. Armed with the confidence the war gave him, Sadat asked the Egyptian mass media to follow an open information policy and to avoid the sensational and exaggerated press reports that had characterized Egypt's statements during the 1967 war.

This policy, however, was followed only during the first days of the war. When the Israeli troops infiltrated to the west of the Suez Canal and encircled the Third Army, Egypt's mass media told the public it was only a minor crossing. According to Egypt's chief of staff during the war, Lieutenant General Saad el-Shazly, the official statements following the Israeli penetration had "succumbed to straightforward lying." In his recently published memoirs, Shazly accused Sadat of hiding the truth about the military setbacks of 1973. He charged that the media continued to spread lies until the end of the war.

The whole world was being told of the encirclement of Third Army — except the wives, mothers, sisters and sweethearts of the men suffering out there. Of course, rumors began to circulate. It was a catastrophe too big to hide. And people in Egypt learned to trust rumor over their press. But the authorities persistently denied the truth. The President even denied it in front of the People's Assembly.(12)

Shazly admitted, however, that he himself faked accounts of two incidents during the war. The first incident took place at the start of the hostilities when Egypt accused Israel of attacking first. The second incident involved publishing fake photographs in the press of the initial crossing of the Suez Cana. Shazly wrote: "Those men in dinghies while the Egyptian flag flies high on the enemy ramparts ahead of them; the soldiers kissing the soil of Sinai; the first tanks streaming over the bridge — all, I regret to say, fake."(13) He said he did not allow photographers into the crossing zone because he expected far bloodier resistance than the Egyptian troops met. He added that he regretted the decision because the photographs produced by the military public relations showed "undisciplined groups, ill-packed equipment, slovenly formations — our men looked more like a mob than an army. I was ashamed of the photographs."(14)

Another example of information management was illustrated when Sadat dismissed Heikal from the editorship of Al-Ahram. In the months following the October war, Heikal became critical of what he regarded as Sadat's excessive dependence on the Americans in seeking a settlement to the Arab-Israeli conflict. In his weekly column in Al-Ahram, Heikal kept up a continuous sniping at Sadat. He opposed the first cease-fire arranged by Henry Kissinger, former secretary of state, and the swift resumption of relations with the United States. He warned Sadat that he was falling into Kissinger's insidious negotiation trap and insisted that there had been no basic change in America's pro-Israeli policy. This was apparently more than Sadat could stand, and on February 2, 1974, he abruptly relieved Heikal of his post as chief editor and chairman of the board of Al-Ahram.(15) Shortly thereafter, Sadat issued a decree abolishing censorship except for military matters. This was seen in Egypt as a symptom of a trend toward a greater freedom for the press.

The lifting of censorship sparked a stormy debate in the press about the negative aspects of the Nasser era. After a silence that had lasted for over two decades, most prominent journalists, writers, and thinkers started revealing the atrocities committed by the past regime toward its political opponents. Such criticism came mainly from journalists and functionaries who were themselves personally affected by Nasser's regime, such as Ali and Mustafa Amin, editors and publishers of Al-Akhbar. Many of the attacks against Nasser involved his repression of political dissent within Egypt. An increasing number of books, articles, and speeches judged Nasser guilty of misrule and injustices. The Amin brothers led the campaign and utilized Al-Akhbar to regularly print their broadsides against the late president. The campaign reached a climax when Galal el-Din Hamamsy of Al-Akhbar alleged in a new book that Nasser had embezzled $15 million.(16)

An official statement by the government denied these allegations, and Hamamsy was reprimanded by the Socialist public prosecutor. The Press Syndicate prepared a statement protesting these "serious accusations" and condemning Al-Akhbar for this planned campaign against Nasser. However, under official government orders, the press refused to publish the statement. An article defending Nasserism by Ahmad Baha' el-Din, a highly respected journalist and a former editor of Al-Ahram, was also rejected on government orders. This led many observers to believe that Sadat and his government stood behind the campaign. Sadat refrained from criticizing Nasser directly, but he also did not take steps to suppress the criticisms.

To Sadat, the freedom he granted the press seemed to have gotten out of hand. While addressing the People's Assembly in March 1976, he rebuked the press for what he called "a conspiracy and a campaign of unfounded criticism, rumors about nonexistent corruption, and even defamation." In emotional tones, he rejected as shameful and absurd the allegations made by Hamamsy against Nasser. He said he did not want to restore press censorship, but it was clear that the press had to be reorganized and that individual editors should no longer have the power to launch harmful campaigns for personal reasons.(17) This was a clear reference to Ali and Mustafa Amin, and in a new press reshuffling the twin brothers lost their positions as chairmen of <u>Al-Akhbar</u>, the newspaper they had founded 30 years before. They remained contributors to the paper, however, and Mousa Sabri, a staunch supporter of Sadat, was appointed as new chairman. Following these changes, an ominous conformity prevailed in the press. Many issues, including Sadat's policies, remained taboo, and freedom to criticize or debate was limited to campaigns against unfriendly Arab states.

The Supreme Press Council

On March 11, 1975, Sadat issued a decree setting up the first press council in Egypt with powers to approve the publication of newspapers and licensing of journalists. Among the council's functions was to draw up a code of ethics, to ensure freedom of the press, and to arbitrate disputes. The first article of the decree announced that the press in Egypt "is an independent national institution whose function is to represent the people in watching over their government through free writing and constructive criticism." The second article provided that 49 percent of the press institutions be owned by persons working in them and that special bylaws be set up in each newspaper to regulate professional rules and salary scales. The decree also granted the new council a right to investigate any violations of the journalistic code of ethics and to refer these violations to the Press Syndicate, which would decide on any legal action to be taken.(18)

At the council's first meeting in May 1975, Sadat said the press should develop into a state institution, but first had to reform itself by adopting a code of ethics "because everything in this world, even freedom, should be controlled." Concluding, he said the press should deepen, confirm, and consolidate state institutions and "should point out mistakes without exaggeration and avoid focusing our lenses only on negative aspects."(19) Soon thereafter, the Supreme Press Council adopted a journalistic code of ethics that called upon all practicing journalists to commit themselves to the following general principles: (1) to liberate Egyptian soil from foreign occupation, (2) to respect religious and spiritual values of Egyptian society, and (3) to protect freedom, democracy, socialism, and national unity. Article 8 of the code demanded that the press not disclose state secrets, as well as be objective when commenting on government officials or public figures.

Emergence of the Party Press

Since assuming power, Sadat has contemplated reorganizing Egypt's political system, including the Arab Socialist Union and its relation to the press. He was eager to liberalize the system but was cautious to keep disruption at a minimum. He said publicly that an abrupt return to the multiparty system after nearly a generation of one-party rule would cause unpredictable strains. On November 11, 1976, however, Sadat surprised the world by announcing the emergence of a multiparty system in Egypt. Appearing before the People's Assembly, he said the three political platforms of the Arab Socialist Union — right, left, and centrist — would form the basis of three separate political organizations. He indicated they would be allowed to operate freely, except that the Arab Socialist Union would remain the dominant political force, controlling their budgets and retaining ownership of the press "so that these important organs will be kept away from private ownership." Sadat also called on the press to allow the three political organizations to express their views in print.(20)

Following the emergence of political parties, a similar rough division of opinion developed in the Egyptian press. The principal rightist publications, Al-Akhbar and Al-Mussawar, called for unbridled free enterprise and a break with the ideology and restraints that prevailed under Nasser. On the left were the weekly Rose el-Yousef and the political monthly Al-Talia', which is written at a high intellectual level but has minority readership. In the center is Al-Ahram, which remains the most influential newspaper in Egypt, although it has lost much of the power it enjoyed under Heikal. The left-wing intellectuals who controlled the political pages of Al-Ahram have been handicapped by the new editors.

Meanwhile a lively debate ensued in the press about its relationship with the new political parties. Many columnists seized this opportunity and called for the liberation of the press from the grip of the Arab Socialist Union. Other voices called for keeping the existing newspapers and periodicals as independent media of expression and allowing the parties to establish newspapers of their own. Sadat expressed his willingness to permit the parties to publish their own papers and proposed that the Arab Socialist Union support these papers financially. Initially, the parties rejected this suggestion to avoid falling under the influence of the government. In mid-1977, however, each of the parties had its weekly newspaper. The left platform — the National Progressive Unionist Party — launched its party organ Al-Ahaly (The People) in February 1978. Fifteen weeks later, however, this weekly ceased publication under government pressure for its attacks on Sadat and his peace treaty with Israel. Khaled Mohieddin, head of the party and editor of the paper, is a Marxist who was one of Nasser's Free Officers. In his writings, he advocated closer ties with the Soviet Union and reliance on class struggle.

Incapable of supporting full-time editors and reporters, Al-Ahaly had to depend on contributors from the ranks of the left party, including 64 journalists who worked for the government-controlled press. Another problem facing Al-Ahaly was the lack of a strong financial base. Revenues came largely from contributions of party members and supporters. From the outset, Al-Ahaly took a highly critical position on Sadat and his "open door" economic policies. In its weekly editorials, the paper attacked the ruling party on issues ranging from Sadat's peace initiative to Egypt's economic ailments and official ineptitude, along with insinuations of corruption and nepotism. Al-Ahaly reportedly increased its circulation from 50,000 to 135,000 in its 15 weeks of existence. According to the Times of London, Al-Ahaly built up a readership estimated at around half a million.(21)

From the first, Al-Ahaly was under fire from the government. State-controlled press organizations gave orders to their members not to work for the party press. To escape official retaliation, most contributors to Al-Ahaly submitted unsigned articles. Another form of avoiding government penalty was to publish personal interviews with noted writers and journalists. This was demonstrated when Al-Ahaly invited Mohamed Hassanein Heikal to contribute to its columns. It was the first time since he left Al-Ahram that Heikal broke a long silence on internal affairs and wrote for an Egyptian newspaper. In a pair of articles framed as an interview to avoid the writing ban, Heikal charged that the Sadat regime had misrepresented the Nasser era and said that Sadat's peace initiative had failed. Soon Heikal became the target of the state-controlled press, which promptly accused him of speaking on behalf of what it described as "his masters in the Kremlin."

Sadat's Crackdown on Critics

In November 1977 Sadat stunned the world by going to Jerusalem in search of peace with Israel. The initial popular reaction to this initiative was enthusiastic. Many Egyptians believed that Sadat's trip to Israel would bring peace and lead to a solution of Egypt's economic problems. But complaints among Egyptian intellectuals about a steadily deteriorating domestic situation were mushrooming in various forms, including the People's Assembly and the press. Critics of Sadat's peace initiative, however, were not allowed to express their views in the state-controlled press, but some were able to air their views in foreign news media. One of those was Heikal, who warned in the London Times that Sadat's initiative would lead to a deep and lasting rift between Egypt and the rest of the Arab world. He said that peace reached under such circumstances would be a "weak fabric, a cardboard peace."(22)

Opposition to Sadat's peace initiative in Egypt was largely confined to left-wing intellectuals who expressed their views in Al-Ahaly. In May 1978, stung by growing criticism, Sadat began a set of procedures to purge his most troublesome critics from the press and political life. Speaking at the People's Assembly, he complained that the country was "full of rumors" and blamed opponents in the assembly and the press for trying to exploit Egypt's domestic difficulties for their own political ends. He said he was determined to crush his opponents on both the left and the right "by using democratic means" and announced that he would hold a referendum to ask the people if these critics should be banned from the political process.

The referendum, set for May 21, asked Egyptian voters to endorse the banning from politics and journalism of anyone with "atheist and corrupt ideologies," code words in Egypt for Communists and some politicians active both before and after the 1952 revolution. A few days before the referendum, Al-Ahaly carried a front-page editorial urging readers to vote no on the referendum. The newspaper was confiscated by police just as it was going to the press, although a few copies reached the streets. The seizure was upheld by a court on the grounds that Al-Ahaly was inciting a boycott of the referendum. Editor Khaled Mohieddin said in a news conference that his newspaper was only asking its readers to vote against the referendum, not to disrupt or boycott it. He added that the seizure violated Egyptian law because each party had a legislative, constitutional right to express its viewpoint on the referendum.

As expected, Sadat won an overwhelming majority (98.2 percent) in the referendum, which gave him a mandate to curtail political dissent and criticism in the press. On June 1, 1978, the People's Assembly approved a draft law aimed at silencing Sadat's critics. Among other things, the law prohibited "propaganda which aims to oppose the principles of the 1952 revolution, or to spread theories aimed at undermining the rule of democratic socialism." Article 6 of the law stipulated that "one means of corrupting political life and exposing national unity and social peace to danger is considered to be the publication, writing, or transmission of articles or false rumors within the country or abroad, with a view to attacking the national interests of the state or to propagating the spirit of defeat or provocation about matters of social peace and national unity." The law also called on the press "to respect, in all that is written and diffused, the laws controlling the press and publications, as well as the code of conduct for journalists."(23)

Among those who spoke against the law in the People's Assembly were members of the rightist New Wafd Party and the left-wing coalition who warned that this law could put an end to party life and political activities in Egypt. Less than 24 hours after the passing of the law, the New Wafd Party voted unanimously at a meeting in Cairo to disband in protest against the measure. The left-wing alliance followed suit and announced a freeze on all its activities and the closure of its newspaper Al-Ahaly. In a bitterly worded statement handed to foreign correspondents in Cairo, the Nationalist Progressive Unionist Party said that it would keep its activities suspended until the new law was revoked. The statement accused the government of liquidating Egypt's democratic experiment while it was still in its infancy. The statement also said the new law breached the article in the constitution guaranteeing equality regardless of race, religion, or political beliefs.

Sadat's clampdown on his critics began with an order to 30 Egyptian journalists working in foreign countries to return home immediately to face unspecified charges of "defaming their country abroad." According to Al-Ahram, the accused journalists worked for Arabic-language newspapers in Lebanon, Iraq, Britain, and France. Copies of their articles and tape recordings of their broadcasts critical of Sadat were referred to the Socialist public prosecutor, a political post created by Sadat to investigate political offenses. These journalists were requested to report to the nearest Egyptian embassy or be tried in absentia. The purge against critics at home began when five leading journalists, including Heikal, were barred from leaving the country pending investigation of charges of defaming Egypt in the foreign media and writing articles in the domestic press aimed at "dissension and threatening social peace." These writers had been prevented from writing for publication in Egypt and had turned to markets abroad. Heikal was included on the list for criticizing Sadat in his interviews in Al-Ahaly and two other interviews in the Times of London and the New York Times. He told the New York Times that "the whole thing is bizarre because Sadat wanted a sort of democracy and I think that what he got was more than he wanted."(24)

Angered with the foreign news media coverage of his drive against his critics, Sadat summoned foreign correspondents in Egypt to a country residence outside Cairo and rebuked them. "I am not happy with what I have read in your papers," he told them, "because you are supposed to be the link between us and your people." He singled out the Times of London and the British Broadcasting Corporation (BBC) for particular criticism. Sadat said he was not curtailing free expression but was moving only against those leftists who sought to exploit the liberalization policies for their own ends. The Times of London and the BBC were rebuked for their long interviews with Heikal. Without naming him, Sadat denounced Heikal, likening him to the notorious Lord Haw Haw (William Joyce) who broadcast Nazi propaganda to Britain from Berlin during World War II. The next day, attacks on Heikal in the state-controlled press gathered momentum. Al-Gumhouria carried a front-page photograph of Heikal and a short account of Lord Haw Haw's career, including his execution for treason when captured at the end of the war.

To make the press conform to the state line and support his peace initiative, Sadat resorted to threats and public criticism of journalists. In his speeches and press conferences, he repeatedly attacked journalists, friends and foes alike, for failing to grasp the new developments in Egypt and explain them to the public. In a meeting with Egyptian newsmen in Alexandria in August 1979, he launched a sharp attack on the Press Syndicate and accused the press of committing crimes against the people for "failing to publish all the facts." He criticized the press for ridiculing the deteriorating status of the public transportation system and the telephone system in Egypt, and threatened to jail journalists who wrote about student and worker unrest, corruption among government officials, unemployment or inflation. He said that dissemination of information about these topics was against Egypt's national interest.(25)

Another form of censorship used by Sadat was closure of papers critical of his peace treaty with Israel. In May 1979 the government closed down two publications of the Islamic opposition in Egypt. Both publications, Al-Da'wa and Al-I'tisam, printed bitter attacks against the Camp David accords and the peace treaty with Israel. The editor of Al-Da'wa, the organ of the Muslim Brotherhood in Egypt, said in an editorial that "recognizing the usurpation of our land by Israel is inconsistent with heavenly laws," and warned that opening the doors to Israel would lead to Jewish manipulation of the Egyptian economy.(26) Sadat's tolerance of the Muslim opposition groups in Egypt ended in the wake of Iran's Islamic revolution under Ayatollah Khomeini. Realizing the growing threat to his regime by extremist Muslim groups, he declared in a public speech that "there will be no ayatollahs in Egypt" and that he would not allow the mixing of politics and religion.(27)

Meanwhile, opposition to Sadat's treaty with Israel had grown among dissident Egyptian journalists living abroad. In summer 1979 a group of prominent journalists living in London announced the publication of a weekly magazine to serve as a forum for Sadat's critics in exile. Mahmoud el-Sa'dani, editor of the new magazine 23 Yulyo (July 23), said in an interview that the purpose of the weekly was to "expose Sadat's lies and help topple his regime."(28)

In recent years, the exodus of writers, intellectuals, and journalists has been on the rise. To avoid risking jail or loss of work, those who stay in Egypt cannot speak against the treaty with Israel or against government corruption. Many prefer silence or avoid politically sensitive issues. But it was domestic criticism in the party press that clearly upset Sadat. On several occasions since the signing of the treaty with Israel, police have raided the offices of the National Progressive Unionist Party and seized editions of Al-Taqadum, an internal bulletin for party members only. Police also confiscated printing presses, typewriters, and documents from the archives of the party's headquarters. In an act of defiance to the normalization of relations with Israel, the party flew a Palestinian flag from its headquarters in Cairo and held more rallies to publicize its views. At the same time, the Socialist Labor Party, the only party with seats in the People's Assembly, urged the people in its newspaper Al-Shaab to boycott all forms of the new Israeli presence in Egypt. The Press Syndicate also pledged to refrain from having professional contacts with Israeli journalists.

The Law of Shame

Feeling that his critics were posing a genuine threat to his regime, Sadat came up with a new idea to curb opposition at home and abroad. In January 1980, he proposed a "law of shame" to punish Egyptians who disparaged their government. He urged the People's Assembly to adopt legislation on ethics to curb critics, mostly Nasserites and leftists, who criticized his policies through publications and broadcasts supported by other Arab countries opposed to Egypt's peace with Israel. Soon after a draft of the proposed law was published in Al-Ahram, it was sharply attacked by the opposition parties. Journalists and lawyers called the draft law unconstitutional and undemocratic.

To justify the law, Sadat said it was necessary because of those in Egypt "who are exploiting freedom and democracy" and propagating rumors and false information designed to undermine the security of the state. Observers inside Egypt, however, believe that Sadat needed to persuade other Arabs that his policies had unanimous backing from the Egyptian people. At the same time, they suggest that Sadat wanted to show the West and the United States that he was replacing Nasser's authoritarian regime with a pluralistic democracy.(9) Sadat said repeatedly that Egypt was entering a crucial stage of its development with billions of dollars in economic aid expected to flow in from foreign sources. Therefore, he believed, the government should be spared the burden of dealing with political criticism and internal subversion. He told the People's Assembly that there was a need "to cut every person down to size if he doesn't know shame. I would say that whoever doesn't know what shame means should be isolated before the people."(30)

In April 1980, despite the strong opposition from the press, the judiciary, and the opposition parties, the People's Assembly passed the Law of Shame (Qanoun el-Aib) "to protect the basic values of society from shameful conduct." The law made antisocial behavior an indictable offense and imposed harsh punishment for committing vague crimes. The law also set up an extrajudicial court of values and gave the Socialist public prosecutor a stronger role. The Law of Shame stipulates that "citizens advocating opposition to, hatred of or contempt for the state's political, social or economic systems will be held accountable." Journalists "broadcasting or publishing false or misleading information which could inflame public opinion, generate envy or hatred or threaten national unity or social peace" will be liable for prosecution. Those found guilty under the law could be deprived of all avenues of political expression for up to five years.(31)

The reaction of the opposition to the new law was strong. The weekly Al-Shaab of the Socialist Labor Party devoted a full issue under the banner headline "No to the Law of Shame," with critical reactions from prominent journalists and writers. The paper charged that the law would simply be used to shield the Sadat regime from any criticism and would genuinely threaten freedom of expression in Egypt. An independent member of the People's Assembly was quoted as saying the new law "closes all the windows of freedom." The real outcry, however, came from lawyers, who objected that the new law would regulate ethical behavior and set up a parallel judicial system in which legislators rather than judges would have the majority decisions.(32)

By the end of 1980, Sadat was having second thoughts about the role of the opposition parties in Egypt. He thought the parties had failed to play "a constructive role of opposition parties in Egypt's political life." As his critics grew bolder in their criticism of his foreign and domestic policies, Sadat began taking subtle steps to blunt them. Heading the list was the Socialist Labor Party, which Sadat once backed as a symbol of Egypt's move toward democracy. Known in Egypt as the "tame party," the Socialist Labor Party was widely expected to be only a symbolic opposition, with little more than a token show of dissent. But when the party newspaper and the party chairman, Ibrahim Shukri, vigorously attacked normalizing relations with Israel and accused the president of planning to divert some of the Nile's water to Israel, Sadat was stung to the point of uncontained anger. He lashed back in a speech in November

1980 that these writings were nothing but "hatred and ignorance," and dismissed an editorial in Al-Shaab as "unethical and filthy." This upset the Socialist Labor Party and prompted its vice-chairman, Mohamed Hilmi Murad, to take the unusual step of filing a libel suit against Sadat, asking token damages from the president. "If any other politician in Egypt used such terms," said Ibrahim Shukri, "he would be punished under the Law of Shame." In May 1981, however, a Cairo court dismissed the case and ruled that it did not have jurisdiction to try the president.(33) Meanwhile, Al-Shaab was targeted for harassment by the government and Shukri came under steady attack by the government-controlled press. The newspaper was told that the government-influenced Al-Ahram Publishing House could no longer supply it with newsprint. The cutoff forced the party to buy newsprint from the market at 20 percent higher cost and reduce the size of the 90,000 circulation weekly from 16 page to 12.(34)

By mid-1981, Sadat was considering dissolving the opposition parties in Egypt and replacing them with a "genuine and constructive opposition." He said he was planning to introduce a bill in the People's Assembly to form new and strong opposition parties along the lines of the two-party systems of Great Britain and the United States. At this point, Sadat's experiment with democracy seemed to have placed him in a political quandary. He was eager to promote the organization of opposition parties and allow freedom of the press to flower. But when criticism of these parties and their newspapers grew bolder and sharper, Sadat unceremoniously cut them off. Sadat's attitude clearly reflected a conviction that as the head of state, he knew what was best for the country, and that any criticism of his policies must be regarded as an act of subversion.

POSTSCRIPT

A peculiar era in the history of the Egyptian press ended on October 6, 1981, when President Anwar el-Sadat was assassinated in Cairo by a group of Muslim fundamentalists. Before his assassination, Sadat had become aggressive in his crackdown on opposition parties and dissident journalists. Just one month before his death, Sadat stunned Egypt by arresting 1,600 people in the strongest crackdown of his 11 years in power. Those arrested were journalists, lawyers, professors, members of opposition parties, and Muslim and Coptic fundamentalists. Sixty-seven print and broadcast journalists were dismissed from their jobs, and seven publications were closed down in September 1981. These included the daily Al-Shaab, the paper of the opposition Socialist Labor Party, and Al-Da'wa, the magazine of the Muslim Brotherhood in Egypt. These publications and journalists had become more assertive in their criticism of Sadat and his policies.

Among those detained were prominent journalists and political figures such as Mohamed Hassanein Heikal, former editor of Al-Ahram, Ibrahim Shukri, leader of the Socialist Labor Party, and Khaled Mohieddin, leader of the National Progressive Unionist Party. Sadat accused Heikal of distorting the image of Egypt abroad. He said that those detained had abused the freedoms he introduced to Egypt. A government statement said that those detained had "indulged in irresponsible and suspicious acts under cover of religion."(35) Many of those arrested, however, were not known for their religious activities, but were outspoken critics of Sadat's regime. Khaled Mohieddin accused Sadat of "trying to cover the sectarian strife by blaming it on the parties."(36) Sadat was particularly stung by critical reports and editorials in the foreign press that accused him of no longer tolerating dissent and drastically restricting Egypt's democracy. In a press conference with foreign correspondents in Cairo, Sadat accused them of distorting news coverage of Egypt, but assured them that there would be no censorship of their reports. The next day, however, an American television reporter for ABC News was expelled from Egypt for interviewing outspoken critics of Sadat.

Following Sadat's death, a new era has begun under his successor, President Hosni Mubarak, whose style and personality contrast sharply with those of Sadat. Less than two months after taking power, Mubarak released 31 of the September detainees, including the leadership of the Muslim Brotherhood and members of the opposition parties and dissident journalists. This move was seen as a gesture of reconciliation by Mubarak toward the detainees who, for their part, promised to support the new president.

NOTES

1. Hamid Mowlana, "Mass Communication, Elites and National Systems in the Middle East," paper presented at the AIERI International Scientific Conference, Karl Marx University, Leibzig, East Germany, September 1974.

2. For a comprehensive look at the press in the Arab countries, see William A. Rugh, The Arab Press: News Media and Political Process in the Arab World (Syracuse, N.Y.: Syracuse University Press, 1979).

3. Al-Ahram, May 27, 1975.

4. Law No. 33 of 1978, Article 6.

5. Mohamed Hassanein Heikal, private interview, July 6, 1976.

6. Ministry of Information, Qanoun Al-Matbou'at Wal-Sahafa (Laws of Printed Materials and the Press) (Cairo, n.d.).

7. Ibid., p. 8.

8. Adnan Almaney, "Government Control of the Press in the United Arab Republic, 1950-1970," Journalism Quarterly 49, no. 2 (Summer 1972): p. 347.

9. Robert Springborg, "Professional Syndicates in Egyptian Politics, 1952-1970," International Journal of Middle Eastern Studies 9 (1978): 275-95.

10. Law No. 76 for 1970, Article 3.

11. New York Times, February 5, 1973, p. 2.

12. Saad El Shazly, The Crossing of the Suez (San Francisco: American Mideast Research, 1980), p. 293.

13. Ibid., p. 291.

14. Ibid.

15. For a complete account of Heikal's dismissal, see Munir K. Nasser, Press, Politics, and Power: Egypt's Heikal and Al-Ahram (Ames: Iowa State University Press, 1979).

16. Galal el-Din Hamamsy, Hiwar Wara' El-Aswar (Dialogue Behind Walls) (Cairo: Al-Maktab Al-Masri Al-Hadith, 1976), pp. 189-90.

17. Al-Ahram, March 13, 1976.

18. Al-Ahram, March 12, 1976.

19. Al-Ahram, May 27, 1975.

20. Al-Ahram, November 12, 1976.

21. Times (London), June 6, 1978.

22. Times (London), December 12, 1977.

23. Index on Censorship 7, no. 6, November/December 1978.

24. New York Times, May 30, 1978.

25. Al-Ahram, August 8, 1979.

26. Christian Science Monitor, May 31, 1979.

27. Ibid.

28. Al-Thawra (Baghdad), May 11, 1979.

29. New York Times, February 21, 1980.

30. Christian Science Monitor, March 14, 1980.

31. Index on Censorship 9, no. 4, August 1980.

32. New York Times, February 21, 1980.

33. Asharq Al-Awsat (London), May 27, 1981.

34. Los Angeles Times, December 29, 1980.

35. New York Times, September 5, 1981.

36. Ibid.

CHAPTER 9

Black African States

BY DENNIS L. WILCOX

PRESS CONTROLS IN SUB-SAHARA AFRICA

Fewer daily newspapers are published in the 38 independent black nations of sub-Sahara Africa than any other region in the world. In an area more than twice the size of the continental United States with a population of 330 million people — 10 percent of the world's population — about 90 dailies are published.(1) Put another way, Africa (excluding the Arab states) has only 1 percent of the world's daily newspaper circulation and an average of 13 copies of a daily newspaper per 1,000 population. For comparison, it is also noteworthy that the paucity of mass media is further defined by the fact that continental Africa has only 3 percent of the world's radio receivers and 1 percent of the world's television sets and publishes only 1.4 percent of the world's book titles.(2)

More important, from the standpoint of controlling the flow of information, the black nations of Africa do have the dubious distinction of having more government ownership and control than any other major geographical area of the world. About 90 percent of black Africa's dailies are operated and owned by the government or government corporations. And, in at least half of the nations, no privately owned, commercial press of any kind exists.(3)

Dr. Wilcox is author of Mass Media in Black Africa: Philosophy and Control (1975) published by Praeger. This chapter is an update of his systematic, comparative analysis of the independent black nations south of the Sahara.

The great majority of government-owned daily newspapers in the 38 nations of independent black Africa are directly under the ministry of information or a similar government agency. A good example is the Daily News of Botswana, a four-page tabloid published by the Ministry of Information. It has an estimated 14,000 circulation and is distributed free, primarily in the capital city of Gaborone and the surrounding area.(4) Yet, it is the only daily newspaper published in a country of nearly a million people. In addition, there is only one printing press in the nation — located in the government printing office.

The Botswana example is fairly typical of most black independent nations in Africa. Fourteen nations have only one daily newspaper, and they are owned by their respective governments. In such nations, it is also fairly typical that the printing capacity of the entire nation rests with one somewhat antiquated printing press, usually located as part of the government printing office. Commercial job printers are rare. Botswana and the other 13 nations have mass media poverty, but they are still a step up from the five nations in black Africa — Chad, Gambia, Lesotho, Rwanda, and Swaziland — that have no daily newspaper published within their borders.(5)

The second most popular form of government ownership in black Africa, after direct control by a ministry of information, is the government-organized corporation. Under such an arrangement, the newspaper is theoretically somewhat insulated from the whims of cabinet ministers and is supposed to be financially self-supporting. In several cases, the government corporation owns controlling interest but relies on the investment of individuals or foreign companies to provide the necessary capital. Recently, in Zimbabwe, the government purchased 45 percent controlling interest in the nation's four major publications after forcing the South African Argus Group to divest itself of controlling interest.(6) The government of Zambia, in recent months, has also purchased controlling interest of the Times of Zambia from the Lontho Group.(7)

The government corporation is most identified with West Africa, where, a decade ago, the Nigerian government purchased 60 percent controlling interest in the Daily Times, black Africa's highest circulation daily.(8) Even before that, the governments of Senegal and Ivory Coast had moved to control the primary daily newspapers while, at the same time, retaining French investment groups as minority stockholders. Ghana, for a number of years, has also operated the Daily Graphic and the Ghanaian Times through government corporations. The boards of directors are appointed by the government, and their autonomy, as in all cases, has varied over the years according to whether a military or civilian government was in power. Government corporations are also found in Liberia, Sierra Leone, and Tanzania.

The third most popular form of government control is through the formal one-party system. In Guinea, for example, Horoya has always been the official organ of the Parti Democratique de Guinee (PDG). The Sudanese Socialist Union operates the major dailies in that nation. Nations with strong Marxist-Leninist leanings like Ethiopia, Benin, the Congo, and Mozambique attempt to follow the Soviet example by having newspapers owned by the government and others owned by the formal one-party apparatus, although actual ownership and control gets somewhat blurred in these particular situations.

A distant fourth in the typology of ownership in black independent Africa is the privately owned, commercial daily newspaper. The number of newspapers in this category can easily be counted on the fingers of one's hand. Kenya, for all practical purposes, is the last remaining bastion of the privately owned commercial daily newspaper in black Africa. To add to the anomaly, Kenya's three dailies are probably the last to be owned by foreign interests.

And the future doesn't seem to bode well for the continued existence of a private daily press in Kenya either, despite that nation's strong support of free enterprise and Western capitalism as a model of economic development. Increasingly, Kenyans are becoming restless, primarily over the foreign ownership question, and leading journalists, as well as top government officials, are hinting that it is time for Kenyan ownership — despite the fact that the nation's three dailies have exclusively utilized Kenyan editors and staff for a number of years. The ultimate solution may be relatively autonomous government corporations or even sales of stock to individual Kenyans, thus effectively reducing the control of outside interests.

One portent of Kenya's approach to future press ownership is the formation of public nonprofit trusts. Such a trust was recently formed for the Weekly Review and the Nairobi Times, weeklies owned by Kenya's leading journalist, Hilary Ng'weno. In this arrangement, Stellascope, Ltd., the holding company, became the Press Trust of Kenya with President Daniel Moi as a major patron and with power to appoint two of the seven directors.(9) Press experts wonder, perhaps with good reason, just how independent the publications will be now from government official policy.

Dailies owned by private interests also exist in Nigeria and Cameroon, but they must compete for readership, newsprint, and advertising revenues with the larger, better financed dailies owned and operated by the government. The price of newsprint in the Cameroon, for example, is extremely high, with a 12-page newspaper having to sell at about double the price of a 40-page newspaper in London.(10)

Nigeria, the most populous nation in black Africa with 75 million people, perhaps offers the greatest variety of mass media ownership. Several dailies are still privately owned despite the trend for the state governments in this federal system to take control of the daily press. David Williams, a former editor for West Africa magazine, has written, "With the exception of Lagos, every state now either has a newspaper of its own or is part owner of one."(11) Of the 11 dailies in Nigeria, at least 7 are now state-owned. On the other hand, the federal government controls television broadcasting. Rounding out the mixed ownership pattern is a host of weeklies and magazines that are commercial operations.

Government ownership of the print media and broadcasting facilities, of course, is the ultimate control exerted on the mass media of any nation. Such control, in essence, removes the need for such authoritarian measures as draconian laws, extensive pre- and postpublication censorship, licensing of journalists, and extensive national security legislation. It is a closed-loop system where the press already functions as an integral part of the national government. Such ownership and control strongly resembles the Soviet Communist model in the respect that the press, ideally, is harnessed for national development and mass education in a socialistic system, like Mozambique. Yet it is also the ultimate form of authoritarianism in such nations as Kenneth Kaunda's Zambia, where the emphasis appears to be on suppression instead of enlightenment.

Government ownership in Africa apparently seems to know no particular ideological pattern. It appears in the Marxist-Leninist governments of Ethiopia, Benin, and the Congo as well as in the functioning democracies of Nigeria, Zimbabwe, and Botswana. It is also found in the formal one-party states of Tanzania, Malawi, and Angola. It exists in the military regimes of the Central African Republic, Equatorial Guinea, and Mauritania. It is even found in a nation like Senegal, where, in recent years, opposition parties have been allowed to form, although only along the guidelines set down by Leopold Senghor.

For what it's worth, government ownership doesn't occur in two of the last remaining monarchies in the world — Lesotho and Swaziland — where the pattern of control is more traditionally along the lines of authoritarianism with a series of press laws and sedition and preventive detention for matters involving nation security.

In sum, government ownership is not particularly tied to ideological beliefs in black Africa so much as it is to economic realities. Arguments are often advanced that if the government did not operate the mass media, it wouldn't exist. This is because Africa has more than its share of the world's poorest nations, and there is insufficient private capital or potential for advertising revenues to support a private press. In addition, the potential readership is still somewhat limited because about 80 percent of the African peoples are still illiterate, according to UN surveys.

Another theme, expressed by African leaders for almost two decades now, is the idea that a developing nation — in a battle for its very economic survival and political stability — cannot afford the luxury of a "free press" as defined by Western standards. In sum, the press should be national "cheerleader." According to Willie Musarurwa, the editor of the Sunday Mail in Zimbabwe, "We are in a formative stage. If we take an irresponsible line, we can destroy the nation we spent 20 years struggling for." He gets no disagreement from Robin Drew, the white editor of Zimbabwe's Herald before it was taken over by the government, who says, "Criticism can be far more destabilizing here than in an older country."(12)

It should also be pointed out that Africa has never had a role model for a free and privately owned press. The colonial governments of England, France, Portugal, and Belgium — up until giving independence to their colonies in the 1960s and 1970s — also operated an essentially government-owned or government-controlled press. To this day, draconian press laws from the colonial period are still on the books in many independent African nations. Perhaps one scholar summed it up best by observing that the government gazette operated by the colonial power was the "Adam and Eve" of African journalism.

Ownership of the press is an important factor in a comparative analysis of press control, but it does not completely measure the full extent of such control in Africa. Some nations, like Nigeria, Zimbabwe, Ghana, and Botswana, also have functioning political parties with a strong tradition of judicial independence. In these nations, government tends to be more liberal and tolerant of the press and journalists, although this is not to say that there are no occasional crackdowns, harassment, and veiled government threats.

One must then systematically analyze nations on a number of "press control" scales to ascertain the degree of press control in any given situation. For such purposes, one may wish to utilize the following criteria or points of reference:(13)

- Newspaper ownership. Government ownership of all daily newspapers in the country.
- Printing ownership. Over 50 percent government ownership of the nation's printing presses for newspapers and magazines, thus limiting access.
- Budget allocation. Newspapers and magazines supported by direct government subsidies.
- Newsprint allocation. Priority of government publications over private publications for allocations of newsprint.

- Censorship. Prepublication review of a nation's newspapers and magazines by government officials. This is inherent in a wholly owned government press.
- Suspension. Existence of government policy to ban, suspend, seize, or confiscate newspapers and magazines.
- Opposition publications. Publications of opposition political parties are banned. This includes formal one-party states where only one party is constitutionally permitted.
- Licensing. Required government certification and licensing of working newsmen.
- Licensing publications. Required registration or licensing by government of private newspapers and magazines.
- Judicial appointment. Judiciary subject to dismissal on political grounds.
- Independent judiciary. Lack of judicial review concerning constitutionality of laws and regulations.
- Preventive detention. Existence of preventive detention acts to detain journalists and other citizens without charge or trial.
- Imprisonment. Fine or imprisonment for journalists who imply "disrespect" or criticize the nation's leaders and policies.
- Harassment. Pattern of incidents where journalists and editors are beaten, publicly humiliated, interrogated by police on a regular basis, or where newspaper offices are subject to unannounced searches.
- Bond. Requirement that privately owned newspapers and magazines post bonds to cover any potential libel or sedition judgments.
- Libel laws. Nations with broad-based and highly restrictive libel and sedition laws.
- Broadcasting. Source of primary funding, degree of control exerted by the executive branch of government, criteria for selection of personnel.
- Film censorship. Foreign entertainment films screened by government for political content.
- Foreign periodicals. Incidents of foreign periodicals being confiscated or banned.
- Visa requirements. Special visa requirements imposed on foreign journalists, as opposed to foreign visitors in general.
- Cables. Foreign journalists requested to submit stories to government officials before getting approval for transmission.

● Foreign news agencies. Government has exclusive con-
tractual agreements with international news agencies.

By applying this list of reference points where press control
can be exerted, one can document a pattern of pervasive press
control in the 38 independent black nations of sub-Sahara Africa.
The exact number of nations, at any given time, that utilize
these press controls has the major disadvantage of being out of
date almost before the number is calculated, but continual
monitoring of the African continent over a period of years does
show that the pattern of control remains somewhat static.

NEWSPAPER OWNERSHIP

It already has been stated that about 90 percent of black
Africa's daily press are owned or controlled by government. In
at least half of the nations, the government has total control
over all publications and broadcasting facilities.

PRINTING PRESS OWNERSHIP

For all practical purposes, the dominant reality in independent
black Africa is for government control and ownership of printing
facilities. More than half of the governments already own more
than 75 percent of the printing facilities in their nations now.
Such ownership, as previously suggested, tends to restrict and
control any nondaily or nongovernment access to the mass media.
Ethiopia's monarchy exercised ownership over all printing
presses as early as World War II, and the present military
government has continued the tradition to the present day.
Other governments having a high percentage of control over
printing presses include Guinea, Ivory Coast, Sierra Leone,
Sudan, Angola, Mozambique, and Somalia. In most cases, the
presses were nationalized along with other major industries. One
must remember, too, that many African nations only have one
printing plant for the entire country.
In Africa today, Kenya probably remains the only nation
where less than 10 percent of the country's presses are owned
by the government. A thriving commercial press supplements the
printing plants of the nation's three commercial daily newspapers.

GOVERNMENT SUBSIDIES

Most governments of the world consider the flow of
information a vital part of national life. Consequently, a variety
of policies are implemented to encourage the circulation of
newspapers and magazines.

In some countries, as in the United States, the encouragement is indirect by permitting reduced postal rates for printed matter, although the degree of this "subsidy" has steadily declined in recent years. In many Third World countries, where there is a lack of private capital, however, the encouragement may be more direct in the form of government budgetary allocations.

In Africa, the primary method of financing the press is through direct government subsidy to pay for salaries, production, and administrative overhead. About two-thirds of the 38 independent black nations provide such direct subsidies. This high figure is not unusual, given the fact that most daily newspapers are operated by government in the first place. Although privately owned newspapers rarely share in this form of government encouragement, many do share the financial assistance of official government advertising, which often makes the difference between profit and bankruptcy.

About half of the African nations do support the press through official government advertising. Such advertising includes legal notices, proceedings of government bodies, government employment opportunities, requests for bid offers on contracts, and pleas for support of national developmental goals. Although providing additional revenue for government newspapers, government advertising also is a powerful economic weapon over private publications on the borderline of economic solvency.

A third of the nations do have policies giving a reduced postal rate for periodicals, but some do not extend the privilege to nongovernment publications. Tanzania is a good example.

Loans for printing equipment are less known in black Africa, and most governments claim that it is not part of official policy. In the case of newspapers operated by government corporations, as in Ghana, the national government tends to point out that the corporation should finance its own equipment expenditures.

Guaranteed purchase of bulk copies is even more rare in Africa. Less than 10 percent of the nations have such policy, mainly because direct governmental allocations often include the free distribution of copies to various governmental offices. Such is the case in Botswana. Togo, several years ago, did have a system where each government ministry ordered bulk subscriptions. This, in effect, spreads the cost of operating the daily press among a number of government departments.

NEWSPRINT ALLOCATIONS

Most Third World nations, due to foreign exchange considerations, have policies regulating the amount of imported newsprint. The outflow of hard currency for foreign goods is a serious problem in terms of balance of payments; but the other edge of the sword can be the deliberate attempt to withhold newsprint from dissident publications. Accordingly, it is important to look at the allocation of newsprint as a possible government control of the nongovernmental press in a country. Do government publications, for example, have priority over those in the private sector?

As indicated earlier, about half of the African nations have a wholly owned government press; no private, commercial publications are in existence. Consequently, the question of newsprint allocation never comes up. In those remaining nations that have some semblance of a private, commercial press — be it bulletins, weeklies, or magazines — official government policy makes no distinction between the newsprint needs of a private versus government publication.

In some nations, however, allocation of newsprint is on a proportional basis according to the publication's circulation. Ghana, for a number of years, has utilized this system. Neighboring Nigeria, on the other hand, has no fair share allocation system. All newsprint purchases are done on competitive bidding and any newspaper can buy as much as it can afford.

Tanzania's press is now primarily state-owned, but there are a few private publications. All newsprint orders must go through a subsidiary of the State Trading Corporation, and that can be a tedious process, subject to refusal at any point. The process is described as follows:

> The red tape involved in importing paper is wearisome and time consuming; after a pro-forma invoice is obtained from a supplier, an import license is issued; then follows a pre-shipment inspection at the paper factory abroad; a certificate of price of goods at market value is then issued, against which payment in foreign exchange can be made.(14)

CENSORSHIP

The most direct form of government press control is the prepublication review (censorship) of newspapers and magazines. Almost 60 percent of the nations in independent black Africa exert this type of control. In most of the countries, it is the logical extension of a press totally owned and operated by the government. Such a situation makes prepublication review an inherent part of the press system in these countries.

The Central Africa Republic, for years, has had an "editing and information control service" to examine all information before it is printed or broadcast. This system was begun by Emperor Bokassa in 1965, when he seized power in a military coup. It was continued by President Dacko after seizing power in 1979 and is probably being continued by the military regime that toppled Dacko in 1980.

Current evidence indicates that Cameroon's less formalized system of prepublication review of several years ago — the first copy of all privately owned newspapers must be given to the local district officer — had tightened in recent years. According to reports, all newspaper stories must now have the approval of the government censor before they are printed. It is not uncommon for blank spots to appear, not because the articles were considered sensitive but because there is shortage of censors in the Cameroon and all the material has not been read.(15)

Several African nations had laws in the past requiring government approval of all news stories in advance of publication, but these edicts have been revoked or fallen into disuse with the advent of a completely owned government press in those countries. This is the case in Mali, Mauritania, Niger, and Togo, which once required delivery of copy to government officials from 4 to 24 hours prior to publication. Today, the editors are trusted government employees and such review is carried on within the newspaper office.

The remaining nations in black Africa have no government prepublication review of newspapers; but many African journalists contend that indirect pressures are effective substitutes. In Kenya, for example, no prepublication review exists but it is not uncommon for government officials to talk with editors about the content and treatment of major news stories before publication. There are also instances of high government officials publicly attacking the press for certain articles and threatening legislation to prevent further irresponsibility. Thus, there is a great deal of self-censorship throughout the African continent.

SUPPRESSION OF PUBLICATIONS

Another form of direct government press control is postpublication censorship. In many nations, governments ban, suspend, seize, or confiscate any newspaper or magazine when officials feel that the content threatens public order and safety — a classical authoritarian response.

Independent black Africa is no exception to the concept that government can and should prohibit published articles that are considered detrimental to national plans of development and tribal unity. In addition, a great many of the African nations, by culture and tradition, do perceive that criticism of a leader is the same thing as an attack on the integrity of the nation-state, of which the leader is the living embodiment. The passion for unity is also a factor, as exemplified and manifested in the Soviet Communist theory of the press.

About three-fourths of the African governments have policies that would enable officials to engage in postpublication censorship. In other words, a publication that violated government sensitivities could easily find street copies confiscated and the door of the newspaper padlocked by sundown. This was true during the last years of the Smith government in Rhodesia, and the law still applies in Robert Mugabe's coalition government.(16)

The deliberate use of "policy" indicates that individual governments often assume prohibitory powers, although it is not provided for in the constitution or legislation. This is especially true in nations where a military regime has suspended the constitution and publications exist at the whim of officialdom. In other countries, there is no substantial body of written law or case law to protect the press against arbitrary executive action. One might argue that all governments have the ultimate authority to restrict the circulation of printed materials. This discussion, however, deals with governments that have announced policies or have shown that the policies exist by past suppression of publications for other reasons than libel, pornography, or specified sedition laws.

It is interesting that the reported incidences of suppressed publications within countries have somewhat declined in recent years. Again, the advent of a wholly controlled government press in many of the African nations probably has made this form of control less necessary. In addition, the constant threat of suppression has taught other editors and journalists the fine art of self-restraint. One Botswana journalist says, "There are limitations, not written but understood." Says a Kenyan journalist, "There's a lot of self-censorship for fear of government reprisals."

Sometimes, censorship after the fact is the basis of future restrictions. In Ghana, for example, the government of President Hilla Limmann ordered the Daily Graphic to stop publishing editorials.(17)

OPPOSITION PUBLICATIONS

An opposition party press often provides citizens with a dissenting viewpoint regarding the government's plans and policies. At best, it serves the valuable function of being a skeptic and watchdog of government officials and programs. At worst, a party press provides emotional polemics that offer few alternatives to solving the nation's problems.

The history of press development in other countries shows that an active party press was often the first step in the evolution of a diverse and relatively independent press system. The opposition press of Africa, however, seems to have been in existence only before independence when mimeographed flyers and broadsheets, or the "bombs of independence," rallied the people against continued colonial domination.

Today, throughout independent black Africa, there are few newspapers and magazines owned and operated by opposition parties. For all practical purposes, pluralistic political activity is found in only 5 of Africa's 38 independent states — Gambia, Botswana, Zimbabwe, Nigeria, and Ghana. Almost 90 percent of the nations either have a military government, a formalized one-party state, or a de facto one-party state. Liberia used to have a token opposition political party before the seizure of the government by Sergeant Samuel Doe in 1980. At present, all political activity is banned.

LICENSING OF JOURNALISTS

Government ownership of periodicals and printing facilities is one form of restricting citizen access to mass media channels, but another equally important press control is the licensing and certification of journalists who work on these publications. Such control, claim many African governments, simply assures that working journalists are competent and qualified to handle the dissemination of information to millions of people. Advocates of the libertarian press concept, however, claim that such licensing and certification procedures are tantamount to controlling access to the press. A working journalist, dependent upon government permission to earn a living, is less likely to serve as a public watchdog or uncover stories potentially embarrassing to government officials.

As near as can be determined, about half of the 38 independent nations in black Africa now require licensing or certification of journalists, based on professional training (apprenticeship) or a litmus test of loyalty and support for a particular political ideology. Spain, under the Franco regime, was an outstanding example of this authoritarian approach to certifying journalists.

In the Sudan, journalists cannot be employed unless they have formal journalism training, talent, and membership in the nation's only political party, the Sudanese Socialist Union. The Sudanese Press Corporation, which directs operation of the country's print media, registers and certifies all journalists for employment.

Certification of journalists, according to one report, is "dependent upon an ideological framework considered appropriate to the goals of national and social development."

The government-owned press of Zaire also requires formal training in journalism. A prospective employee on a newspaper or magazine must attend the country's Institute of Journalism for a specific period of time. In the Cameroon, working journalists must have a press card, subject to revocation if the writer becomes "irresponsible" in coverage of government activity.

The remaining nations in black Africa have no formalized method of licensing journalists, per se; but because so many have a government-controlled press, perhaps it is a moot point since journalists have already been certified as loyal government employees. Even in the case of government corporations, as in Ghana and Nigeria, there is often overt government meddling in personnel matters. A good case in point is the Daily Times of Nigeria. After the change to civilian rule, the newspaper staff wrote stories and commented on the salaries of the new government officials. The government reacted by quietly suggesting a change of editor and staff.(18)

The privately owned, commercial press of Kenya also occasionally feels the heat of government pressure to demote an editor or fire a staff reporter when top government officials have taken a dislike to someone. Yet, there is no formalized licensing of journalists; a work card is required, but all employed people are required to have one.

LICENSING OF PUBLICATIONS

Nongovernment newspapers and magazines being subjected to registration and licensing by the state has been used as an index of press controls in several worldwide press freedom studies. Libertarians contend that any form of license to permit publication can also be withdrawn if the periodical becomes too critical or skeptical of government policies and officials. The concept of press control is inherent in any licensing or registration mechanism; but, in Africa, the criterion appears to lose much of its relevance and descriptive quality. In the first place, half the nations have a completely owned government press, so licensing is a moot point. Second, in those nations where there is mixed ownership, licensing is a standard requirement for all businesses in the country. It is not so much for possible suppression, but for the purposes of establishing financial accountability and collecting taxes.

Registration, or licensing, also serves the same purpose as it does in Western democracies in terms of postal regulations. In Nigeria, to use an example, all newspapers must be registered and a signed copy of every issue must be deposited with the government. The name and address of the publisher and editor must appear in every issue — a somewhat common requirement around the world.

Although periodicals conceivably could have their publishing license revoked by the government, most informants in Africa say that such a situation is unlikely. In most cases, they say, the government has other powers at its command to close a publication for political reasons. Direct suppression can be done in most nations on the basis of ill-defined sedition laws, the public order and safety, or the national interest.

JUDICIAL APPOINTMENT AND JUDICIAL REVIEW

A number of press scholars have come to the conclusion that a nation's press system is free, not necessarily because of constitutional guarantee (almost every national constitution in the world has a clause regarding press freedom or freedom of speech), but because an unintimidated judiciary protects the press against government encroachment. Consequently, it is important to find out if the judicial systems of independent Africa are free from manipulation and control by the executive and legislative branches of government.

Two indexes are used. The first is the criterion dealing with the appointment and dismissal of judges. It is not uncommon for the head of a country to appoint judges, but the critical point is whether these same judges also can be removed by the executive at will. In other words, are there adequate safeguards to prevent the removal of judges who become politically unpopular with a current government? The second criterion is the judiciary's authority to determine the constitutionality of government laws and regulations. In many countries, this is not a power bestowed upon the judicial system. If the right of review is not guaranteed and denied, the judicial mechanism has little authority to dissuade governments who wish to suppress publications by legislation and executive orders despite free press guarantees in the nation's constitution.

Put in this context, an independent judiciary with power to rule on the constitutionality of government legislation and executive orders is a rarity in sub-Sahara Africa. Between 70 and 80 percent of the 38 independent nations have no independent judiciary as it is understood in Western terms. Of these nations, about 10 have military governments where the constitution has been suspended. Another group are formal one-party states where the ruling hierarchy exerts a great influence on judicial appointments and dismissals. In Mauritania, for example, the ruling political party appoints judges and determines their tenure on the basis of political loyalty. Guinea has a similar system, where the central political bureau has complete power to appoint and dismiss judges.

Kenya presents a less clear concept of executive power to dismiss judges. Kenyan journalists agree that the president has the power to dismiss judges, but others say this power is somewhat diluted because he first must receive cabinet approval. Because the nation is a de facto one-party state, this doesn't seem to be a major drawback.

Judicial review, which could protect the press against government abuse or suppression, is presently found in only a few nations — Nigeria, Ghana, Gambia, Botswana, Zimbabwe — the same nations that rank high (by African standards) as pluralistic political systems. Nigeria and Ghana give evidence of an operating judicial system now that both have been returned to civilian rule by the military. In Nigeria, the high court ruled in an editor's favor when the Nigerian senate questioned the right of a journalist to protect his sources, but the editor was eventually demoted to an obscure position on the newspaper anyway.[19] In Ghana, when President Hilla Limmann appointed a supervising editor to curb the Daily Graphic's criticism of his government, the newspaper cited constitutional guarantees and asked the supreme court to make a ruling.[20] It is not known whether this appeal to judicial authority was effective in curbing the government's attempt to impose additional controls on a government corporation.

PREVENTIVE DETENTION OF JOURNALISTS

The lack of an independent judiciary to review effectively the constitutionality of government actions also permits the existence of preventive detention legislation. These laws enable a government to detain citizens for lengths of time without charge or trial. The presence of such legislation creates a chilling effect on the free flow of information, because a government official becomes the sole arbiter of determining which published stories are prejudicial to the national interest. For journalists wishing to stay out of jail, preventive detention policies are a pervasive control on the press.

The majority of African governments have executive or legislative detention acts on the books. In some cases, preventive detention is only used after a state of emergency has been declared. Or, in the case of Nigeria, all citizens were subject to arrest without warrant and detention without trial during the 13 years of military government, from 1966 to 1979. Arbitrary detention of journalists is almost becoming a standard occupational hazard in Nigeria, and it has not abated much since the civilian government was formed. The International Press Institute (IPI) recently reported, for example, that the editor of the New Nigerian was detained by police for over a week for alleged contempt of a state judge.(21) The detention of journalists, or even their harassment, in Nigeria seems to be at the state level instead of the federal level. In Ibadan, the head of the Nigerian Tribune was placed under police guard for two days for "dissemination of falsehood and incitement to public disorder."(22)

In Uganda, in 1981, the Uganda Times editor was detained after he reported army rampages in the country's remote East Madi district. No charges have been filed, but he, at last report, was still at the police station.(23)

Kenya has a preventive detention act dating to 1966 in which the government has broad powers to detain citizens and censor newspapers. Although rarely invoked, it was in 1981, when six Kenyan journalists from the Daily Nation spent three days in detention. The arrests followed President Daniel Moi's accusation that the Daily Nation had misled Kenyans over a strike by government doctors. The government statement following the arrests said, "The persistent rebellious attitude of those concerned with the selection of editorial matters within the Nation newspapers cannot be viewed as being in the interests of the state. They can only be described as sectarian and tribally motivated."(24)

IMPRISONMENT OF JOURNALISTS

A press-control criterion closely related to preventive detention is the government's arbitrary power to fine or imprison journalists whom officials feel have shown disrespect for the country's institutions and leadership. Such "disrespect" is interpreted rather broadly in some countries as a threat to the nation's unity and harmony. This means that journalists can be punished for any number of broad concepts that are generally outside the usual grounds of libel, pornography, or even sedition laws. In black independent Africa, a monitoring of the press will show that most fines and imprisonments are directed at journalists who have questioned or criticized government policies.

Officially, journalists can be fined or imprisoned for criticism of the government in about three-fourths of the countries. It, however, is a rarity now in terms of actual practice. There are several reasons for this. First, the majority of journalists in Africa are government employees and most stories are screened by government-appointed editors. Second, in the case of mixed ownership, journalists have learned the fine art of self-control;

most know exactly how far they can go without incurring government censure.

HARASSMENT OF JOURNALISTS

Harassment of journalists is a time-honored authoritarian way of dealing with the press, dating back to the Middle Ages. It takes many forms — verbal threats by government officials, beatings by unidentified assailants, poison pen letters, smashing of press equipment, rocks thrown through windows, unannounced police searches, difficulty in securing permits for purchase of equipment, withdrawal of government advertising, and so forth.

Incidences of harassment can be found in any country, and Africa is no exception. In Nigeria, the office of the Nigeria Standard in Jos was ransacked by police who wanted some "vital documents."(25) The editor of the Sunday Standard and a one-time activist in the Nigerian Union of Journalists was beaten up by a legislator in the Gongola State Assembly.(26) During 1981, it was also reported by IPI that Nigerian legislators, on more than one occasion, had trooped into newspaper offices and radio stations to harass journalists. They even interrupted news broadcasts and seized tapes from the radio stations.(27) In neighboring Ghana, a television talk show host for the Ghana Broadcasting Corporation resigned because of unwarranted government harassment. A program about a former head of state was not telecast because of a "technical" difficulty.(28)

Journalists in Uganda are practically an extinct species because of harassment. During Amin's reign of terror, many journalists and editors disappeared without a trace or were found later floating in the river or in burned-out cars. The toppling of Amin, however, has not brought much improvement in conditions. Before the last national election when Milton Obote resumed power, pamphlets were circulated to journalists suggesting death if they did not follow the line set forth by the pamphlet. To underscore the seriousness of the threat, a television personality was shot shortly after receiving the pamphlet.(29)

Another form of harassment is financial. In Ghana, the Daily Graphic is in serious financial trouble because the government has not paid its bills for official advertising.(30)

POSTING OF BOND

The requirement of nongovernment newspapers and magazines to post a bond as an integral part of permission to publish dates back to the colonial era. At that time, British administrators in East and West Africa found bonds a good way to discourage the proliferation of newssheets by aspiring nationalists. A large bond not only discouraged many would-be editors but also had the effect of making the existent press more cautious, as many editors could not afford to lose their posted bonds.

The required posting of large bonds, however, has now virtually disappeared in independent black Africa. One reason is the advent of a wholly owned government press in half of the nations. It is reported that Gambia and Kenya still require a bond to be posted, but they are exceptions.

LIBEL AND SEDITION LAWS

A common press control throughout the world are libel and sedition laws. Every nation has laws to protect citizens from press abuse and to safeguard national security. Consequently, the very existence of such laws in a nation is not really a good index to how these laws, in reality, affect the operation of the press. One can argue, however, that some nations have very restrictive laws, while others have allowed such legislation to gather dust. Independent black Africa is no exception. A survey several years ago asked African journalists about their perception of libel and sedition laws in their nation.(31) The nations of Central African Republic, Ethiopia, Gabon, Malawi, Mauritania, Somalia, Uganda, and Zaire were perceived as having highly restrictive laws. Fairly restrictive laws were recorded for Benin, Gambia, Kenya, Liberia, Nigeria, Rwanda, Sudan, Swaziland, and Upper Volta. Some of these nations have a wholly owned government press, but the laws remain on the books.

On the other hand, nations with a wholly owned government press saw no relevance in the question. As a Togoese representative said, it is practically impossible to sue a government newspaper and it is unthinkable that a government organ would violate sedition laws.

Malawi, which has a mixed press ownership, gets a "highly restrictive" rating because there is a law (dating from 1973) making the publication of a false report punishable by life imprisonment. In addition, it is a capital offense to pass false information to journalists.(32) President Banda is the arbiter of whether the report is true or false.

BROADCASTING

Radio broadcasting probably is the most universal form of mass communication in independent black Africa. Cheap transistor radios have brought the spoken word to millions of rural Africans, and broadcasting has broken the barriers of illiteracy and poverty. Given Africa's great oral traditions, many observers say that radio and television are the continent's only true mass communication media.

All 38 nations have their own radio transmission facilities, and about half now have television. In all cases, general audience broadcasting is the exclusive province of the state. Such total ownership and control should be considered in the context of press-government controls because access to broadcasting facilities and alternative programming by nongovernmental interests is nonexistent.

The extent and degree of government control over broadcasting facilities can be indexed in several ways: what is the source of financial support; who is directly responsible for policy formulation; and how personnel are selected.

The primary source of financial support is government funds, either as a line item in the national budget or through a budgetary allotment from a ministry of the government. Most nations have no objections to commercial advertising as a source of funds, but such revenues are extremely low in the Third World. A third source of income is license fees, much like that found in Western and Eastern Europe.

Although the concept of a relatively autonomous public corporation (like the BBC) was introduced by the British colonials in Africa, the idea didn't remain after independence. Rosalynde Ainslie, writing in 1966, noted:

> African broadcasting . . . tends away from the concept of broadcasting as a function independent of government, such as was envisaged by the British . . . in colonial days. The tasks of radio have emerged as so much part of, and essential to, the politics of government, that many of the countries that inherited with independence a statutory corporation in charge of broadcasting, have legislated the bringing of radio and television back under direct ministerial control.(33)

In sum, only three nations among the 38 independent black African nations now claim to have somewhat autonomous public broadcasting corporations — Nigeria, Ghana, and Liberia. And in the case of the latter, the military government of Sergeant Doe may have altered its status in recent months. In the overwhelming majority of the nations, the minister of information has direct control of the broadcasting services. Broadcast personnel, however, tend to be part of national civil service and only the top administrators change when there is a coup or government shake-up.

FILM CENSORSHIP

The film industry in Africa is still in its developmental stage, and so almost 100 percent of the entertainment films come from foreign sources. Governments are concerned about political content, as well as violence, obscenity, and nudity. Consequently, about 90 percent of the independent black nations have some form of formalized government preview of foreign films. The most pervasive censorship is based on concepts of morality and violence, but political content gets a close review in such nations as Ethiopia, Guinea, Benin, Congo, and Mozambique — all states with Marxist-Leninist leanings.

CONFISCATION OF FOREIGN PERIODICALS

The lack of a diverse, well-developed press in independent black Africa has created a healthy market for foreign newspapers and magazines among the educated elites of the 38 nations. These elites, speaking either French, Portuguese, or English, rely heavily on the publications of former colonial powers for news and information. Time and Newsweek also make their impact, as well as Pan-African publications like Drum and Jeune Afrique.

These newspapers and magazines often are the only source of nongovernment information in a country, and it is important to document their relative freedom to circulate. In general, foreign media are not subject to the same strictures that hinder the local media. One reason is the content, which usually deals with issues outside the country. Another reason is the fact that the majority of people in any one country do not speak English, French, or Portuguese. Finally, only the educated elites (usually less than 10 percent of the population) can afford or understand the foreign periodicals.

Yet, it is not uncommon for foreign newspapers and magazines to be banned or seized for a variety of reasons, but political considerations are the most prevalent criterion. In the early 1970s, about three-fourths of the nations had banned or confiscated foreign publications in the previous two years. By the beginning of 1981, however, there were fewer reported incidences of foreign publications being banned or confiscated. In some instances, as in Ethiopia, the ban may be de facto, but the majority of nations tend to be more liberal about foreign publications.

Recently, Kenya banned a Libyan publication for blatant political content. The Sudan, which charged Libya with trying to undermine its government, has also banned Libyan publications. Perhaps the best recent example of banning is Equatorial Guinea. It has not only barred all Spanish journalists but has also banned all Spanish newspapers and magazines from the country. In addition, heavy sentences are promised for anyone caught in possession of such publications. If convicted, a fine of $1,400 and six months in jail could be levied.(34) This is nothing new: Spanish publications were also banned immediately after independence in 1968.

VISA REQUIREMENTS FOR FOREIGN JOURNALISTS

Independent Africa, as a whole, doesn't exercise excessive control over the admission of foreign journalists to a country, but African leaders still display a great deal of sensitivity regarding how their nation is portrayed abroad. Any restrictions on foreign journalists, of course, inhibit and control the type of information the rest of the world receives about a specific nation. Some nations are infrequently covered in the world press simply because foreign journalists rarely get permission to visit the country. The Congo, for example, bans foreign journalists as a class. Guinea rarely issues tourist visas, to say nothing of permission for foreign journalists. Few journalists have also visited Ethiopia, Benin, or Equatorial Guinea in recent months.

It is somewhat ironic that the nations that often get the most unfavorable coverage in the world press are the ones that do allow foreign journalists to visit. Although the Republic of South Africa is not covered in this discussion, its apartheid system is well known throughout the world because of relatively easy access for foreign journalists. On the other hand, Equatorial Guinea banned foreign journalists for years while it went about extensive human rights violations, some even say genocide. Yet the world doesn't know much about the crimes committed there. Uganda, under President Amin, also saw the destruction of entire tribal groups, but foreign journalists were not around to witness it.

Zimbabwe, one of the few functioning democracies in Africa, has recently revived its requirement that journalists must get permits for 24 hours at a time. This, according to the government, is an effort "to improve what it regards as a contentious and negative reporting of the country."(35)

Generally, the pattern now in Africa is simply to expel foreign journalists if the government doesn't like what they transmit abroad. Recently, a Reuters correspondent was arrested in the Central African Republic for an article that displeased the government.(36)

SUBMISSION OF CABLES

As with visas, most African governments have abandoned the idea of officially approving the cables of foreign journalists. This is probably because transmission or telecommunications services are manned by loyal government employees and because it is relatively ineffective. Foreign correspondents, faced with the prospect of censorship, may merely file their stories after they leave the country. On the other hand, foreign correspondents continue to report that stories that are particularly sensitive to a government often meet with unusual "technical difficulties" in their transmission.

CONTRACTS WITH NEWS AGENCIES

Although the majority of African nations complain about large international news agencies dominating world communications, it is interesting that three - fourths of these nations already effectively control all external information coming into the country. They can do this because the government has the exclusive contract with AP, UPI, Reuters, or AFP. In other words, the national news agency or a similar government office receives all incoming foreign news and distributes it to local media.

Such an arrangement in most of the independent African nations gives the government unlimited power to filter, screen, and control the public's knowledge of foreign news events. News items can be edited, changed, or deleted to complement the government's foreign and domestic policies. The other danger of exclusive contracts with international news services is the feeling of many newsmen that a wire service cannot maintain objectivity and independence when the principal client in the country is the government itself.

CONCLUSIONS

A systematic review of press controls in the 38 independent nations of Africa south of the Sahara shows dominant government ownership and control of the mass media. Almost 90 percent of the nations fall into this category. The majority of the nations also subscribe to an authoritarian press concept, which is manifested in a number of controls to prevent any criticism or public debate of a nation's policies or leaders.

Most of the countries exercise some form of prepublication censorship, inherent in government ownership. At least three-fourths have policies that empower government officials to ban, confiscate, or seize any newspaper or magazine. An independent judiciary is an alien concept in three-fourths of the nations, and the majority of the governments have preventive detention laws in which citizens can be held without charge or trial.

Broadcasting is becoming more professionalized but still remains the exclusive province of the ministry of information in most nations. Foreign periodicals are often confiscated or banned, and about three-fourths of the nations have exclusive government contracts with international news agencies.

It is doubtful that the present profile of press ownership and restraints in independent black Africa will change in the near future. Most nations are still finding some sense of nationhood and lack the self-confidence to permit a robust discussion of public issues. In addition, most have opted for a formal one-party state, which precludes the formation of a legitimate opposition press or party.

The lack of capital also remains a serious problem, and government will remain the only institution in most nations that is large enough to amass the kind of capital necessary for press development.

NOTES

1. World Communications: A 200 Country Survey of Press, Radio, Television, Film (Paris: UNESCO, 1975).

2. Sean MacBride, Many Voices, One World: Report by the International Commission for a Study of Communication Problems (Paris: UNESCO, 1980), pp. 125, 127.

3. Dennis L. Wilcox, Mass Media in Black Africa: Philosophy and Control (New York: Praeger, 1975). The percentages and numbers presented throughout this chapter reflect the continuing research of the author from 1971 through 1981. Percentages and numbers in the original text have been updated to reflect 1981 situations.

4. "The World's Most Modest National Daily," IPI Report, June 1979, p. 14.

5. World Communications, op. cit. (country listings).

6. "Zimbabwean Official Assails Takeover of Newspapers," New York Times, January 6, 1981. See also June Kronholz, "In Africa, Tribal Power Wanes, but Still Rivals Government at Times," Wall Street Journal, June 15, 1981.

7. "Zambia Tightens Its Grip," IPI Report, November 1980, p. 3.

8. "Freedom Review," IPI Report, December 1980, p. 12.

9. "Trust Buys Stellascope, Ltd.," IPI Report, June 1981, p. 3.

10. "Smuggled Newsprint Prices Hit Private Papers," IPI Report, June 1979, p. 2.

11. David Williams, "Power in Restraint: Nigeria's Press Prepares for October," IPI Report, June 1979, pp. 6-7.

12. Krunholz, op. cit.

13. Wilcox, op. cit. This list of criteria was developed by the author to compare systematically nations on press-control scales.

14. Michael Traber, "Kiongozi of Tanzania: Development for Self-Reliance," Tanzania Episcopal Conference (Kitwe, Zambia, 1973), p. 32.

15. "Smuggled Newsprint Prices Hit Private Press," op. cit.

16. Kronholz, op. cit.

17. Ibid.

18. "Freedom Review," op. cit.

19. Titus Ogunwale, "A Rough Time for Nigeria's Newsmen," IPI Report, September 1981, pp. 14-15.

20. "Freedom Review," op. cit.

21. Ogunwale, op. cit.

22. Ibid.

23. "Editor Held in Uganda," IPI Report, May 1981, p. 4.

24. "Six Freed After Police Round Up," IPI Report, June 1981, p. 3.

25. Ogunwale, op. cit.

26. Ibid.

27. Ibid.

28. "TV Newsman Quits in Anger," IPI Report, June 1979, p. 2.

29. "Freedom Review," op. cit.

30. "Help Us Plea Over Machinery," IPI Report, June 1979, p. 2.

31. Wilcox, op. cit. This survey of African journalists and informants was taken in 1973.

32. Richard Harwood, "Hard Work and Obedience: An African Success Story," Manchester Overseas Guardian, weekly edition, June 28, 1981, p. 17.

33. Rosalynde Ainslie, The Press in Africa: Communications Past and Present (New York: Walker, 1966), p. 174.

34. Briefs, IPI Report, September 1981, p. 4.

35. "Zimbabwe Revives Permits," IPI Report, November 1980, p. 3.

36. "Freedom Review," IPI Report, December 1980, p. 4.

PART IV
EXTERNAL CONTROLS
OF DOMESTIC MEDIA

CHAPTER 10

The Censorship Operation
in Occupied Japan

BY JUN ETO

Exactly nine years ago, in August 1971, John W. Hall of Yale University presented a paper at the Fukuoka UNESCO Conference on U.S.-Japan relations. In the essay, entitled, "Pearl Harbor Thirty Years After — Reflections on the Pathology of War and Nationalism," he states the following:

> Pearl Harbor through the smoke and anguish of Vietnam takes on a new look. Our current disillusionment over American policy in Asia, and our newly gained understanding of the Japanese military mind, lead to a clear conclusion: that we need to rethink the causes of the Pacific War from what can best be described as a tragic view, one which takes no comfort in scapegoats and offers no sanctuaries for private or national claims of moral righteousness, but rather admits that as two nations are drawn into violent conflict, something very tragic in human affairs is taking place.

Hall's proposition that one should take a tragic viewpoint is not only applicable to the reassessment of Pearl Harbor but also to the study of the American Occupation of Japan as well. On the American side there is still a notable tendency to look back to the Occupation period as something colored in a rosy aura — a successful and benevolent Occupation under the able leadership

Presented at the Amherst Conference on the Occupation of Japan, August 21-23, 1980. A Japanese translation of this article will appear on <u>Tenno ga Baiburu o Yonda Hi</u>, Ray A. Moore, ed. (Tokyo: Kodansha, 1982).

of General Douglas MacArthur in which the victorious Americans guided the oppressed Japanese from feudalism into the glorious path of freedom and democracy. On the Japanese side, some have simply complied with the American picture, whereas some others have tried hard, consciously or unconsciously, to forget about it — perhaps only because one does not like to recall the time of misery and hardship once one is finally rid of it.

In terms of psychology, all of these three attitudes are quite understandable — a bit of self-complacency for the Americans and perhaps a well-meaning wish on the part of the Japanese to play an American game on this matter, coupled with an equally conceivable forgetfulness of the average Japanese. Yet, a closer look at this particular period would instantly reveal a less rosy reality. Hall pointedly states in his paper:

> we have all too easily taken on the role of the protector of "Civilization," equating our private national interests with the higher aims of history. The sense of moral superiority (which was the certitude of our missionaries) and of technological superiority (which is our national faith) combine in our minds to give a particular aura of inevitability to our actions in Asia . . . . The Occupation was too easy a chance "to realize the ethnocentric American sense of mission" to remake our enemy in our image. And unhappily for us, Japanese behavior in the postwar years only reinforced our predilection to play the "big brother." Japan has our approval so long as it plays our game and minds its own business.

Perhaps for the very reason brought forth in the Hall paper, the six and a half years of the American Occupation of Japan, which officially began on September 2, 1945, and terminated on April 28, 1952, had to become another example of what Jack Hall terms a "tragic" encounter of two totally different cultures. It could otherwise have been a fascinating instance of cross-cultural contact, in which two different cultures met with one another on much more equal terms to discover each other.

Yet, despite the fact that in no other instance in its history have the Americans experienced closer contact with Japan and "things Japanese," this did not by any means result in a deeper understanding of Japan and its people, let alone the complexities inherent in its long cultural heritage.

In this sense, perhaps, the American occupiers in the mid-1940s were less prepared to understand the Japanese than their more cautious predecessors had been in the 1850s. Commodore Perry at least led his flotilla to meet the Japanese, whereas MacArthur and his men landed at Atsugu airfield for the explicit purpose of remaking their enemy in their own image. What they intended was not so much to discover as to transform and reorganize almost everything they happened to encounter in the occupied island empire. And, needless to say, in order to remake and reorganize in haste, it is always best for one not to understand what one is remaking.

Thus the American occupiers committed themselves to the total remaking of Japan with unprecedented zeal and yet a characteristic sense of mission. It does not necessarily follow, however, that they were entitled to do so without compunction. As Ray A. Moore of Amherst College points out in his article "Reflections on the Occupation of Japan," (Journal of Asian Studies, Fall, 1979) there exists some evidence that even General MacArthur himself somehow realized "the limitations on American action implicit in the Potsdam Proclamation." Evidence is found in his cable to General Marshall, dated September 3, 1945, referring to the preliminary draft of a directive he was to receive, in which he states: "I feel I must express my opinion to you, particularly since the proposed directive appears to me to go in certain respects far beyond the principles set forth in the surrender terms and the Potsdam Declaration."

It is all too natural that these "limitations on American actions" were more keenly perceived by the occupied Japanese. According to an article by Taoka Ryoichi entitled "The Legal Status of Japan After the Cessation of Hostilities," which was presumably written in January 1946, at the request of the Treaties Bureau of the Japanese Foreign Office and declassified on July 31, 1978, it is evident that the Japanese government interpreted Japan's defeat not as a defeat by conquest as perceived by the Americans, but nothing more than a defeat by agreement, as one which came as a consequence of a contract reached between Japan and the Allied Powers, the terms of which were either explicitly or implicitly stated in the Potsdam Proclamation as incorporated in the Instrument of Surrender.

The fact that there existed such fundamental conflict of perceptions between the Japanese and the Americans with respect to the "limitations on American actions" is in itself another aspect of the tragic cross-cultural encounter inherent in the American Occupation of Japan. The Japanese perception that the defeat was nothing but a defeat by agreement implies that they were at least entitled to ask for a deeper understanding of Japanese heritage on the part of the occupiers, whereas the American assumption of a defeat by conquest flatly excluded any such possibility, bringing forth a sharp discrepancy never to be entirely resolved until the very end of the Occupation, or, for that matter, even to this day.

Whether the defeat was by agreement or by conquest, however, the occupiers were firmly determined to remake Japan in their own image. Censorship operations enforced by the Civil Censorship Detachment during this particular period illustrate one of the most meticulous endeavors on the part of the Occupation authorities and were aimed at transforming not only Japanese thinking but even the deeply seated memories of the Japanese mind itself. In this regard, it is worthwhile to note that very little mention has been made by Japanese writers of Occupation censorship until very recently. For instance, the sixth and supplementary volume of the Kodansha Nihon Kindai Bungaku Dai Jiten (Kodansha Encyclopedia of Modern Japanese Literature), published in 1978, carries a detailed chronology of books and authors censored by the Japanese authorities dating from the fourth year of Keio. But, strangely enough, practically no mention whatsoever is made of the censorship operations enforced by the Civil Censorship Detachment, thus virtually leaving the Occupation period blank in terms of discussing media control by outside authorities.

Several reasons may be given for this flagrant lack of reference to Occupation censorship. First of all, the compiler of the chronology must have been lacking information on various aspects of the Occupation censorship. There is perhaps also a more complicated psychological reason. In order to clarify it, one should be reminded of the fact that the Occupation censorship was enforced despite the explicit provision of the Potsdam Proclamation guaranteeing "freedom of speech, of religion, and of thought" under the provisions of Paragraph 10. At the same time, one should also note the fact that the Occupation censorship was enforced in spite of Paragraph 2, Article 21, of the 1946 constitution of Japan, which prohibits any form of censorship operation in that country. In other words, the Occupation censorship was carried out in flagrant violation of both the Potsdam Proclamation and the 1946 constitution — which was, ironically enough, drafted by no other party than the American Occupation authorities.

Perhaps for this very reason, then, any mention of the censorship operations was strictly prohibited in the Japanese media throughout the whole Occupation period. The impact on all forms of media was both actual and latent. There was also the fantastic charade that no such thing as Occupation censorship ever existed, carried out to the point where this forced pretense finally had become an integral part of the psychological reality by which Japanese came to live in the immediate postwar years. Intentional or unintentional elimination of books and authors suppressed by the Occupation censor in the Kodansha chronology must have to do with this forced pretense so characteristic of the Occupation period or, for that matter, of the postwar Japan up to this day.

By way of illustration, in the meantime, let me mention several historical facts with regard to the Occupation censorship. The Civil Censorship Detachment, or CCD, which had been established under G-2, the Chief of Counter-Intelligence, GHQ, AFPAC, in January 1945, began its operation in Japan on September 3, 1945, on the day following Japan's surrender to the Allied Powers. And throughout the greater part of the Occupation period — between September 1945, and November 1949, to be exact — the CCD enforced a very thorough and stringent censorship operation over all Japanese media of expression: newspapers, radio scripts, motion pictures, dramatic productions, phonographic records, books, magazines, and pamphlets. Not even slides and kamishibai, a paper picture-card show for children, could escape the scrutiny of the Occupation censors.

Although the CCD had five other divisions — Postal, Telecommunications, Travellers Documents, Special Activities, and Information and Records — under its command, I should like to concentrate my account exclusively on the Press, Pictorial and Broadcast Division, as it was this division that was "responsible for the censorship of all news disseminating media and motion pictures within Japan" according to the revised AFPAC Basic Plan for Civil Censorship in Japan, dated September 30, 1945.

Even before that date, on September 19, 1945, the Press Code for Japan, which set forth the basic principles of censorship, was issued as SCAPIN 33, and under this press code, a 30-point operational guideline was provided. According to a CCD document that I found at the National Record Center in Suitland, Maryland, it runs as follows:

Press, Pictorial and Broadcast Division

Monthly Operation Report
Annex I   25 November 1946

Following is a brief explanation of the categories of deletions and suppressions as listed on the form attached as Annex I to monthly report:

1. Criticism of SCAP:
This is any general criticism of SCAP and criticism of any SCAP agency not specifically listed below.
2. Criticism of Military Tribunal:
This is any general criticism of the Military Tribunal or specific criticism of anyone or thing connected with this Tribunal.
3. Criticism of SCAP Writing the Constitution:
Any reference to the part played by SCAP in writing the new reference to the part played by SCAP in

writing the new Japanese Constitution or any criticism
of the part played by SCAP in the formation of the
Constitution.

4. Reference to Censorship:
Indirect or direct references to censorship of press,
movies, newspapers, or magazines fall into this
category.

5. Criticism of the United States:
Any criticism, direct or indirect, of the United States
falls into this category.

6. Criticism of Russia:
(ditto)

7. Criticism of Great Britain:
(ditto)

8. Criticism of Koreans:
(ditto)

9. Criticism of China:
(ditto)

10. Criticism of Other Allies:
(ditto)

11. General Criticism of Allies:
Criticism of the Allies, not directed at any specific
country, falls into this category.

12. Criticism of Japanese Treatment in Manchuria:
Criticism referring specifically to treatment of
Japanese in Manchuria falls into this category. These
are not to be listed under criticism of Russia or China.

13. Criticism of Allies' Pre-War Policies:
Any criticism of any policies of the Allies, singly or
together, which existed prior to the war falls into this
category. If criticism falls into this category, it will
not be listed under criticism of any specific country.

14. Third World War Comments:
Deletions made on the subject of the Third World War
will be included here, rather than under criticism of
any particular country.

15. Russia vs. Western Powers Comments:
Comments on the situation existing between the
Western Powers and Russia fall into this category, and
will not be listed under criticisms of Russia or any
other Western Powers.

16. Defense of War Propaganda:
Any propaganda which directly or indirectly defends
Japan's conduct of and in the war will fall into this
category.

17. Divine Descent Nation Propaganda:
Propaganda which either directly or indirectly claims
divine descent for either the Nation of Japan or the

Emperor will fall into this category.

18. Militaristic. Propaganda:
This will embrace all propaganda strictly militaristic in nature, which is not included under Defense of War Propaganda.

19. Nationalistic Propaganda:
This will embrace all propaganda strictly nationalistic in nature, but will not include militaristic, defense of war, or divine descent nation propaganda.

20. Great East Asia Propaganda:
This will embrace only propaganda relating to Great East Asia, and will not include militaristic, nationalistic, defense of war, divine descent nation, or other propaganda.

21. Other Propaganda:
This will include all other types of propaganda not specifically included above.

22. Justification or Defense of War Criminals:
Any justification or defense of war criminals will fall under this category. It will not include criticism of the Military Tribunal, however.

23. Fraternization:
This will include stories dealing strictly with fraternization. These stories will not be included under criticism of the United States.

24. Black Market Activities:
Reference to black market activities will fall into this category.

25. Criticism of Occupation Forces:
Criticism of the Occupation Forces will fall into this category, and will not therefore be included under criticism of any country.

26. Overplaying Starvation:
Stories overplaying starvation in Japan will be under this category.

27. Incitement to Violence and Unrest:
Stories of this nature will be included here.

28. Untrue Statement:
Statements palpably untrue will fall into this category.

29. Inappropriate Reference to SCAP (or local units)

30. Premature Disclosure

A mere glance at these guidelines will give one an insight into the very comprehensive nature of censorship operations. With its national headquarters located in Tokyo and two other district offices in Osaka and Fukuoka, at the height of its operations CCD consisted of 66 officers, 63 enlisted men, 244 Department of the Army civilians, and 148 non-Japanese foreign nationals supplemented by 5,658 Japanese employees. As is clearly seen from these figures, from the very outset the CCD suffered a chronic shortage of Allied personnel with sufficient command of the Japanese language. This inevitably led them to employ Japanese nationals as the lowest-ranking examiners, who worked under the supervision of American officers.

In the case of the Press, Pictorial and Broadcast Division, which began operations in Tokyo on September 10, 1945, the procedures covering precensorship of the press and publications were as follows: Publishers were requested to submit two galley proofs of all materials to the PPB station prior to publication. These proofs were given to Japanese examiners who had been instructed to scrutinize them according to the guidelines that I have mentioned, while superiors checked the headlines of newspapers and the complete table of contents of magazines translated into English by the examiners in advance.

Whenever examiners discovered materials that fell into one of the categories indicated in the guidelines, they were requested to report the matter to a supervisor who was then to review the tentative translations prepared by the examiners and send them on for briefing. At the Briefing and Translation Unit, which consisted exclusively of non-Japanese personnel fluent in both Japanese and English, the officer in charge reviewed the briefs and indicated items requiring full literal translation for censorship action. All literal translations were accomplished by the U.S. Army Nisei personnel.

Once a final decision had been made on a given item, censorship action was marked on both pages of the proof. One copy was returned to the publisher, and the other was retained for comparison with the published product. Passed materials were stamped with a censorship seal; passages to be deleted and suppressed materials were marked in red and labeled as such. Publishers were required to keep these proofs for a certain specific period of time as evidence of authority for publication. In the one month of September 1947, for example, 335 news items were deleted and 321 suppressed out of a total of 160,147 items submitted for precensorship. In regard to magazine articles, 140 were deleted and 33 suppressed out of 653 total issues examined during the same period. Also, out of 1,691 books place on precensorship in that month, 85 were determined to require deletions and 9 were suppressed.

In this manner, precensorship of all books published in Japan continued until October 15, 1947. More than 1,200 major magazines were precensored until December 15, 1947, and nearly 70 major newspapers, including such nationwide dailies as the Asahi, the Mainichi, and the Yomiuri, were placed on precensorship until July 25, 1948. Even after that date, 14 publishers who specialized in ultra-right and ultra-left materials were retained on the watch-list for precensorship. Postcensorship of all printed matter, as well as radio scripts, motion pictures, and other publications, was enforced even after the CCD operation was terminated in November 1949. This is evidenced by the fact that the Press Code in Japan was never revised or abolished until after the Allied Occupation of Japan itself was terminated as of April 28, 1952. Moreover the Communist Party organ Akahata (Red Flag) was suspended twice in the summer of 1950, together with 561 affiliated minor leftist newspapers.

In the meantime, if one looks at the categories of deletions and suppressions as listed in the CCD guidelines, one should instantly become aware that they fall into three categories: (1) suppression of any criticism of the Allied authorities, including SCAP; (2) prohibition of any kind of so-called "propaganda"; (3) suppression to be more efficaciously put into effect in the future — long after the end of the Occupation — such as criticism of SCAP writing the constitution and references to censorship.

Given these proscriptions, it is clear that any Japanese writer could suffer from CCD censorship once he sat down and tried to write what he had in mind in a way satisfactorily honest to himself. In actuality, however, some suffered less and others suffered more. In the case of Yoshida Mitsuru, his work had to be suppressed not only once but three times during the Occupation period simply because it was regarded as an example of "militaristic propaganda."

The work in question was a poem en prose entitled The Last of the Battleship Yamato, which Yoshida wrote shortly after he had been demobilized from the Imperial Japanese Navy. During the war, Yoshida had been commissioned as an ensign upon his graduation from Tokyo University and had served in the capacity of a radar officer on board the Yamato, the nation's largest and most powerful battleship at that time. The Yamato, however, was attacked repeatedly by American bombers while en route to the Battle of Okinawa, and after a particularly long and fierce battle, it was sunk off the southern coast of Kyushu. Out of a full crew of some 3,000, Yoshida was among the scant 200 men to survive the doomed vessel.

He returned home like a man deprived of his own soul when the war ended. He felt as though he had lost practically everything — the nation, the Yamato, and his pride and identity as a young officer in the service of His Imperial Majesty — everything, that is, until he realized that he still had one inviolable thing in his possession. That was his memory — an all too vivid memory of his comrades-in-arms who had fought so valiantly aboard the Yamato and were sleeping now in the depths of the sea off the island of Tokunoshima. He realized that only by evoking and describing his departed shipmates could he restore his shattered identity as a man. For Yoshida Mitsuru, the act of writing was another way of mourning their departed souls. So he decided to write this moving account, which in fact he composed almost overnight in a notebook he had kept from his college days.

The most unfortunate thing for the author, however, was the fact that The Last of the Battleship Yamato was interpreted by the Occupation censors as nothing but a "militaristic" piece of propaganda. In my view, as in the eyes of most Japanese readers, The Last of the Battleship Yamato is essentially a requiem for the dead, like a Noh play in which the ill-fated Heiké heroes are fondly evoked from the land of oblivion and reproduce the battle scene in which they took so valiant a part. What is central to the work is not so much the militarism, let alone "propaganda," as much as a wish to relieve and appease the tortured souls that passed away without being mourned by the people for whom they dedicated their lives. This wish on the part of the author was not appreciated by the Occupation censor who wrote in a comment sheet:

> Here is given in the form of a prose-poem a detailed description of the battle fiercely fought by the Yamato by the pen of a young officer who was on board the ship and himself fought with "all his might and main."
>
> The story begins with the preparation of the fleet for starting on the new action, and the main part is of course devoted to the description of how the adamantine battleship together with the following ships was attacked repeatedly by the American bombers and how it was at last sent to the bottom of the sea to the south of Kyushu. Toward the end the author, who was saved while floating on the waves, dwells on his reflection on life and death, but in the last two lines he closes his record with these words, "Over three thousand were the number of the crew, of which the survivors were only two hundred and something. Who could surpass their ardent fighting spirit? Who could doubt their excellent training? Glorious be their last in the eyes of all the world!"
>
> The main idea through the full sixteen pages is of course that of admiring that blind tension which has been enjoyed by so many Japanese when they plunge into danger without "discussing the matter." Here is an instance of the Japanese militaristic spirit being viewed from inside.
>
> The simple attitude of the author and the vivid style of the poem as well as the extremely impressive contents themselves cannot fail to arouse in the mind of the readers something like deep regret for the lost great battleship, and who can be sure than the warlike portion of the Japanese do not yearn after another war in which

they may give another Yamato a better chance?   Anyhow, if such a work of thorough militaristic effect, though a good piece from a certain viewpoint, be passed even with drastic deletions, the censorship principle of C.C.D. must be considered to have undergone some revolutionary reform. Suppression recommended.

The original suppression occurred in November 1946, when the editor of a quarterly magazine Sogen submitted the galley proof of Yoshida's work for the CCD censorship. The CCD suppressed it again in October 1948, when the editor of the same quarterly tried to persuade the censor to give them permission to publish it for the second time. At the third suppression, which occurred in July 1949, Yoshida was summoned to the CCD district office and reprimanded "in no certain terms that any further attempt by him to smuggle suppressed material into publication is likely to be embarrassing to him and to his publisher whom he inveigles into the deal."

Mainly because of these successive events, Yoshida had to give up his literary career practically before he had ever started it. He became instead a banker by joining the Bank of Japan. Throughout his successful banking career however, Yoshida, as the author of The Last of the Battleship Yamato, has been troubled as to why the Occupation authorities were endowed with the power to suppress a memory and a wish on his part to mourn the dead.   This fundamental question in the end led him to a conversion to Roman Catholicism from his original Jodo Shinshu Buddhism, and again into Protestantism from the Catholic faith.

In my view, Yoshida's spiritual quest was an effort basically originating from his desperate desire to find some other impartial censor who could have passed a fair judgment on his own work, a dispassionate censor who could have appreciated the importance of a memory as something so vital and precious to human existence that its suppression could become tantamount to a kind of spiritual death.   This effort on Yoshida's part was also a quest for the image of a God that could embrace both Yoshida and his departed shipmates.   It may only have been a coincidence that a Catholic priest, who had been deeply moved by a chance reading of The Last of the Battleship Yamato draft, was the person to lead Yoshida to his baptism into Catholicism. And yet it appears to me quite logical that Yoshida looked for the invisible and impartial censor in a Western, rather than indigenous, faith, because the censor who suppressed his work was the Occupation, and therefore a Western, censor.

Although Yoshida reconverted himself into Protestantism when he became engaged to a Protestant girl, and was still a Protestant when he died of cancer in September 1979, he nevertheless found it hard to participate in the protest movement against the government-proposed Yasukuni Shrine Act (a protest jointly made by the Christian churches in Japan), for the very reason that it would sever him from his dead comrades, who are enshrined at Yasukuni Shrine irrespective of the faiths to which they belong.

For Yoshida, the protest certainly seemed a betrayal to his fellow crew members — a betrayal that he himself could never tolerate. It was not only a betrayal but also a denial of his cherished memories, memories that he had so persistently sustained despite the Occupation censorship. They were saved when he finally got The Last of the Battleship Yamato published in book form in August 1952, four months after the Allied Occupation of Japan had in fact come to an end.

If the CCD censorship suppressed an individual memory as in the case of Yoshida Mitsuru's The Last of the Battleship Yamato, it also tried to suppress a collective memory: that of the people of Japan, as expressed in the form of Shintoism. In the Gordon Prange Collection at the McKeldin Library of the University of Maryland, I found one day a deleted galley proof of Yanagida Kunio's Ujikami to Ujiko (The Tutelary Deity and the People under His Protection). Needless to say, Yanagida was truly a great scholar of Japanese folklore, the forerunner in this field along with Orikuchi Shinobu. The article in question was originally a series of lectures by the author given at the Yasukuni Shrine, of all places, in July 1946. In it Yanagida criticized the Occupation policy toward Shintoism as entirely irrelevant to the real nature of Shintoism, which is, according to Yanagida, derived from the spontaneous ancestor cult of village folk and has actually nothing to do with the misconceived idea of state Shintoism so persistently held by the Occupation authorities. Let me quote two deleted paragraphs out of the total of seven deletions in this particular work:

> A SCAP Directive on the Japanese shrines issued in December last year was so surprisingly rough and reckless that the village folks in a remote countryside who worship local deities in tiny shrines in their respective villages would certainly lose the sense of where to turn to. For me it appears, however, that even an incident like this may give us a good chance of educating ourselves.

This is a deleted paragraph in Chapter I, entitled "Mirai no Shigaku" (A Study of History in the Future). The next one is a part of Chapter XXX, entitled "Tanjun ni Shizen ni" (Pure and Simple):

> From the time of the nation's founding, Japan has continuously approved the inherent faiths of its people.

It has seldom exerted any restriction on their respective developments, and since the Middle Ages, it has picked up a couple of denominations and placed them under special official protection. The fact that these long practiced customs have been wiped away by the Occupation authorities is in itself a considerable intervention in the people's spiritual, it not material, life. By this act of the Occupation authorities, the mind of the people has been shaken and intimidated. It would require several decades at least before it regains peace and composure. In order to meet this kind of challenge, the best way would be to let everything go as it goes, never trying to take hold of things dying out of themselves. The only concern that we should be aware of would be to take the precaution not to twist or destroy the wishes of the innumerable common people that are coming up spontaneously from the bottom of their hearts. I have heard that even among the Japanese there are some people these days who propagate the idea of a total conversion of Japan into Christianity. I wonder whether or not it is conceivable under these circumstances. I am even curious to see if they could really do that.

As a result of a textual study, I have found out that the text included in Vol. XI of Teihon Yanagida Kunio Shu (The Definitive Works of Yanagida Kunio) does not carry these two deleted paragraphs, nor other five deletions, all of which were filled up by rather vague, ambiguous and attenuated statements amounting to the exact number of deleted words, apparently provided by the author himself at the persuasion of the publisher, who himself had been instructed by the CCD never to reveal the existence of censorship by crossing out the deleted sentences.

What Yanagida tried to advocate in Ujikami to Ujiko is the importance of a collective memory for the ordinary Japanese populace — a collective memory as embodied in Shintoism, which is, according to Yanagida, none other than an accumulation of the Japanese way of life from time immemorial and has little, if anything, to do with "militaristic" or "nationalistic" propaganda. Therefore, for him, the Occupation policy toward Shintoism appeared a ruthless amputation of a people's link with their own ancestors, the fond memory of whom is the very source of vitality in their daily lives.

At this juncture, let me turn to another aspect of the CCD, that is, its operation with regard to the prohibition of any criticism of, or reference to, the actual problems involving the Occupation. In this respect, perhaps, the substantial deletions made by the CCD on a feature film entitled Senso to Heiwa (War and Peace) may illustrate the case in point. According to the G-2, GHQ, Inter-Office Memorandum, dated June 12, 1947, the film, which was originally produced at the request of the Constitution Popularization Society, was submitted to the CCD censorship on May 20, 1947, by the Toho Motion Picture Company. It was in fact, however, produced by a labor union in Toho under a form of production control, with Kamei Fumio as its director and the scenario written by Ito Takeo, both of whom were known in those days as prominent Communist members. The memorandum states:

1. The film, intended to help popularize the new Japanese Constitution, was produced at the request of the Constitution Popularization Society. Contents of the film were not specified by the society, which now is worried about a leftist slant in the film, according to a minor official of the society. Present Japanese Foreign Minister Ashida was chairman of the Constitution Popularization Society.
2. The film contains several Communist propaganda lines, e.g., glorification of demonstrations, identification of the Emperor with discreditable groups, overplaying post-surrender starvation in Japan and decadence in morals.
3. This film falls into a "sensitive" category, similar to Nippon no Higeki (The Tragedy of Japan), which was reviewed after censorship action had been taken and withheld from distribution.

The incident referred to in the memorandum was the one in which a Nichiei documentary film Nippon no Higeki (The Tragedy of Japan) was suppressed in July of the previous year on the ground of "incitement to unrest." In the case of Senso to Heiwa (War and Peace), although the film was passed with deletions after having been held up for a month, it was deleted in as many as 16 places on the grounds of "incitement to violence and unrest, overplaying starvation, criticism of Allied Nations and SCAP, and leftist propaganda." The PPB Memorandum for Record, dated June 5, 1947, recommends the following action to be taken:

It is recommended that Toho's new production Senso to Heiwa (War and Peace) be passed with the following deletions.
Reel 1.
    a. Scenes of wreckage after bombing of Japanese Army transport, prominently showing floating box with Red Cross insignias.

Reason for deletion. Criticism of Allies. Inference made that Allies showed no regard for the Red Cross insignia.

Reel 4.

a. Realistic air-raid scenes.

Reason for deletion. Incitement to unrest and criticism of U.S. Viewing of realistic bombing scenes will cause resentment against U.S.

b. Scene of ex-soldier who goes insane and yells "Tenno Heika Banzai" (Banzai for the Emperor).

Reason for deletion. Criticism of SCAP. SCAP has recognized the Emperor system, and the scene is an attempt to belittle the system by inferring that only ex-soldiers who have gone insane ever think of their Emperor.

c. Emperor's Surrender Speech.

Reason for deletion. Incitement to unrest. Realistic reproduction of speech may be taken for the real thing, and further objectionable because scenes portrayed are not consistent with the actual situation that existed at the time of the speech.

Reel 5.

a. Scene of young children selling pictures of nude foreign woman.

Reason for deletion. Criticism of Allies.

b. Scenes of Japanese women policemen being ridiculed.

Reason for deletion. Criticism of SCAP-supported project.

c. Scene of man negotiating for date with streetwalker, both using the sign language. [sic]

Reason for deletion. Criticism of Allies. Man has face well hidden, and both using the sign language, infers that Allied personnel is involved.

d. Scene of dead ex-soldier in subway, who had died of starvation, and policeman reading his unfinished diary.

Reason for deletion. Overplaying starvation and criticism of SCAP. Unfinished diary states that dead man was former Army officer and Emperor believer, who upon repatriation could not find a home to live in or enough food to live. Inference that all Emperor believers will end in like manner is made.

Reel 7.

a. Promiscuous kissing scenes at cabaret; (1) two women acrobatic dancers going into a passionate embrace and kiss at the end of their act, (2) men patrons kissing their women partners. (3) Jitterbugging scenes in which dancers feet contrast with "marching laborers" feet.

Reason for deletion. Criticism of U.S. Suggestive that such display of public affection is due to American influence.

Reel 8.

a. Statement made by ex-army officer, who remarks at cabaret scene that "as long as we are humans there will be wars, and there is no power on earth that can stop nations from going to war."

Reason for deletion. Criticism of Allies and incitement to unrest.

b. Marching scenes of strike demonstrators.

Reason for deletion. Incitement to unrest and criticism of SCAP. Demonstrators carrying banners and posters such as "Freedom of Speech," "Let us who work eat" and watchers cheering and joining the marchers, etc. are suggestive of criticizing SCAP censorship and encouraging labor strife.

Reel 10.

a. Bar-room scene with walls covered with pictures of Joan Crawford, Jean Harlow, and nude foreign women.

Reason for deletion. Criticism of U.S. and/or Allies.

Reel 11.

a. Scene showing close-up of wording of pledge signed by one of principal characters in picture at time he joined strike-breakers group, which reads, "I Goto Kenichi, being an ex-soldier and believing in the Emperor system, etc."

Reason for deletion. Incitement to unrest. Suggestive that ex-soldiers and Emperor system believers are members of strong arm, strike-breakers' groups that are against labor group.

b. Scene of group of strike-breakers invading a factory yard and attempting to break up a meeting of labor group on strike, with guns and swords.

Reason for deletion. Incitement to unrest and violence.

c. Scene of Goto Kenichi being held up and beaten by strike-breakers.

Reason for deletion. Suggestive of American "gangster" methods and subtlely-intended criticism of U.S.

In addition to the 15 scenes enumerated above, the deletion of the sound track Song of the Wanderer wherever it was playing was also ordered by the CCD for the reason that the song "can be taken as applying to present conditions in Japan."

Thus the PPB Memorandum not only clearly reveals the points of concern for the Occupation censors but sometimes reveals them in a somewhat curious way. The fact that they ordered the elimination of pictures of such Hollywood stars as Joan Crawford and Jean Harlow, as well as those of other nude foreign women, from the scene, for example, attracts our particular attention in this regard. The PPB review sheet, dated June 13, 1947, suggests that the pictures of nude foreign women be changed to those of Japanese women (not nude), and the pictures of Hollywood stars be substituted for those of Toho stars. This of course implies that the censors were not merely extremely puritanical, but also had an amazingly subtle sense of racial discrimination. They could tolerate the scene of young kids selling pictures of Japanese women, or that of bar-room walls covered with Japanese movie stars, but they could never tolerate the pictures of women belonging to the same race to be exposed to curious Japanese eyes. As Jack Hall points out in the article cited earlier, Japanese producers as well as audiences had CCD approval so long as they kept their business in mind, never to trespass over the forbidden boundary.

It goes without saying that of all media of expression, that of the motion picture industry, in a sense, was the one most directly affected by CCD censorship. This is evident when one considers the large sum of investments that are required to get a production off the ground. In the case of Nichiei, the suppression of the documentary film Nippon no Higeki cost the company as much as 1,364,053.99 yen, including 556,753.99 yen for direct cost of production and 807,300.00 yen for expected revenues from distribution of the film. This amounts to approximately a 120 billion yen loss to the company (equivalent to about 600,000.00 yen if the inflation rate is taken into account). Due to this tremendous financial loss, Nichiei nearly went bankrupt and was only bailed out by Toho after the former agreed to distribute its newsreels exclusively through the latter. And Toho's 1st Studio, which had spent 7 million yen (approximately 210 billion yen with the inflation rate taken into account, which amounts to more than $1 million) for the production of Senso to Heiwa, exercised great pains in checking on all scenes or dialogues that they felt might be objectionable before shooting. The result was that by February 1948, a full eight months after the suspension of Senso to Heiwa occurred, all pictures submitted to the censor had been passed in toto without any deletion at all.

In this particular case, moreover, the influence exerted by the CCD censorship action was even more far-reaching than the apparent loss of money on the part of motion picture companies. Because of this incident, Kamei Fumio, director of **Senso to Heiwa** and codirector of **Nippon no Higeki,** was unable to direct any picture, for fear on the part of Toho that he might again produce another picture of a similar, objectionable nature. Thereupon, to the great disappointment of leftists and their followers, the "production control" of Toho's 1st Studio, otherwise known as Kinuta Studio, previously assumed by the labor union, was rapidly taken over by the management.

In this way and in others, the CCD meticulously and very effectively eliminated any attempt on the part of Japanese writers and media to surpass and circumvent the suppressions imposed upon them. It should be noted, at this point, that the Occupation censorship also attempted to conceal the real identity of the nation's most fundamental law, that is the fact that SCAP had drafted the 1946 constitution of Japan. We have seen that in No. 3 of the CCD guidelines provided by SCAP mention of this should be either deleted or suppressed. We have also taken note of the fact that No. 4 of the CCD guidelines prohibits any reference to the existence of the Occupation censorship. If we combine these two prohibitions and analyze their structure, then we will light upon the deeply hidden secret of why the present constitution of Japan in general, and the so-called "no-war" provisions of Article 9 in particular, have been functioning for such a long time as an inviolable taboo that rejects any criticism by the Japanese regarding its authenticity.

It is evident that the taboo consists of a dual structure of prohibitions, namely, prohibition of the fact that SCAP drafted the present Japanese constitution, and also of any criticism concerning this matter, which is supplemented with another prohibition not to disclose the very existence of such prohibitions. Through these carefully contrived psychological devices, the part played by SCAP in the formation of the present Japanese constitution has been totally obliterated.

By the same token, the Occupation authorities succeeded in fabricating a fictitious framework for the postwar Japanese to live under and to believe in, namely, that the 1946 constitution of Japan was drafted by no other party than the Japanese government itself, and that then Prime Minister Baron Shidehara, rather then General MacArthur, had proposed the "no-war" clause of Article 9, to the gratified amazement of the supreme commander.

This was indeed a surprisingly ingenious psychological gimmick on SCAP's part in that it has so far exerted an overwhelming influence — long after the occupation of Japan terminated and the CCD ceased its existence. During the course of the past 35 years, the taboo imposed upon the Japanese mind by an exogenous authority has been transformed and internalized to such an extent that it has eventually become a kind of pseudo-conscience for the Japanese at large, functioning to guide and control Japanese thinking.

Thus the "remaking" of Japan was achieved by the American occupiers. It is no wonder, then, that Paragraph 2 of the Preamble of the present Japanese constitution so faithfully reflects the image of the world as fabricated by the CCD censorship in suppressing any criticism of the Allies, such as the United States, the Soviet Union, Great Britain, China, and others. Let me quote that specific paragraph as my concluding remark:

> We, the Japanese people . . . have determined to preserve our security and existence trusting in the justice and faith of the peace-loving people of the world.

In this light, it should be pointed out as ironic that some American friends these days appear somewhat irritated by a Japan that they have so thoroughly remade and transformed. I wonder whether they are prepared this time to meet Japan and its people to discover them on equal terms, or do they just simply want once again to remake Japan in their own image, only to start once more that tragic vicious circle. In any case, I must make it clear that we Japanese are willy-nilly still living in the shadow of the Occupation, although it has been almost three decades since its official termination.

CHAPTER 11

Conclusion: Media Management
and Political Systems

BY JANE LEFTWICH CURRY

No political or social system exists with a totally free flow of information. Control over information and ideas is inherent in the very nature of human society — the human desire to conform; the natural coloring of events by the observers' preconceptions; the necessary bureaucratic pressures and interests involved in journalistic work; the monopoly of bureaucrats over information; and the needs of politicians and officials to ensure their own legitimacy with and penetration of their societies. These forces limit and structure the content of the mass media everywhere far more than do laws and explicit practices of directing and censoring the mass media. In fact, as Gertrude Robinson has pointed out, "it is entirely too simpleminded to evaluate a country's information system as more or less democratic by merely recording the presence or absence of censorship practices."(1)

In all systems, the primary controls over the content of the mass media, then, are inherent in the process of media production. And no matter under what conditions the media are produced, the imperatives and process of media production are basically the same. Therefore, the variations are far more with the controllers than in the process itself. For journalism, wherever it is done, is both a profession that rewards individual actors and one that requires conformity to protect the interests of the bureaucracy and its owners.(2) Individual journalists in all systems control their own work to appeal to their three constituencies: fellow journalists, their readers, and the "power elite." Their work is further controlled through the natural constraints of a bureaucratic setting, time and resource constraints of scheduled production, and the perceptions of editors. Finally, whether they are part of a political or an economic elite, the "owners" of the means of communication have interests in the media that are similar to their colleagues' outside the media establishment.

Beyond this, political and economic forces have an entire set of protective barriers to protect themselves from negative images appearing in the mass media. These are insurance beyond the libel and slander laws found in most societies to protect citizens from unjust and damaging attacks. In some cases, there are also laws to protect the position and interests of specific groups in a society. In others, there are structures of review designed specifically to keep the media in line with the political elite. However, in most cases, the barriers are far less clearly articulated. They are outgrowths of an elaborate interlocking directorate of individuals and organizations (both political and economic) with common interests and personnel. Or they are the result of natural controls that bureaucracies and bureaucrats, in competition for scarce resources of power and materials, put on any information that might give them a negative image. Often, they are the products of unspoken inducements or potential sanctions that the government or other organizations are assumed to be prepared to use. And, finally, the broader pressures that political and economic forces can and do exert on a society — ranging from advertising to summary arrests and executions — affect the media and their personnel.

The control over the information and ideas in the mass media, whether inherent in the media process and the political system in which they exist or articulated into laws, involves a complex matrix of variables: (1) who owns the mass media; (2) where or for what sector of society the media are controlled; (3) what information is managed; (4) how media management is done; and (5) at what point in the production process information is controlled. In each society, the variables form a different pattern in the matrix. They are determined by national historical and cultural experiences; the leadership's perception of its own legitimacy and success in penetrating the society and making it loyal; the level of popular expectations and the ability of the system to fulfill these expectations; and the goals of the dominant ideology.

As these variables change over time and from leadership to leadership, the qualitative nature of external media controls changes as well. It is, therefore, impossible to speak of unidimensional correlations. Instead, one can only note tendencies of variables to cluster around certain poles in various types of political systems and the relationship between historical and political factors and the media systems that result. Finally, the nature of media control is a determining factor in the ability of the political leadership to penetrate the population and ensure its own legitimacy.

In any society, pressures on the media come not only from the ruling elite but also from groups and institutions throughout the society that are concerned about how they appear to the rulers and to their public. No national medium is controlled by only the top political leadership. This book and this chapter, to an even greater extent, focus on the relationship between the dominant political powers and the media. That focus was inherent in the nature of our concerns. But, as some of the chapters note, similar informal pressures are placed on the media by nonruling groups in any society. And, particularly in states with economies based on private enterprise and profit, economic institutions try to control their images in the mass media through informal pressure on the newsmakers as well as formal advertising.

The systemic variables and the media control patterns that result from them form, even in the best of circumstances, a highly complex and multilevel pattern of media control. In fact, so many elements are involved that no scholar or observer can be expected even to see and record all of the elements involved in any one system's control of the media. In part, as Joan Dassin pointed out in her introduction, this reflects the different priorities of scholars growing out of their interests and disciplinary preconceptions. In part, this is also an accurate reflection of different emphases of political systems. This chapter is an attempt to highlight the various elements that can be considered in analyses of media control and direction; to look at what appear to be the significant elements of political systems in determining patterns of media control; and to raise the questions that have to be addressed in assessing the obverse, the impact of media control on political systems.

THE DETERMINANTS OF MEDIA CONTROL PROCESSES

The ultimate irony in this book on the media control process is that, in systems with ideologies and political realities ranging from the most democratic to the most repressive, the differences are more quantitative than qualitative. This is not to say that the media of the United States or Great Britain are comparable to those of the Soviet Union or the repressive systems of Asia and Latin America, both Communist and non-Communist. It is to say that there are inherent barriers in the media production process that, when used by those who want to determine at least what will not appear in the mass media, control media messages without any formal censorship. In fact, formal censorship is unusual rather than common. The imposition of explicit control and direction occurs when a political leadership sees itself as not totally penetrating and controlling its population and the journalism profession. What happens in most systems is that, whatever the nature of the political processes, the media are controlled and directed through informal contract between journalists and their subjects.

Key elements in determining the extent of media control are the goals of the ruling ideology and the position of the political leadership vis-à-vis its own population. In turn, the leadership's perception of its own position is a reflection of the compatibility between the ruling ideology and national historical and cultural traditions and the leadership's sense of its ability to fulfill the promises of the ideology and the expectations of the population. So the need to control or direct the media actively is directly proportional to the gap between the ideology and reality.

The ideological base on which a political system is built determines the focus of pressures on the media. While all political, economic, and social institutions and leaders in a society try to influence the messages transmitted in their societies, their ideologies differ as to what the role of the media should be. A commitment to an ideology of change and popular mobilization involves the political leadership in controlling the media's messages and directing their content. This tends to be true for Communist systems when the leadership is committed to bringing society closer to the Marxist-Leninist ideal of a "new Communist man." This pressure to direct as well as to control also comes from leaders in developing countries who are committed to national development and modernization. In authoritarian regimes where the leadership took over to stop rapid social transformation, the emphasis tends to be more on limiting what the media prints than on using it as a tool for change. Such a pattern of emphasis is characteristic of most regimes in the Third World (including most military juntas), as well as nondemocratic regimes in Western and Eastern Europe where the emphasis is not on changing but on maintaining the status quo. It is characteristic even of cases like Brazil where national security policy also involves propagandizing abroad and engaging in domestic advertising campaigns. American military censorship of occupied Japan functioned in the same way. In these cases, though, the media were allowed to submit to restrictions without giving support to the government.

The leaders of democratic systems do not, under normal circumstances, engage in either direction or control against the will of the media. On the other hand, the potential for both direction and control always exists. Normally, in these systems, the political leadership's actions are more understated than those of authoritarian and mobilizing regimes. The emphasis is on restraint and suggestion by appeals (largely indirectly made) to common values and symbols. The effectiveness of these appeals is influenced by the alternative pressures placed on the mass media. In this way, democratic systems tend to be different from either authoritarian or Communist systems: Equally strong pressures on the media come from institutions and individuals other than the political leaders, including economic and social institutions as well as opposition parties.

The differences in media management (be it direction, control, or restraint) depend on the security of the leadership. Political leaders or institutions that are successful in achieving their goals and being accepted by their populations have less need to exert control over the media and their messages than those that have failed to reach their goals and are not accepted. In situations where the ruling ideology is a continuation of national traditions and historical experiences, the individuals who produce the mass media are more likely to share the views of the leaders or institutions concerned with media images. And the public they contact is more likely to see the leadership or the institutions involved as legitimate than in situations where there has been the imposition of a new ideology and new institutions. Deliberate control and direction are thus unnecessary. But in postrevolutionary situations when new cadres have been brought in to run the mass media, as in the Communist takeovers, the new cadres and the world in which they work are products of earlier times and ideologies, so the media must be monitored and directed to see images as the leadership wants them to be seen. Even after years of rule, systems like the Soviet Union or many military dictatorships do not have rational media that can be trusted naturally to picture the world as the leadership would have it seen. Reality for journalists and even editors simply is not consistent with the images that the political leadership wants presented.

It is in systems where the leadership fails to meet its goals, whatever the declared ideology, that formalized and active press control emerges. So when leaders even in democratic societies feel besieged by policy failures or criticism, they tend to move toward more active press control and direction. In the United States, for instance, as the events of Watergate unfolded, the Nixon administration attempted to stem media attacks by counterattacking, catering to favorable journalists, and cutting off access to information for all but trusted journalists. In the case of France, where there has been a tradition of popular pressure against the leadership, laws have been put in place that limit public criticism, however true, about the government leadership. In Communist and authoritarian systems, when policy is not successful and readily accepted by the population, formal media control is necessary. Ironically, as is clear in overtly repressive systems in Africa, Latin America, East Germany, and Rumania, the existence of formal media control is also necessitated when terror is reduced over the society as a whole. So, although formal media control is normally treated as a critical indicator of totalitarianism or repression, it is in fact a sign of the weakness of the leadership's actual control.

As a result, few media systems have regular, separate formal institutions of censorship. Those that have, like Brazil, Poland, Czechoslovakia, Israel, and Allied-occupied Japan, tend to be systems in which the authorities do not have the full support of their populations or feel they are at war with either their domestic or foreign audiences. The most ironic case is that of the Soviet Union. Some 65 years after the Communist takeover, a complex of formal censorship structures is still at work culling out prohibited material and encouraging journalists to follow directions. This is a reflection of the failure of Soviet policies to reach the goals they have set. It is also a reflection of the continued failures of Communist rule to socialize completely that population. And for journalists and writers who have been censored for their entire lifetimes, it is a useful shield that allows them to try and evade controls.

In systems like the Soviet Union and other states trying to mobilize their populations, censorship is not the best mechanism to ensure that the media aid the leadership. Censorship is merely the final control over what appears. It only indirectly determines what is prepared because it occurs at the end of the production process. In this sense, it occurs as journalists learn from experience what will be rejected. But to guide fully what is produced, the leaderships must provide incentives and directions as to what should appear. If and when reality is consistent with the messages the leaders seek, repression makes opposition in any form untenable, or when journalists become so socialized into the ruling ideology that they follow it automatically, then formal censorship is no longer necessary.

But where it exists, formal censorship most often has become a crutch for journalists and writers. It gives them a shield to protect them from making errors in what is published. This allows them to have greater leeway in their decisions. It also provides a foil for explaining the gaps in information. Journalists and editors do not take the responsibility themselves. But in all of the cases where formal censorship exists, what censorship institutions have done is reduce the pressure on journalists to learn the rules and rely on their own skill at self-censorship to remove any unacceptable information that might slip through the net of informal and bureaucratic control. As a result, the removal of formal censorship without its replacement with other effective informal controls uncaps a bottle of formerly unacceptable information.

Inconsistencies in the causes for stricter or looser media control and for differences in emphases on direction, control, or restraint are only part of the picture. In large part, they cross ideological boundaries. The leadership or institutional sense of selves and position in society provides the imperatives for media control or direction. How this occurs is, in part, built into the media production process and into the dynamics of any society. There is no single pattern that fits a group of countries. Instead, various mechanisms and special control and direction institutions have grown out of immediate needs and resources, ideological tenets, and systematic features.

ELEMENTS IN MEDIA CONTROL AND DIRECTION

The prime element in traditional discussions of media control and the role of the mass media in political systems has been the question of ownership. Western scholars distinguish between private ownership and public or state ownership. In doing this, they equate private ownership with the freedom to "inform, entertain, sell," as well as "to help discover truth and to check on government" or "to raise conflict to the plane of discussion." Private ownership is seen as insurance that, even if access was limited to those with the economic means to buy media, the need to compete for users in order to make a profit forces "the self righting process of truth" in "free market place of ideas." Public or state ownership is equated with the media being used only to support and advance the policies of a government or party. Under public ownership, access is assumed to be limited to those loyal to the rulers and all other controls were said not to exist.(3)

Marxist scholars have drawn the same dividing line but have seen its impact quite differently. As the Soviet constitution phrases it:

> In conformity with the interests of the working people, and in order to strengthen the socialist system, the citizens of the USSR are guaranteed by law; . . freedom of the press . . . These civil rights are ensured by placing at the disposal of the working people and their organizations, printing presses, stocks of paper, public buildings, the streets, communications facilities and other material requisites for the exercise of these rights.(4)

The media are thus protected, as Lenin said, against the control of the bourgeoisie over the means of communication and exhortation as workers are protected from their control over the means of production. Their theory assumed that there is no absolute truth but that all facts are colored by those who use or present them. Their concern is with the media as a political resource for its "owners."

In fact, although it is clear that the Soviet media are not organs of the working people but of the Communist party elite, current research in this book and in earlier studies has shown that state ownership does not necessarily taint and restrict information, nor does private ownership guarantee its freedom. In the United States, the economics of the media permit only large corporations or very wealthy buyers to own the media. Others simply cannot afford the technology to establish and operate media. As a result, not only do these individuals or corporations have the potential for influencing the selection and reporting of news to fit their worldview and their needs; but there is also a more significant tendency for media monopolies to develop simply because the costs of operation limit the number of papers that can survive in any one area.(5) This both increases the stress on making a profit and the likelihood of a journal's having a monopoly on information and readers in their target region. The news reflects a bias toward the class groups with which the publishers and journalists associate, class groups most often closely connected with the political and economic power elite. It also, as Gaye Tuchman has pointed out, reflects the necessary bureaucratic imperatives required to make newspaper production profitable. This reinforces the natural bureaucratic imperatives of journalism work. It also makes certain kinds of news less reportable.

The Western European cases further modify the starkness of the dichotomy drawn in American media theory between public and private ownership. On the one hand, although the British Broadcasting Company is state-owned and did cooperate with the government in the handling of the hostage taking in the Iranian Embassy, its behavior was not significantly affected by its state ownership. Other media were equally co-opted by the "emergency." And, in fact, it has been consistently more critical than privately owned media in France, for instance. Thus, at least in some cases, state ownership of broadcast media, the norm for Western Europe, does not mean a state takeover of information.

Equally as significant in the impact of private ownership of the print media in Western Europe is the tradition of ownership by political groups or parties. There, before there was even a press produced by private concerns to turn a profit from circulation and advertising, myriad journals were printed by various political groupings all over Western Europe to inform and convince those parts of the small literate population they could reach. Their success at advocacy rather than their profitability and mass appeal remains the measure of their success. These journals are the traditional models for Western European journalism. As a result, this journalism is normally deliberately biased and engaged in its presentation of information. So, in Western Europe, as long as various political groupings are allowed to exist and argue their cases, private ownership means that information will be politically tainted.

National legal traditions like those in France can be and are used to protect the government against media criticism even as the ownership remains in private hands. In addition, as the Brazilian case demonstrates, private ownership does not ensure freedom from control. Under the authoritarian regimes, a private press existed. But because of fear of reprisals, as well as the interest of the media elite in working with the leadership to protect its own viability, the media consistently followed the line of the leadership even after the ending of military control. The cases of Egypt and Brazil further demonstrate that, whatever the independent perceptions of the private owners of the media, they cannot force their independence on a government bent on ensuring a positive press.

For the Third World, the question of state ownership is an economic necessity as well as a political issue. Many sought to end foreign control of their media and public information in order to end colonial influence. In recent years, this has been a primary impetus for the Third World demands for a new world information order. It has also resulted in many of these states legally barring foreign ownership of mass media in their countries. The lack of domestic investors with the necessary economic resources to set up and maintain even periodicals and the increase in the number of authoritarian regimes concerned with controlling their populations has resulted in a decrease in the number of totally privately owned media in the Third World in the last 20 years. Even where the print media have remained privately owned, their financial survival has required substantial government subsidies and, in turn, substantial government involvement and control. One such case discussed in this book, for instance, is Egypt. Or private control has been so tenuous that fines or confiscations have been continuing threats to the very survival of papers.

The character of information control is also very much a product of the public to which it is addressed. Nations differ both in the extent of literacy and the accessibility of the media to that literate population. In Africa and much of Asia, widespread illiteracy results in print media that in all but a few more developed nations are nothing more than informations sheet for the tiny literate urban population. In most of Western Europe, on the other hand, the print media are accessible to all portions of the population. Finally, in some cases, the issue of the domestic audience is complicated by the question of who abroad has access to information.

The importance assigned to addressing various groups in a national audience varies. Normally, the larger an audience, the broader the potential impact of the message, whether it is radio broadcasts in Africa or advertising campaigns in the United States. As a result, in every system, state involvement and concern tend to be greatest in the most mass media, the broadcast media of radio and television. Who is licensed to use the airwaves is, therefore, both a domestic and an international issue with political overtones, even in the United States where broadcast media are privately owned.(6) Elsewhere, the airwaves are considered public property. In much of Western Europe, this has meant the establishment of public corporations kept at a greater or lesser distance from immediate political control. In the Third World, the domestic broadcast facilities are government instruments as they are in the Communist world. Given the problem of illiteracy in the Third World and, at an earlier date, in much of the Communist world, as well as the importance placed on education in both of these regions, the broadcast media are the most heavily funded and carefully used.(7)

On the whole, this has meant that where there is a literate population to support print media, those media also exist more separately from the state than the broadcast media. The extent of this independence and separation, in turn, depends on the size of the audience and the significance of that audience to the ruling political or economic elite. As a result, in Communist and non-Communist systems, the more limited the readership and esoteric the subject, the less control and direction.

Where exceptions to this rule have occurred, as in some of the examples used in articles in this volume, they have been notable reflections of specific sensitivities of the political leaders. In the case of the takeover of the Iranian Embassy, for instance, broadcast coverage was carefully advised — not because of its mass audience but because of its potential effect on its audience among a handful of terrorists in the embassy. Sadat's battles with critics from the elite media over his decisions on an Egyptian-Israeli peace accord were a result not of a concern with a mass public able to force a reversal of his decision but of Sadat's concern with elite opposition to his decisions as evidenced in an elite press. That was the group with whom Sadat felt weakest. Similarly, in national security states like Brazil, journals addressed to the small, literate urban population were closely watched because that was the population most opposed to military control from which a viable opposition could have developed. In these national security states as well as Communist states, there has also been an element of concern with how information from the media will be used by interested foreign powers.

WHAT INFORMATION IS MANAGED

The question of what information is controlled is one of the most interesting and revealing aspects of media control. It provides evidence as to the priorities and weaknesses felt by those who control the media in each system. It is also one of the least articulated areas of media management. Aside from laws that are general enough to handle various cases and far less significant in determining what appears than the unarticulated agendas and pressures built into media production, little on this is stated explicitly.

Laws regulating what information is made public and transferred exist in every political system. Normally, there is some legal provision for handling libel and slander. Beyond this, the laws vary not only in their stringency but also in their intent. There is

> a distinction between censorship which is censorship of political information by the government, which wishes to impose its own view of events or to withhold information which might lead to views which are disagreeable to it and censorship that is designed to protect, in an ancient phrase, taste and morals.(8)

The former is generally a part of the legal system, if actual legal provisions exist, of Communist and authoritarian regimes. It is necessary because of the incongruity between reality and the image leaders wish to create. It also reflects the sense of the leadership that it has failed to penetrate its own society. Legal provisions or administrative directions with similar intent also exist in democratic societies. As Charles Eisendrath pointed out, the French elite is explicitly and amply protected by law from most direct criticism. Even in Britain where press freedom is carefully protected, policies for handling national emergencies can be used to curb coverage where the government organization involved feels it necessary. The protection of taste and morals, on the other hand, is a part of the legal code of all states. It is more often used in states where there is less political regulation and the media are geared to sell to the public. This control, while not really discussed in this volume, has been a political cause in the West where restrictions on pornography have raised constitutional questions as to freedom of the press and public morals.

Other less accessible codification of what may not appear also exists. In the cases of Poland, Brazil, and occupied Japan, we have specific listings used by those responsible for the content of the media — either external censors or editors — to make their decisions. What is surprising, given the divergent ideological positions of the sources, is the similarity of the restrictions. And, although there is little hard data, indications from those involved in other societies with clear media directives are that regulations, both explicit and implicit elsewhere, concentrate on similar categories:

1. Images of the authorities that they have not themselves approved, especially those revealing dissension within their ranks or failures of their policies;
2. Any potentially negative reflection on allies or potential allies;
3. Encouragement of mass political action by any demonstration that individual problems are actually societal; that they should or could take on authority for their own decision; or that other groups or individuals are successful in defying a system; and
4. Censorship itself.

Beyond these system–shielding prohibitions, there is an even more critical set of guidelines: those that are acted on almost totally unconsciously by journalists.   These are difficult to research because they demand that the researcher analyze voids even journalists and editors are not conscious exist. As a result, there is little scholarly research done in this area, particularly for systems where other explicit regulation exists, which, as Jun Eto contends, leaves in its wake compelling but unarticulated limits. Gaye Tuchman's article in this book is one of the few explicit discussions of these kinds of prohibitions. In the cases she cites, such limits grow out of natural class biases and journalists' own professional values as to what is acceptable and salable. Such biases are dependent on the tenor of the time and place in which journalists find themselves. They are also dependent on the journalists, editors, and publishers who produce the media. In addition to journalists' natural inclinations, the explicit controls gradually inculcate journalists and editors with unconscious prohibitions and create a climate in which broader media decisions are made.

Other legal controls over the media are far more widespread. Aside from the specific legal regulations on the content of the mass media already discussed, there are a number of general rewards and sanctions that encourage media personnel to consider the authorities' positions on the issues they present. The most common are the creation of an employer–employee relationship by the payment of subsidies to journalists — to say nothing of situations where journalists and editors are state employees — and financial aid for media organs and the licensing are not done on an explicitly political basis, the regulations as to who can own and edit a paper, what documentation is required, and what funding is required and available have a potential effect on who can publish. Without being deliberately used for political ends, these "aids" favor more establishment papers. And when the political authorities elect to use subsidies and licensing to benefit groups they support, such formal requirements become highly political.

Beyond the general involvement, there are also incentives for cooperation. Journalists whose work pleases government officials or special interests such as industries can receive benefits ranging from increased access to information to special awards and gifts. Journals, similarly, may receive additional access, increased paid advertisement from the government or special interests, or other special support. And when journals or journalists enter into conflicts with these institutions or individuals, they often are not only publicly attacked but also sanctioned by decreased access, fines, and the removal of all special support. To survive, journals then have to cut back on earnings or coverage.

For much of the Third World and authoritarian states in the Western camp like Israel, Franco's Spain, and Salazar's Portugal, media control is furthered by the state's right to confiscate unacceptable editions or articles or to suspend journals' licenses to publish. The very threat of their use is often enough to cause journalists and editors to restrain themselves, as these sanctions can mean economic destruction. Usually, the threat is carried out only when a new issue is introduced about which journalists and editors have no "sixth sense" or specific instructions so they misjudge what the appropriate response is. On an issue, an editor or a journal takes a risk because it feels strong enough to avoid confiscation or suspension. All of these personnel and economic controls, like their counterparts in the Communist world (nomenklatura and institutional guidance), lead journalists and editors to consider what is acceptable before they ever begin to research and prepare articles. These elements thus have a far more overwhelming, if less explicit, impact on the content of the media because they influence its very conception by leaving journalists and editors to anticipate all possible reactions.

To supplement these negative guidelines, most systems have avenues for directing media coverage. One of the most common avenues for guidance in every system is simple personal interaction between sources and journalists based on personal and professional ties. In addition, specific instructions and suggestions come from government authorities and various special-interest groups through regulations on information access, press releases, and press conferences or private interviews. Whether or not these are couched as suggestions or as explicit orders depends on the tradition of the system. But however they are couched, they have an effect on coverage. In systems where guidance is given openly, press councils of government and media representatives are often organized.

Such guidance is given most explicitly in Communist systems where state ownership of the media and the means of production as well as control of all jobs make criticism in the media an attack on one's employer. The importance of guidance given by both party and government authorities is heightened by the fact that conflicting directions are the exception rather than the rule. As was clear in Hungary, Poland, and Czechoslovakia, conflicting directions growing out of elite divisions liberate the media from the limits normally placed on the mass media. Finally, Communist systems concern themselves with ensuring that specific issues are raised. In most situations, journalists are expected to rely on their own caution and sensitivity to the political atmosphere around them rather than on minute directives on what to say and what not to say. Such enforced self-censorship is far more restraining than clearly declared limits, as the variations in Eastern European systems illustrate.

Ultimately, however, these media-specific control and direction mechanisms merely supplement journalists' and editors' sense of the broader political and social climate. Everywhere journalists and editors are citizens and also parts of state or private bureaucracies with specific interests of their own. Where media are state-owned, journalists are employees of a state bureaucracy. Where the media are privately owned, journalists work is molded to fit the needs of the bureaucracy for speed and cost-effectiveness as well as for salability. Where the media are owned by political or special interests, journalists tend to be selected for and guided by the needs of the organization in which they work. Whatever the nature of their organizational involvement and the societies in which they live, journalists' and editors' personal worldview and understanding of events color their impressions of those events. Those views are the product of their own personal experiences and social group identities. This occurs in every system.

The ultimate restraint built into a system is the terror that exists in some societies. In many of the cases discussed here, the specific sanctions the government is empowered to enact over the media pale in comparison to this terror. For many of the journalists in Africa, Asia and Latin America, as well as China, Eastern Europe and the Soviet Union under Stalinism, the real threat is not of professional sanctions but fear of firings, fines, arrests, or, in some cases, even torture and death for those who cross the rulers. For journalists, this involves the "mishandling" of information in the eyes of the leadership and political criticism. Because such terror affects the whole society and not just journalists, it keeps journalists from writing and being published and also keeps sources from providing information.

PUTTING DOMESTIC CONSTRAINTS INTO
AN INTERNATIONAL ENVIRONMENT

All of these various elements of media control affect not only
the character of the domestic media but also the nature of
information transferred from one country to another. The media
are seen as an extension of the government by most states.
They also perceive of their image abroad as important to their
international position. As a result, all states have provisions to
aid foreign correspondents and distribute positive information
abroad. States that actively control their own media go further.
They feel foreign news should be controlled. So varying
impediments and pressures placed by these governments on the
work of foreign correspondents. Such states also pressure their
own citizens to dissuade them from creating negative impressions
in their contract with foreigners. And to counter negative
publicity abroad about their policies, some of these states,
including Brazil and the Soviet Union, have special active
propaganda campaigns to condemn their detractors and improve
their images. In part, all of this is done to create positive
images abroad in order to encourage travel and investment and
counter human rights pressures. In part, too, it is an attempt
to keep information away from foreign media, especially
broadcast media, accessible to their own populations but beyond
their control and direction. The most celebrated and contested
of these stations is Radio Free Europe/Radio Liberty, which is
funded by the United States to broadcast into nations in the
Soviet bloc. But while nations in the Soviet bloc have targeted
this station, broadcasting to nations abroad is a normal part of
state propaganda for almost all industrial states.

On these concerns, there has been a clear convergence of
interests between Communist bloc leaderships and those of much
of the Third World. It has led to long battles in the United
Nations over the meaning and viability of the so-called new world
information center. For the Third World and, for different
reasons, the Soviet bloc, this involves legalizing the use of many
domestic control mechanisms on an international scale (licensing
and instructing, for instance). It also involves aid for Third
World development of state media resources and regional news
agencies. The underlying assumption of these demands is that
the media is a tool in politics — both domestic and international
— and truth culturally subjective. Western responses to these
proposals have, on the whole, been negative. Such regulations
and financial aid violate basic ideological tenets about good and
bad media work. But they also would hurt Western press
agencies' financial interests. All of this leaves the proponents
and opponents of the new world information order to odds. Their
conflict is merely an outgrowth of the importance of the mass

media to all systems and the variations in the need to control as well as in domestic assumptions and practices.

FINAL QUESTIONS YET TO BE ASKED

No discussion of censorship can fairly ignore the impact of censorship on the political systems that determine its character. The relationship is two-way. The failure of the media to be allowed to address the important questions for the society and to reflect reality leads to disbelief not only of the media but of the controllers of the media. The control that a leadership imposes to maintain itself thus often serves to weaken that leadership further.

On a broader level, as Jun Eto pointed out, the limitation of the messages that appear in the media distort social discourse. Issues and perceptions are removed from public conscience. Language is cast to take on new, often unnatural meanings. And because of their experiences with censorship and rejection on substantive grounds, writers and journalists develop a sixth sense of self-censorship. As this occurs, they often cease to be aware that they are censoring themselves. Eventually, when censorship (however it is done) works smoothly and consistently over a long period, writers and journalists even stop trying to communicate some issues and ideas.

How this occurs and with what effect are questions that have only been touched upon in passing in this chapters. They are not less important issues than the relationship between the political system and media control. They are difficult questions to answer. Much of the empirical data cannot be collected in societies where outright media control occurs. Much fits in the realm of psychology, and much remains undefined, as the societies are unaware that their information is managed. What is needed is another volume to look at this intertwined but obverse relationship.

In all of the questions of censorship, this volume is merely an introduction of the issue. Grand theory and fully developed models must wait until more research has been done in this area. Given that the media are citizens' and scholars' major source for information, the small amount of research that has been done on where the media come from and how they are controlled is tragic. This volume is an attempt to collect the best studies from a broad spectrum of situations and perspectives. That is not the end of the job. What it provides is a resource for further thinking and research as well as an initial introduction to the variables involved in the media control process and in the political dynamics that mold the process.

NOTES

1. Gertrude Joch Robinson, Tito's Maverick Media (Urbana: University of Illinois Press, 1977), p. 61.

2. For a more detailed discussion of the journalism profession, see John W. C. Johnstone, Edward Slawski, and William W. Bowman, The News People (Urbana: University of Illinois Press, 1976), and Penn Kimball's more journalistic account of the specific character of journalism as a profession: "Journalism: Art, Craft, or Profession?" in The Professions in America by Kenneth S. Lynn, ed. (Boston: Beacon Press, 1963), pp. 242-60.

3. Fred S. Siebert, Theodore Peterson, and Wilbur Schramm, Four Theories of the Press (Urbana: University of Illinois Press, 1956), p. 7.

4. Ibid., p. 125.

5. Benjamin M. Compaine, ed., Who Owns the Media? (New York: Harmony Books, 1979).

6. Therefore, radio and television broadcasters are required by the Federal Communications Commission to file reports demonstrating their public service programming and, in the case of political campaigns, ensure equal access to all candidates. These and other regulations provide the government with ultimate means for influence.

7. One of the groundbreaking studies in this area was that done by Wilbur Schramm, Mass Media and National Development (Stanford, Calif.: Stanford University Press, 1964).

8. Stuart Hampshire and Louis Blom-Cooper, "Censorship?" Index on Censorship 6, no. 4 (July-August 1977): 5.

INDEX

Adie, Kate: 50-51
affirmatory rituals: 36
Afrique: 228
Agayants, I.: 94
Agence France Presse (AFP):
    73, 230
agitprop: 90
Al-Ahaly: 199, 200, 201, 202
Al-Ahram: 192, 195, 196, 197,
    199, 202, 204, 207
Ainslie, Rosalynde: 227
Akahata (Red Flag): 243
Al-Akhbar: 197, 198, 199
Algeria: 188
Alves, Márcio Moreira: 163
American-Vietnamese War: 11,
    12
Amin, Ali: 197
Amin, Mustafa: 197
Angola: 212, 215
Angry Brigade: 35
apology, defined: 66
Arab Socialist Union: 189, 192,
    193, 194, 195, 199
Argentina: human rights
    propaganda, 150-51;
    military takeover in, 149
Arns, Dom Paulo Evaristo: 169
Asahi: 242
Asahi Shimbun: 137
Ashida: 248
Associated Press (AP): 73, 230
Atkins, Humphrey: 40
Auby, Jean Marie: 66
"authoritarian statist" form of
    rule: 32

Balcombe Street siege: 38
Banda: 226
Bay of Pigs invasion: 3
beat, disbanding of: 16
Benin: 211, 212, 226, 228, 229

Bernstein, C.: 15
Beuve-Méry, Hubert: 77
Bill of Rights: 12
Bittencourt, Dona Niomar: 163
black African states:
    broadcasting, 226-27;
    censorship, 217-18; film
    censorship, 228; foreign
    periodical confiscation,
    228-29; formal one-party
    control, 211;
    government-organized
    corporation control, 210;
    government ownership,
    212-13; government
    subsidies, 215-16;
    harassment of journalists,
    225; imprisonment of
    journalists, 224-25; judicial
    appointment and review,
    222-23; libel and sedition
    laws, 226; licensing of
    journalists, 220-21;
    licensing of publications,
    221-22; ministry of
    information control, 210;
    news agency contracts,
    230; newspaper ownership
    in, 215; newsprint
    allocations, 216-17;
    opposition publications,
    219-20; posting of bond,
    225-26; preventive
    detention of journalists,
    223-24; printing press
    ownership, 215; privately
    owned press, 211-12;
    submission of cables, 229;
    suppression of publications,
    218-19; visa requirements
    for foreign journalists, 229
de Bloch, Richard: 173

271

ABOUT THE EDITORS

DR. JANE LEFTWICH CURRY has written on Polish journalists as professionals, their participation in the policy process, and the role of the media in Communist countries. She has done in-depth interviews in Poland and Western Europe with Polish journalists, editors, and former censorship officials. She is currently heading a consortium of scholars on the roots of the Polish crisis and working on a comparative study of the role of specialists and professionals in the policy-making process of Communist societies. She has also completed <u>The Black Book of Polish Censorship</u>, based on internal Polish censors' documents from 1974 to 1976 that were smuggled to the West.

Dr. Curry is a member of the Political Science Department at Manhattanville College, a Research Associate at the Institute on East Central Europe at Columbia University, and a Social Science Consultant for the Rand Corporation. Her field is political science. She has held various fellowships to pursue her research, including a Rockefeller Humanities Fellowship, a Fulbright Fellowship and two fellowships from the International Research and Exchanges Board.

DR. JOAN R. DASSIN has published a book in Portuguese on Brazilian literature and has written on the Brazilian press, film, and theater, as well as on contemporary European and American literature. She is currently completing a monograph on censorship and the military state in Brazil, based on extensive archival research and interviews with Brazilian journalists, editors, and scholars.

Dr. Dassin is a member of the Communications Department at Fordham University and is a Research Associate at the Institute of Latin American and Iberian Studies at Columbia University. Her fields are communications and Latin American studies. For her research, she has held several post-doctoral fellowships, among them grants from the H. V. Kaltenborn Foundation, the National Endowment for the Humanities, the Social Science Research Council, and the Tinker Foundation. She also held a Fulbright Professorship in Brazil from 1976 to 1977.

LIST OF CONTRIBUTORS

Jane Leftwich Curry is a member of the Department of Political Science, Manhattanville College, New York, and a Research Associate at the Institute on East Central Europe of Columbia University.

Joan R. Dassin is a Research Associate at the Institute of Latin American and Iberian Studies of Columbia University and a member of the Communications Department at Fordham University, Bronx, New York.

Lilita Dzirkals is a Soviet specialist in the Social Science Department of the Rand Corporation, Los Angeles.

Charles Eisendrath is a professor in the Department of Communication at the University of Michigan at Ann Arbor.

Jun Eto is affiliated with the Center for Humanities and Social Sciences at the Tokyo Institute of Technology, Tokyo.

Lu Keng is a Chinese journalist who left the mainland for Hong Kong in 1979.

Munir K. Nasser is a member of the Department of Communication at the University of the Pacific in Stockton, California.

Gaye Tuchman is a professor in the Department of Sociology, Queens College, and the Graduate School and University Center, City University of New York.

Philip Schlesinger is the head of the Division of Sociology at Thames Polytechnic, London, England.

Dennis L. Wilcox is a professor of journalism at San Jose State University, San Jose, California.